HPE GREENLAKE ADMINISTRATOR ESSENTIALS:

498 PRACTICE QUESTIONS FOR CERTIFICATION SUCCESS

Test Your Knowledge with Realistic Scenario-Based Questions, Configurations, and Detailed Explanations to Master HPE GreenLake Operations

Q1: Scenario-based Question Your company, GlobalTech Solutions, has recently transitioned to a hybrid IT environment and is using HPE GreenLake to manage its resources efficiently. As the administrator, you are tasked with ensuring smooth operations and resource allocation across multiple departments. The marketing team has requested additional compute resources to support a new campaign, while the finance department is concerned about budget constraints and wants to monitor cloud spending closely. You need to allocate resources without exceeding budget limits and ensure that both teams have visibility into their resource usage and costs. How would you effectively manage these requirements using the GreenLake portal?

A) Allocate additional resources to the marketing team without any restrictions and inform the finance department to adjust the budget.

B) Use the GreenLake portal to set up resource pools for each department and enable budget alerts for finance monitoring.

C) Request manual reports from the GreenLake support team to provide budget updates to finance.

D) Increase the overall budget limit in GreenLake to accommodate marketing's needs and notify finance.

E) Implement a third-party tool for budget tracking and resource allocation outside of GreenLake.

F) Deny the request from marketing until a formal budget approval is obtained.

Answer: B

Explanation: The GreenLake portal provides robust tools for managing and monitoring resources efficiently. By setting up resource pools, you can allocate specific resources to the marketing team while ensuring that the finance department can track cloud spending through budget alerts. This approach allows both teams to have the necessary resources and visibility into their usage and costs without exceeding budget constraints. The use of in-built features such as resource pools and budget alerts within GreenLake allows for seamless integration and real-time monitoring, thus negating the need for manual interventions or third-party tools. This strategy balances operational needs with financial oversight, aligning with the company's hybrid IT management objectives.

Q2: True/False Question Access to different services within the HPE GreenLake portal can be managed through role-based access controls.

A) True

B) False

Answer: A

Explanation: True. HPE GreenLake uses role-based access controls (RBAC) to manage user access to various services and resources within the portal. This system allows administrators to assign specific roles to users, defining what actions they can perform and what data they can access based on their roles. RBAC provides a structured way to enforce security and ensure that users have the appropriate permissions aligned with their responsibilities. This is crucial for maintaining operational security and managing resources effectively in a shared IT environment.

Q3: Fill-in-the-gap Question In the HPE GreenLake portal, the _____ feature allows administrators to track resource usage and optimize costs by analyzing trends and usage patterns over time.

A) Resource Allocation

B) Usage Analytics

C) Cost Management

D) Service Monitoring

E) Alerting System

F) Dashboard Overview

Answer: B

Explanation: The Usage Analytics feature in the HPE GreenLake portal is designed to provide administrators with detailed insights into resource usage and trends. By analyzing these patterns, administrators can make informed decisions to optimize costs and improve resource allocation. Usage Analytics allows for a comprehensive understanding of how resources are consumed over time, which helps in planning future capacity needs and preventing budget overruns. This feature is integral to effective hybrid IT management, ensuring that resources are used efficiently and aligned with business objectives.

Q4: Standard Multiple-Choice Question Which of the following actions can be performed via the HPE GreenLake portal to ensure compliance with company policies regarding data access and usage?

A) Disabling user access to the portal after business hours.

B) Creating automated compliance reports for audit purposes.

C) Enabling multi-factor authentication for all users.

D) Setting up a secure VPN for remote access.

E) Implementing a ticketing system for access requests.

F) Encrypting all data stored within the portal.

Answer: C

Explanation: Enabling multi-factor authentication (MFA) for all users is a critical step in ensuring compliance with company policies regarding data access and security. MFA adds an extra layer of security by requiring users to provide two or more verification factors to gain access to the portal, thus reducing the risk of unauthorized access. While options like automated compliance reports and secure VPNs contribute to overall security, MFA directly addresses access control, a key component of data security policies. Implementing MFA in the GreenLake portal aligns with best practices for safeguarding sensitive information and maintaining compliance with regulatory standards.

Q5: Standard Multiple-Choice Question What is the primary benefit of using the HPE GreenLake portal's Service Monitoring feature?

A) Reduces the need for manual reporting.

B) Automates the allocation of resources.

C) Provides real-time visibility into service health and performance.

D) Eliminates the need for third-party monitoring tools.

E) Offers predictive maintenance suggestions.

F) Enhances user interface customization.

Answer: C

Explanation: The primary benefit of the Service Monitoring feature in the HPE GreenLake portal is that it provides real-time visibility into the health and performance of services. This feature enables administrators to monitor the status and performance metrics of their IT resources continuously, ensuring that any potential issues are identified and addressed promptly. Real-time monitoring is crucial for maintaining optimal service levels, minimizing downtime, and ensuring that resources are functioning as expected. While other options like predictive maintenance and automation are valuable, the core advantage of Service Monitoring is its ability to offer immediate insights into service operations, thus supporting proactive management and troubleshooting.

Q6: Scenario-Based Question Your company, TechWave Solutions, recently adopted HPE GreenLake to manage its cloud services. As the lead IT administrator, you're responsible for setting up user accounts and permissions across the organization. The finance department needs access to billing and usage reports only, while the development team requires full access to compute resources and data analytics services. Additionally, the CEO should have a high-level overview of all operations without access to detailed technical configurations. How should you configure user roles to meet these specific requirements?

A) Assign the finance department to the 'Billing Administrator' role, the development team to the 'Service Administrator' role, and the CEO to the 'Read-Only Administrator' role.

B) Assign the finance department to the 'Read-Only Administrator' role, the development team to the 'Billing Administrator' role, and the CEO to the 'Service Administrator' role.

C) Assign the finance department to the 'Service Administrator' role, the development team to the 'Read-Only Administrator' role, and the CEO to the 'Billing Administrator' role.

D) Assign the finance department to the 'Data Analyst' role, the development team to the 'Infrastructure Administrator' role, and the CEO to the 'Compliance Officer' role.

E) Assign the finance department to the 'Billing Administrator' role, the development team to the 'Infrastructure Administrator' role, and the CEO to the 'Executive Viewer' role.

F) Assign the finance department to the 'Security Administrator' role, the development team to the 'Data Analyst' role, and the CEO to the 'Service Administrator' role.

Answer: E

Explanation: In HPE GreenLake, roles are designed to align with specific responsibilities. The 'Billing Administrator' role allows users to access billing and usage reports, making it ideal for the finance department. The 'Infrastructure Administrator' role provides full access to compute resources and data analytics services, suitable for the development team. The 'Executive Viewer' role gives the CEO a comprehensive overview without the ability to change configurations, fitting their need for high-level monitoring.

Q7: True/False Style Question In HPE GreenLake, a 'Service Administrator' has the ability to modify user account permissions.

A) True

B) False

Answer: A

Explanation: In HPE GreenLake, the 'Service Administrator' role is designed to manage and configure services, which includes the ability to modify user account permissions. This role is responsible for overseeing the implementation and maintenance of services, which necessitates the capacity to adjust user access to ensure that team members have appropriate permissions aligned with their functional needs.

Q8: When creating a new user account in HPE GreenLake, what is the first mandatory step you must perform?

A) Assign the user to a billing account.

B) Define the user's role and permissions.

C) Verify the user's email address.

D) Set up multi-factor authentication.

E) Configure the user's regional settings.

F) Add the user to a project group.

Answer: C

Explanation: The first mandatory step when creating a new user account in HPE GreenLake is to verify the user's email address. This step is crucial as it ensures that the user is valid and can receive communications related to their account. Email verification is a basic security measure to prevent unauthorized access and to confirm that the contact information is accurate for account notifications and password resets.

Q9: Which of the following best describes a 'Read-Only Administrator' role in HPE GreenLake?

A) Can modify user roles and permissions but cannot view billing details.

B) Can view all aspects of the infrastructure but cannot make any changes.

C) Can access billing details and create new user accounts.

D) Can manage compute resources but cannot access data analytics services.

E) Can perform infrastructure updates but cannot view usage reports.

F) Can access technical configurations and modify service parameters.

Answer: B

Explanation: The 'Read-Only Administrator' role in HPE GreenLake allows a user to view all aspects of the infrastructure without the ability to make any changes. This role is ideal for users who need to monitor and report on system status and configurations without the risk of altering settings or configurations, providing a secure way to oversee operations without affecting them.

Q10: In HPE GreenLake, what is the primary advantage of assigning a user to the 'Compliance Officer' role?

A) Ability to enforce security protocols across all services.

B) Full administrative access to modify all system settings.

C) Capability to audit system usage and generate compliance reports.

D) Permission to manage network configurations and policies.

E) Access to billing and usage data for financial analysis.

F) Rights to configure data storage and backup settings.

Answer: C

Explanation: The 'Compliance Officer' role in HPE GreenLake is specifically designed to audit system usage and generate compliance reports. This role is critical for organizations that need to adhere to regulatory standards and ensure that all operations are within compliance guidelines. By focusing on auditing capabilities, the Compliance Officer can help identify potential issues and ensure that all activities are documented and traceable for compliance purposes.

Q11: Scenario-Based Question Your company, a global retail chain, is using HPE GreenLake to manage its IT resources across multiple regions. Recently, the IT department noticed a spike in resource consumption and unexpected downtime during peak shopping hours. You are tasked with configuring alerts to ensure the IT team can proactively manage these issues. The goal is to minimize downtime and optimize resource usage. Considering the diverse operations across different time zones, you need a solution that allows for customized alerts based on specific thresholds and regions. Which configuration best suits this requirement?

A) Set a global alert threshold applicable to all regions and notify the central IT team.

B) Configure region-specific alert thresholds and assign local teams to manage alerts.

C) Use a single alert configuration with automated responses to all regions.

D) Implement a daily summary alert for all regions without specific thresholds.

E) Create alerts based on historical usage data aggregated over all regions.

F) Set up alerts focusing only on the regions with the highest sales volumes.

Answer: B

Explanation: Configuring region-specific alert thresholds and assigning local teams to manage alerts is the most effective strategy in this scenario. This approach allows for a tailored response to the unique conditions and requirements of each region, ensuring that alerts are relevant and actionable. Local teams can respond more quickly to issues due to their proximity and understanding of regional operations. A global alert threshold might not account for regional variations in usage, and automated responses could lead to inappropriate actions if not carefully designed for each region's needs. Historical data aggregation could inform thresholds but isn't sufficient on its own to manage current events, and focusing solely on high-sales regions might miss critical issues in other areas.

Q12: Standard Multiple-Choice Question Which component of HPE GreenLake allows for the configuration of alerts based on predefined templates?

A) HPE GreenLake Central Console

B) HPE InfoSight

C) HPE OneView

D) HPE CloudPhysics

E) HPE Aruba Central

F) HPE Synergy

Answer: A

Explanation: The HPE GreenLake Central Console is the primary interface for managing and configuring alerts within the HPE GreenLake environment. It provides predefined templates that simplify the process of setting up alerts, allowing administrators to quickly establish thresholds and notifications tailored to their specific operational needs. Although HPE InfoSight and HPE OneView offer insights and management capabilities, the central console is the designated tool for alert configuration in the GreenLake ecosystem.

Q13: Fill-in-the-Gap Multiple-Choice Question In HPE GreenLake, an alert can be configured to trigger notifications via email, SMS, or _____.

A) Slack

B) Telegram

C) Microsoft Teams

D) WhatsApp

E) Discord

F) PagerDuty

Answer: C

Explanation: Microsoft Teams is increasingly integrated into enterprise IT ecosystems, and HPE GreenLake supports triggering notifications through this platform. This integration allows for seamless communication and collaboration among IT team members, ensuring that alerts are seen and addressed promptly. While other messaging and collaboration platforms are popular, Microsoft Teams is specifically supported by HPE GreenLake for alert notifications, enhancing workflow efficiency and response times.

Q14: True/False Question HPE GreenLake alerts can be configured to automatically resolve events without any manual intervention.
A) True

B) False

Answer: B

Explanation: While HPE GreenLake provides extensive capabilities for alert management, including automated notifications and integrations with various tools, the resolution of events typically requires some level of manual intervention or predefined automated actions configured by an administrator. The system itself does not automatically resolve events without any setup. Automation can facilitate the process, but administrators must define the rules and responses to specific alerts.

Q15: Standard Multiple-Choice Question Which best practice should be followed when configuring alerts for HPE GreenLake to ensure efficient event management?

A) Set alerts to trigger for every minor change in resource utilization.

B) Use a single alerting strategy for all types of resources.

C) Regularly review and adjust alert thresholds based on operational changes.

D) Disable alerts during non-peak hours to reduce noise.

E) Rely solely on automated responses for all alerts.

F) Configure alerts to notify only the IT director to streamline communication.

Answer: C

Explanation: Regularly reviewing and adjusting alert thresholds based on operational changes is a best practice for maintaining efficient event management within HPE GreenLake. As IT environments and business requirements evolve, alert configurations must be updated to remain effective and relevant. Setting thresholds too low can lead to alert fatigue, while too high thresholds might miss critical issues. A dynamic approach ensures that alerting remains appropriate to current conditions, enabling proactive management and minimizing downtime.

Q16: A mid-sized IT company, Tech Solutions Inc., has recently migrated its infrastructure to HPE GreenLake to enhance scalability and operational efficiency. The company is interested in integrating their existing monitoring tools with the HPE GreenLake platform to streamline operations. As the lead administrator, you are tasked with ensuring that the integration leverages APIs effectively for real-time data exchange and automation. Which API management tool would be most appropriate for this task, considering the need for secure, scalable, and controlled access to the HPE GreenLake APIs?

A) HPE OneView Global Dashboard

B) HPE GreenLake API Explorer

C) HPE Insight Control

D) HPE Synergy Image Streamer

E) HPE Cloud Service Automation

F) HPE Data Services Cloud Console

Answer: B

Explanation: The HPE GreenLake API Explorer is specifically designed for interacting with HPE GreenLake services through APIs. It provides a user-friendly interface for developers and administrators to explore available APIs, making it ideal for integrating existing tools with the HPE GreenLake platform. The API Explorer ensures secure and controlled access by offering detailed documentation and examples, which are critical for facilitating real-time data exchange and automation. Other options like HPE OneView Global Dashboard or HPE Insight Control cater to different aspects of infrastructure management and do not offer the same API-focused capabilities.

Q17: True/False: The HPE GreenLake CLI is capable of automating resource provisioning and monitoring without the need for additional scripting languages.
A) True

B) False

Answer: B

Explanation: While the HPE GreenLake CLI is a powerful tool for managing resources, it typically requires integration with additional scripting languages to automate more complex workflows. The CLI can execute commands and perform standard tasks, but for comprehensive automation, administrators often incorporate scripting languages such as Python or PowerShell to enhance functionality and create custom automation scripts. This integration allows for sophisticated resource provisioning and monitoring that goes beyond the CLI's native capabilities.

Q18: Which command-line interface tool is specifically designed for managing HPE Synergy components, allowing administrators to automate and streamline workflows?

A) HPE GreenLake CLI

B) HPE Synergy Composer CLI

C) HPE OneView CLI

D) HPE iLO RESTful API

E) HPE Nimble Storage CLI

F) HPE Data Services Cloud Console CLI

Answer: B

Explanation: The HPE Synergy Composer CLI is tailored for managing HPE Synergy environments. It enables administrators to automate and streamline various workflows associated with Synergy components, such as composable infrastructure management. Unlike the more general-purpose HPE GreenLake CLI or HPE OneView CLI, the Synergy Composer CLI is specifically optimized for tasks related to HPE Synergy, providing the necessary commands and features to efficiently manage the composable infrastructure components.

Q19: Fill in the gap: The _____ is an HPE tool that provides comprehensive lifecycle management for server infrastructure, allowing for automation and orchestration of server configurations through an intuitive interface.

A) HPE OneView

B) HPE iLO Amplifier Pack

C) HPE GreenLake Central

D) HPE SimpliVity

E) HPE Cloud Volume Block

F) HPE InfoSight

Answer: A

Explanation: HPE OneView is designed to provide comprehensive lifecycle management for server infrastructure. It enables automation and orchestration of server configurations through an intuitive interface, allowing administrators to streamline operations and reduce manual intervention. HPE OneView integrates with other tools and platforms to offer a holistic approach to infrastructure management, enhancing efficiency and reliability across the IT environment.

Q20: A retail company is planning to implement a centralized management solution for its distributed IT resources across several locations. They need a tool that offers a unified API for managing different hardware platforms, simplifies resource allocation, and enhances reporting capabilities. Which HPE management tool would best meet these requirements?
A) HPE InfoSight

B) HPE Synergy Image Streamer

C) HPE OneView

D) HPE Cloud Service Automation

E) HPE GreenLake Central

F) HPE Data Services Cloud Console

Answer: C

Explanation: HPE OneView is the ideal choice for managing distributed IT resources across various locations. It provides a unified API that supports a wide range of hardware platforms, making it suitable for centralized management in diverse environments. HPE OneView simplifies resource allocation and enhances reporting capabilities by offering a single pane of glass for infrastructure management. This enables organizations to efficiently monitor, report, and manage their IT resources, ensuring consistency and operational effectiveness across different sites.

Q21: Your company, TechSolutions Inc., has recently adopted HPE GreenLake for managing its hybrid cloud environment. You are responsible for ensuring optimal application performance across both on-premises and cloud resources. Recently, users have reported latency issues with a critical financial application during peak business hours. The application is hosted on a mix of local servers and cloud instances. You suspect the issue could be related to resource allocation or network bottlenecks. As an HPE GreenLake Administrator, which of the following actions should you prioritize to diagnose and potentially resolve the performance issue?

A) Increase the bandwidth capacity for all network connections.

B) Utilize the HPE GreenLake Central platform to analyze historical performance data and identify trends.

C) Implement additional cloud instances to handle increased loads.

D) Conduct a manual audit of all server configurations and settings.

E) Engage external consultants for a comprehensive network assessment.

F) Schedule downtime for the application to perform a full system reboot.

Answer: B

Explanation: Utilizing the HPE GreenLake Central platform to analyze historical performance data is the most effective initial step. This tool provides insights into performance trends and resource utilization, enabling you to pinpoint whether the issue is due to resource constraints, network bottlenecks, or other factors. By examining historical data, you can correlate periods of poor performance with specific resource usage patterns or external factors, which is crucial for informed decision-making. Increasing bandwidth or adding instances without understanding the root cause could lead to unnecessary costs and complexity. A manual audit or engaging consultants should be considered only if internal analysis does not yield clear results.

Q22: True or False: Application performance monitoring in HPE GreenLake can automatically adjust resource allocation to optimize performance.
A) True

B) False

Answer: B

Explanation: False. While HPE GreenLake provides comprehensive monitoring capabilities and insights into application performance, automatic adjustment of resource allocation based on performance data is not an inherent feature of the platform. Administrators must analyze the data and make informed decisions about resource adjustments to optimize performance. This approach allows for more deliberate and context-aware resource management, avoiding potential misconfigurations or over-provisioning.

Q23: Which of the following metrics is least relevant when monitoring application performance using HPE GreenLake tools?
A) CPU usage

B) Memory utilization

C) Disk I/O speed

D) User satisfaction scores

E) Network latency

F) Server uptime

Answer: D

Explanation: User satisfaction scores, while important for overall business strategy and user experience, are not directly monitored by HPE GreenLake tools as part of application performance metrics. HPE GreenLake focuses on technical metrics like CPU usage, memory utilization, disk I/O speed, network latency, and server uptime to provide insights into the performance and health of applications and infrastructure. User satisfaction scores are typically gathered through separate surveys or feedback mechanisms and require qualitative analysis outside the scope of technical monitoring tools.

Q24: A company using HPE GreenLake is experiencing a decline in application performance. As an administrator, you decide to use synthetic transactions as part of your monitoring strategy. What is the primary purpose of implementing synthetic transactions?

A) To audit security compliance of applications.

B) To simulate user activity and measure application response times.

C) To back up application data regularly.

D) To automate software updates and patches.

E) To track historical data of application usage.

F) To manage user access control policies.

Answer: B

Explanation: Synthetic transactions are designed to simulate user interactions with applications to measure response times and performance under controlled conditions. This proactive monitoring technique helps identify potential performance issues before they impact real users. By creating consistent and repeatable test scenarios, synthetic transactions provide valuable insights into application behavior and responsiveness, aiding in the identification of bottlenecks or inefficiencies. This is distinct from auditing security, managing data backups, automating updates, tracking historical data, or managing access control.

Q25: During a routine performance review, you notice inconsistent application response times in HPE GreenLake's performance reports. To ensure accurate monitoring, which step should you take first?

A) Reboot all servers hosting the application.

B) Verify that the monitoring agents are correctly installed and configured.

C) Increase the frequency of data collection from once per hour to every five minutes.

D) Migrate the application to a more powerful server.

E) Remove all existing monitoring tools and start from scratch.

F) Conduct a full application code review for performance optimization.

Answer: B

Explanation: Verifying that the monitoring agents are correctly installed and configured is a critical first step. Inaccurate data collection can lead to misleading reports and, consequently, misguided decisions. Ensuring that agents are functioning properly and collecting data at intended intervals is fundamental for reliable performance monitoring. Rebooting servers or migrating applications should be considered only if monitoring confirms the need for such actions. Increasing data collection frequency or conducting an application code review might be necessary later, but these actions depend on first confirming that monitoring data is accurate and complete.

Q26: Scenario-based A medium-sized retail company has been using HPE GreenLake to manage their infrastructure. The IT team is tasked with automating their resource management to reduce operational costs and improve efficiency. They decide to use REST APIs to automate the creation and management of virtual machines (VMs). The team wants to ensure that the automation script they develop can handle the creation of multiple VMs based on specific criteria such as CPU, memory, and storage requirements, and can also provide error handling for any unsuccessful API calls. Which of the following steps should the IT team prioritize to ensure a successful automation setup?

A) Begin by developing a script that sequentially makes API calls without validating the responses.

B) Use POST requests to create VMs and implement error handling to retry failed requests.

C) Implement a monitoring system to manually track API call success rates.

D) Focus on writing API calls to delete VMs first to understand the API's response structure.

E) Develop a script that logs only successful API responses for future reference.

F) Use GET requests to retrieve VM metrics before attempting to create new VMs.

Answer: B

Explanation: The correct step to prioritize is to use POST requests to create VMs, while implementing error handling to retry failed requests. In a REST API context, POST requests are typically used to create new resources, and error handling is crucial for automation because it ensures that temporary issues do not lead to permanent failures of the automation script. Implementing retries for failed requests can help mitigate issues such as network instability or temporary API unavailability. This approach not only ensures a more robust automation process but also aligns with best practices in API usage by accommodating transient faults, which are common in networked applications. Monitoring and logging are also important, but they supplement rather than replace the need for proper error handling.

Q27: True/False When using HPE GreenLake REST APIs, it is mandatory to authenticate each API request with an OAuth token.

A) True

B) False

Answer: A

Explanation: It is true that HPE GreenLake REST APIs require authentication for each API request, typically using an OAuth token. OAuth is a standard authorization protocol that provides secure delegated access, allowing applications to access resources without exposing user credentials. By using OAuth tokens, HPE GreenLake ensures that API calls are authorized and secure, preventing unauthorized access to the infrastructure. This requirement is part of the security model to protect sensitive data and operations within the GreenLake platform.

Q28: Which HTTP method should you use with the HPE GreenLake REST API to update the configuration of an existing virtual machine?

A) GET

B) POST

C) PUT

D) DELETE

E) HEAD

F) OPTIONS

Answer: C

Explanation: The HTTP method PUT is typically used to update an existing resource in RESTful APIs. In the context of HPE GreenLake, if you need to update the configuration of an existing virtual machine, you would use a PUT request. This method is designed for idempotent operations, meaning multiple identical requests should have the same effect as a single request. Using PUT ensures that the resource is updated with the data provided in the request body, making it the appropriate choice for configuration updates.

Q29: While automating task execution in HPE GreenLake using REST APIs, which of the following best describes a 'stateless' operation?

A) An operation that maintains a session state across multiple API calls.

B) An operation where each request from the client must contain all necessary information.

C) An operation that requires synchronization between multiple API requests.

D) An operation that relies on server-side cookies to maintain state.

E) An operation that automatically retries failed requests without client intervention.

F) An operation that uses WebSockets to maintain a real-time connection.

Answer: B

Explanation: A stateless operation, in the context of REST APIs, is one where each individual request from the client must contain all the information needed for the server to fulfill that request. This is a fundamental principle of RESTful architecture, which promotes scalability and reliability by ensuring that each request is independent and does not rely on session data stored on the server. This design allows for simpler server architectures and easier scaling, as the server does not need to track the state of client interactions.

Q30: To ensure secure communication when automating tasks with REST APIs in HPE GreenLake, which protocol should be used?

A) FTP

B) HTTP

C) SMTP

D) HTTPS

E) SSH

F) Telnet

Answer: D

Explanation: HTTPS (Hypertext Transfer Protocol Secure) should be used to ensure secure communication when automating tasks with REST APIs in HPE GreenLake. HTTPS is the secure version of HTTP and uses encryption protocols such as TLS (Transport Layer Security) to encrypt data exchanged between the client and server. This encryption protects sensitive information from eavesdropping, tampering, and man-in-the-middle attacks. Using HTTPS is a best practice in API communication to ensure data integrity and confidentiality, making it essential for secure operations in cloud environments like HPE GreenLake.

Q31: Scenario-Based Question XYZ Corporation recently migrated its core applications to the HPE GreenLake platform. They need to ensure that their data backup and disaster recovery strategies are robust enough to minimize downtime and data loss in case of a catastrophic event. The company operates in a highly regulated industry where data integrity and availability are critical. As the GreenLake administrator, you are tasked with designing a backup solution that not only adheres to industry regulations but also aligns with the company's business continuity plans. Which of the following strategies should you recommend to best meet XYZ Corporation's needs for backup and disaster recovery?

A) Implement a local backup solution using traditional tape storage for weekly backups.

B) Utilize HPE GreenLake's built-in snapshot capabilities for daily backups and keep snapshots for 30 days.

C) Configure a hybrid cloud backup solution with automatic failover to a secondary data center.

D) Set up a third-party cloud-based backup service with end-to-end encryption and daily backups.

E) Deploy an on-premises disk-to-disk backup system with monthly offsite replication.

F) Establish a manual backup process where IT staff perform daily backups to external hard drives.

Answer: C

Explanation: In a highly regulated industry, ensuring data availability and integrity during a disaster is crucial. A hybrid cloud backup solution with automatic failover is optimal because it provides both local and cloud-based data protection, reducing the risk of data loss and minimizing downtime. This approach allows for rapid recovery and business continuity, which is critical for meeting regulatory requirements. Additionally, automatic failover ensures that critical applications remain available even if the primary data center is compromised, aligning with the company's business continuity plans. Traditional methods like tape storage or manual backups do not offer the speed and reliability required in this scenario.

Q32: True/False Question HPE GreenLake's disaster recovery solutions can be seamlessly integrated with existing on-premises infrastructure without requiring a complete overhaul of current systems.
A) True

B) False

Answer: A

Explanation: HPE GreenLake is designed to provide flexible and scalable solutions that integrate with existing IT infrastructure. This capability allows organizations to enhance their disaster recovery strategies without the need for a complete overhaul of their current systems. By utilizing GreenLake's offerings, companies can leverage their existing investments while adopting advanced cloud-based disaster recovery solutions. This integration capability is crucial for organizations seeking to modernize their IT infrastructure incrementally.

Q33: When setting up a disaster recovery plan in HPE GreenLake, which of the following is the most critical factor to ensure minimal data loss and quick recovery times?

A) The speed of the network connection between primary and secondary sites.

B) The geographical distance between the data centers.

C) The frequency of backup data replication.

D) The type of storage hardware used.

E) The number of IT staff available to manage the recovery.

F) The software version of the GreenLake platform.

Answer: C

Explanation: The frequency of backup data replication is crucial for minimizing data loss and ensuring quick recovery times. Frequent replication means that the data at the secondary site is as up-to-date as possible, reducing the amount of data lost in the event of a disaster. While other factors like network speed and geographical distance can affect recovery times, they are secondary to the importance of how often data is replicated. Frequent replication ensures that businesses can meet their Recovery Point Objectives (RPOs) effectively.

Q34: Which HPE GreenLake feature specifically helps in reducing the overhead and complexity of managing backup and disaster recovery operations?

A) Automated billing and usage reports.

B) Built-in AI-powered monitoring and alerts.

C) Centralized data governance policies.

D) Flexible service-level agreements (SLAs).

E) Automated workload balancing across regions.

F) Integrated backup and recovery dashboard.

Answer: F

Explanation: The integrated backup and recovery dashboard in HPE GreenLake simplifies the management of backup and disaster recovery operations by providing a centralized platform for monitoring and managing these tasks. This feature reduces overhead by offering visibility into backup schedules, status, and potential issues, allowing administrators to quickly address any problems. By consolidating management tools, it reduces complexity and helps ensure that backup and disaster recovery processes are efficient and reliable.

Q35: In the context of HPE GreenLake's disaster recovery solutions, what is the primary benefit of utilizing data deduplication during the backup process?

A) It increases the speed of data retrieval during recovery.

B) It enhances the security of stored data.

C) It reduces the overall cost of storage.

D) It improves compatibility with third-party software.

E) It simplifies data compliance management.

F) It decreases the time required for data encryption.

Answer: C

Explanation: Data deduplication reduces the overall cost of storage by eliminating redundant copies of data, ensuring that only unique data blocks are stored. This significantly decreases the amount of storage space required, which is particularly beneficial in cloud-based solutions like HPE GreenLake, where storage costs can accumulate. While deduplication can also indirectly improve retrieval speed and efficiency by reducing the volume of data to be processed, its primary benefit is the cost savings achieved through optimized storage utilization.

Q36: Scenario-Based A mid-sized e-commerce company, XYZ Corp, heavily relies on HPE GreenLake for their IT infrastructure, aiming to scale their operations during high-demand seasons. The finance team has noticed fluctuating monthly bills and is concerned about the lack of clarity regarding cost allocation across different departments such as IT, marketing, and customer service. The IT manager needs to provide a clear breakdown of resource usage and associated costs to ensure each department is accountable for their consumption. Which feature of HPE GreenLake can best assist the IT manager in addressing the finance team's concerns about billing transparency and departmental cost allocation?

A) HPE GreenLake Central Dashboard

B) HPE GreenLake QuickSight Integration

C) HPE Consumption Analytics Portal

D) HPE Cloud Cruiser

E) HPE Resource Pooling Manager

F) HPE Usage Optimizer

Answer: C

Explanation: The HPE Consumption Analytics Portal is designed to provide detailed insights into resource usage and costs. It allows users to break down consumption by different departments or projects within the organization, offering a transparent view of how resources are being utilized. This feature is especially useful for companies like XYZ Corp that need to allocate costs accurately across departments, ensuring accountability and helping the finance team track and manage their budget more effectively. Unlike the dashboard, which provides a high-level overview, the Consumption Analytics Portal offers granular data necessary for detailed analysis.

Q37: True or False: HPE GreenLake's billing transparency features allow users to review real-time usage data and cost estimates, but not to set budget thresholds or alerts.

A) True

B) False

Answer: B

Explanation: False. HPE GreenLake not only provides real-time usage data and cost estimates but also allows users to set budget thresholds and receive alerts when those thresholds are nearing or exceeded. This functionality is crucial for proactive financial management and helps organizations prevent unexpected overspending by notifying stakeholders in advance.

Q38: Which of the following best describes the primary advantage of using HPE GreenLake's usage metrics for enterprises aiming to optimize resource allocation?

A) Provides historical data analysis for financial audits

B) Ensures compliance with regulatory standards

C) Offers predictive analytics to prevent resource shortages

D) Automates the scaling of physical resources

E) Enhances security through detailed access logs

F) Supports multi-cloud environment integration

Answer: C

Explanation: The primary advantage of using HPE GreenLake's usage metrics is the capability of predictive analytics to forecast resource needs and prevent shortages. By analyzing current and historical usage patterns, organizations can anticipate future demands and allocate resources accordingly. This foresight is crucial for optimizing resource allocation, reducing wastage, and ensuring that the infrastructure can handle peak loads efficiently without unnecessary over-provisioning.

Q39: In the context of HPE GreenLake, which of the following actions can help an IT administrator reduce unexpected billing surges?

A) Decrease the frequency of usage data updates

B) Implement detailed tagging of resources

C) Disable underutilized virtual machines manually

D) Increase the default storage capacity

E) Activate automatic scaling without monitoring

F) Utilize third-party billing software

Answer: B

Explanation: Implementing detailed tagging of resources is an effective strategy for reducing unexpected billing surges. It allows for precise tracking and management of resource usage across various departments or projects. By having a clear understanding of which resources are being utilized and by whom, IT administrators can identify unnecessary expenditures, optimize resource allocation, and prevent unexpected billing increases. Unlike decreasing update frequency or disabling VMs manually, tagging offers a proactive and organized approach to cost management.

Q40: Fill in the gap: HPE GreenLake's billing transparency is enhanced through the use of _____, which enables businesses to simulate potential future costs based on current consumption patterns.

A) predictive costing models

B) cost allocation algorithms

C) real-time billing monitors

D) historical usage reports

E) budgetary assessment tools

F) resource management dashboards

Answer: A

Explanation: Predictive costing models are instrumental in enhancing billing transparency within HPE GreenLake. They analyze current consumption patterns and simulate potential future costs, allowing businesses to plan and budget more effectively. This capability aids organizations in anticipating financial needs, avoiding surprises in billing, and making informed decisions about resource allocation. Unlike simple historical reports or dashboards, predictive models provide a forward-looking perspective that is essential for strategic planning and financial forecasting.

Q41: Scenario-Based Question A multinational corporation, TechInnovate, is facing challenges with predicting its IT infrastructure needs across various regions. The company uses HPE GreenLake for its on-premises cloud services. The IT director has noticed significant variations in demand, particularly during product launches and end-of-quarter financial closings, causing either resource shortages or underutilization. To ensure optimal performance and cost efficiency, the director wants to implement a robust capacity forecasting and planning strategy. The company operates in diverse geographical locations with varying market demands and regulatory requirements. Which approach should the IT director prioritize to effectively manage this complexity?   ---

A) Implement a fixed capacity model to ensure resources are always available.

B) Use historical data from the last quarter to set future capacity needs.

C) Develop a dynamic capacity model with real-time analytics and scaling.

D) Rely solely on regional IT managers to report their capacity needs.

E) Increase capacity based on the highest demand observed in any region.

F) Focus on predictive analytics to identify potential bottlenecks before they occur.

Answer: C

Explanation: Effective capacity forecasting and planning in a dynamic and geographically dispersed environment like TechInnovate's requires a flexible and responsive approach. Implementing a dynamic capacity model with real-time analytics and scaling (option C) allows the company to adjust its resources based on current demand, leading to cost efficiency and optimal resource utilization. Fixed models (option A) or static historical data analysis (option B) do not account for unexpected variations in demand. Sole reliance on regional reporting (option D) or planning based on peak demands (option E) could lead to inefficiencies and increased costs. Predictive analytics (option F) is a valuable tool, but alone it may not provide the agility needed without the support of dynamic scaling capabilities.

Q42: Multiple-Choice Question In the context of HPE GreenLake's capacity forecasting and planning, which tool or feature provides the ability to proactively manage resource allocation by predicting future consumption patterns?   ---

A) HPE InfoSight

B) HPE OneView

C) GreenLake Central Dashboard

D) HPE iLO

E) HPE Synergy

F) HPE Cloud Volumes

Answer: A

Explanation: HPE InfoSight is a powerful analytics platform that utilizes AI and machine learning to predict future consumption patterns and optimize resource allocation. By analyzing vast amounts of telemetry data, InfoSight provides insights into capacity trends, enabling proactive management and preventing potential resource shortages. HPE OneView (option B) focuses on infrastructure management but lacks the predictive analytics capabilities of InfoSight. The GreenLake Central Dashboard (option C) provides an overview of resource usage but does not predict future patterns. HPE iLO (option D) and HPE Synergy (option E) are more focused on hardware management. HPE Cloud Volumes (option F) relates to cloud storage services and not specifically to predictive capacity planning.

Q43: Multiple-Choice Question When planning for future capacity needs using HPE GreenLake, which metric is most critical for aligning resource allocation with business goals?   ---

A) Total Cost of Ownership (TCO)

B) Peak Utilization

C) Average Latency

D) Storage IOPS

E) User Satisfaction Index

F) Capacity Buffer Percentage

Answer: B

Explanation: Peak Utilization is a key metric when planning future capacity needs because it indicates the maximum level of resource consumption during a given period. Understanding peak utilization helps businesses ensure they have sufficient resources to handle the highest levels of demand without experiencing performance degradation. While Total Cost of Ownership (option A), Average Latency (option C), Storage IOPS (option D), and User Satisfaction Index (option E) are important, they do not directly inform the alignment of capacity with demand peaks. Capacity Buffer Percentage (option F) is useful for planning but should be informed by peak utilization data.

Q44: True/False Question HPE GreenLake allows organizations to only scale their capacity vertically, meaning adding more resources to existing infrastructure rather than expanding to new infrastructure.   ---

A) True

B) False

Answer: B

Explanation: The statement is false. HPE GreenLake offers the flexibility to scale capacity both vertically and horizontally. Vertical scaling involves adding more resources such as CPU or memory to existing infrastructure, while horizontal scaling involves adding more nodes or instances to the current setup. This flexibility is critical for organizations to efficiently manage varying workloads and demands, ensuring that they can adapt to both increasing and decreasing resource needs.

Q45: Multiple-Choice Question In a scenario where a company using HPE GreenLake experiences unpredictable spikes in workload, what strategy should be employed to ensure cost-effective and efficient capacity planning?

A) Overprovision resources to handle any possible spike.

B) Use a pay-as-you-grow model to align costs with usage.

C) Schedule regular manual reviews to adjust capacity.

D) Implement static thresholds for resource allocation.

E) Utilize a hybrid cloud strategy with predefined limits.

F) Develop a custom AI model to predict spikes.

Answer: B

Explanation: A pay-as-you-grow model is ideal for managing unpredictable spikes in workload because it allows the company to align costs directly with actual usage. This approach ensures that resources are available as needed without incurring unnecessary expenses from overprovisioning (option A). Regular reviews (option C) can be labor-intensive and may not respond quickly enough to sudden changes. Static thresholds (option D) lack flexibility. A hybrid cloud strategy (option E) can be effective but adds complexity. Custom AI models (option F) may provide insights but require significant development and maintenance resources. The pay-as-you-grow model offers a balance of flexibility, cost efficiency, and scalability.

Q46: Scenario-Based Question Your company, a medium-sized e-commerce business, has recently transitioned to using HPE GreenLake to manage its IT resources more efficiently. Over the past few months, you've noticed that your data storage requirements have fluctuated significantly due to seasonal sales spikes. To ensure you maintain optimal capacity without overcommitting resources, you need to develop a strategy to optimize your existing storage capacity while accommodating these fluctuations. You are considering various strategies, including predictive analytics, tiered storage, and data deduplication, to ensure cost-efficiency and performance. Which strategy would be most effective in optimizing storage capacity in this scenario?

A) Implementing predictive analytics to forecast storage needs based on historical data patterns.

B) Increasing overall storage capacity to handle peak demands.

C) Utilizing tiered storage to automatically move less frequently accessed data to lower-cost storage.

D) Regularly archiving data to external storage to free up space.

E) Manual monitoring and adjustment of storage capacity based on current needs.

F) Applying data deduplication to eliminate redundant data across the storage system.

Answer: C

Explanation: Utilizing tiered storage is the most effective strategy in this scenario. This approach allows the business to automatically manage fluctuating storage demands by moving less critical and infrequently accessed data to cheaper storage tiers, thus optimizing costs without sacrificing performance. Predictive analytics, while useful, may not be as effective in managing immediate fluctuations. Increasing overall storage is cost-inefficient, and manual monitoring might lead to delays and inaccuracies. Data deduplication helps in saving space but does not directly address the challenge of fluctuating demand. Regular archiving might not be practical for managing frequent and rapid changes in data requirements.

Q47: True/False Question True or False: HPE GreenLake's capacity optimization strategies primarily focus on increasing the physical storage capacity available to the customer.

A) True

B) False

Answer: B

Explanation: False. HPE GreenLake's capacity optimization strategies are primarily focused on efficient utilization and management of existing resources rather than merely increasing physical storage. Strategies such as predictive analytics, tiered storage, and data deduplication aim to optimize how storage is used, ensuring that businesses can handle their needs dynamically and cost-effectively without unnecessary investments in additional physical capacity.

Q48: When implementing predictive analytics for capacity optimization in HPE GreenLake, which of the following is the most critical factor to consider to ensure accurate forecasts?

A) The current market trends and customer behavior data.

B) Historical data usage patterns and trends.

C) The overall budget allocated for IT resources.

D) The number of IT staff available to manage the systems.

E) The availability of third-party analytics tools.

F) The geographic location of the data centers.

Answer: B

Explanation: Historical data usage patterns and trends are crucial for accurate forecasts when employing predictive analytics. By analyzing past data, businesses can identify patterns and anticipate future needs, allowing them to optimize capacity efficiently. Market trends and customer behavior are secondary factors, as they may not directly influence internal data usage. Budget, staff availability, third-party tools, and geographic location are important considerations but do not directly impact the accuracy of capacity forecasts.

Q49: Which of the following HPE GreenLake capacity optimization strategies directly reduces the burden on primary storage by minimizing the volume of inactive data stored?

A) Real-time data compression.

B) Predictive analytics for workload balancing.

C) Tiered storage management.

D) Regular system audits.

E) Data deduplication.

F) Implementing strict data access policies.

Answer: C

Explanation: Tiered storage management directly reduces the burden on primary storage by automatically moving inactive or less frequently accessed data to lower-cost storage tiers. This ensures that only active and critical data occupies the more expensive high-performance storage, optimizing cost and performance. Real-time compression and deduplication optimize storage space but do not specifically target inactive data. Predictive analytics, system audits, and access policies help in overall management but do not directly manage inactive data storage.

Q50: Fill-in-the-gap: In the context of HPE GreenLake, _____ is a strategy that involves identifying and eliminating duplicate copies of repeating data to optimize storage usage.

A) Real-time analytics

B) Data archiving

C) Data deduplication

D) Predictive modeling

E) Storage virtualization

F) Continuous monitoring

Answer: C

Explanation: Data deduplication is the strategy that focuses on identifying and eliminating duplicate copies of repeating data to optimize storage usage. This approach helps in significantly reducing the amount of data that needs to be stored, thereby optimizing the storage capacity and reducing costs. Real-time analytics, archiving, predictive modeling, virtualization, and monitoring each have their roles in capacity management but do not specifically target the reduction of duplicated data.

Q51: Scenario-Based Question A mid-sized company, TechDynamics, has recently transitioned to HPE GreenLake for its IT infrastructure needs. The company is particularly keen on using the centralized dashboard management feature to streamline its operations. The IT team wants to monitor resource utilization, track performance metrics, and ensure compliance with internal policies from a single pane of glass. However, they are also concerned about data security and ensuring that only authorized personnel have access to sensitive information. The team has been tasked with setting up the dashboard to meet these requirements. Which of the following steps should the IT team prioritize to effectively utilize the centralized dashboard management features while addressing their concerns? ---

A) Integrate third-party security software for enhanced data protection.

B) Set up role-based access controls to limit dashboard access.

C) Customize the dashboard to display only compliance-related metrics.

D) Implement automated alerts for resource utilization thresholds.

E) Schedule regular training sessions for all IT staff on dashboard usage.

F) Develop a custom API to extend dashboard functionalities.

Answer: B

Explanation: When using HPE GreenLake's centralized dashboard management, it is crucial to first establish role-based access controls (RBAC). This step ensures that only authorized personnel can view or modify sensitive information, addressing data security concerns. Role-based access helps in defining clear permissions for different users, thereby reducing the risk of unauthorized access. While other options like integrating third-party software or setting up alerts are beneficial, RBAC directly targets the security concern mentioned in the scenario. Ensuring that staff only have access to the information necessary for their roles enhances data protection and aligns with best practices for managing IT resources.

Q52: True/False Question The centralized dashboard in HPE GreenLake allows for real-time monitoring of all connected devices and services without the need for additional configuration. ---

A) True

B) False

Answer: B

Explanation: The statement is false because, while HPE GreenLake's centralized dashboard does provide extensive monitoring capabilities, it often requires initial configuration to tailor the monitoring to specific business needs. Users must configure the dashboard to integrate with their existing IT systems and set up the necessary metrics and alerts to ensure effective real-time monitoring. This process includes defining the scope of monitoring, setting up data sources, and customizing the views to reflect the organization's operational priorities.

Q53: Which of the following features of HPE GreenLake's centralized dashboard management is most critical for a company looking to optimize its IT spending?

A) Real-time performance analytics

B) Predictive analytics for resource allocation

C) Automated compliance reporting

D) Integration with third-party applications

E) Network traffic visualization

F) User activity logs

Answer: B

Explanation: Predictive analytics for resource allocation is the most critical feature for optimizing IT spending. This feature provides insights into future resource needs based on current and historical usage patterns. By forecasting demand, companies can adjust their resource allocation proactively, minimizing wasteful spending and ensuring resources are available when needed. Real-time performance analytics and other features are valuable but do not directly address the cost optimization aspect as effectively as predictive analytics.

Q54: When configuring the centralized dashboard for a multinational corporation, which of the following customization options is most important to ensure effective global IT operations management?   ---

A) Language localization

B) Time zone synchronization

C) Multi-currency support

D) Customizable user interfaces

E) Region-specific compliance metrics

F) Integration with global communication tools

Answer: B

Explanation: Time zone synchronization is essential for a multinational corporation managing global IT operations. It ensures that all data and alerts are displayed in a consistent manner, regardless of the user's location. This synchronization simplifies coordination across different regions and ensures that performance metrics and alerts are accurately interpreted in the context of local operations. While other options like language localization and compliance metrics are important, time zone synchronization directly impacts the operational efficiency and accuracy of global IT management.

Q55: In HPE GreenLake, which feature of the centralized dashboard can significantly enhance decision-making by providing visual representation of data?

A) Text-based reports

B) Heatmaps

C) Tabular data views

D) Email notifications

E) Static graphs

F) System logs

Answer: B

Explanation: Heatmaps are a powerful feature in HPE GreenLake's centralized dashboard that significantly enhance decision-making by providing a visual representation of data. They offer a quick, intuitive way to identify trends, anomalies, and areas of concern across the IT infrastructure. By visualizing data in a color-coded format, heatmaps enable IT administrators and decision-makers to quickly assess the status of various systems and make informed decisions. While other features like text-based reports and graphs provide valuable information, heatmaps offer an immediate visual impact that aids in faster interpretation and action.

Q56: Scenario-Based Question A large retail company, RetailCorp, has been using HPE GreenLake for managing their IT infrastructure across multiple locations. Recently, they decided to integrate a new e-commerce platform to enhance their online presence. This integration requires updates to existing workloads and the deployment of new resources. The CIO emphasizes that these changes should not disrupt daily operations or compromise security. You are tasked with managing this change process. What is the most effective first step to ensure a smooth transition?

A) Immediately deploy the new resources during peak business hours to test their impact.

B) Conduct a comprehensive risk assessment and develop a change management plan.

C) Inform all stakeholders about the changes after they have been implemented.

D) Test the new e-commerce platform in a production environment to ensure compatibility.

E) Disable existing workloads temporarily to facilitate the integration.

F) Assign a single team member to oversee the entire change process without additional support.

Answer: B

Explanation: In any change management process, especially in a critical business context like RetailCorp's integration of a new e-commerce platform, the first step should be to conduct a comprehensive risk assessment. This involves identifying potential risks associated with the changes and crafting a detailed change management plan. This plan should outline the steps required to integrate the new platform, the resources needed, and the potential impacts on existing operations. This strategic approach helps ensure that the integration does not disrupt daily operations or compromise security, aligning with the CIO's priorities. Immediate deployment or testing in a production environment without prior assessment can lead to significant operational risks and security vulnerabilities.

Q57: True/False Question Change management in HPE GreenLake environments strictly follows ITIL (Information Technology Infrastructure Library) guidelines without any customization to specific organizational needs.
A) True

B) False

Answer: B

Explanation: While ITIL provides a comprehensive framework for IT service management, including change management, it is not a one-size-fits-all solution. In HPE GreenLake environments, change management processes can be customized to meet the specific needs and circumstances of the organization. This customization allows organizations to incorporate unique business requirements, regulatory considerations, and operational priorities that ITIL guidelines might not fully address. Therefore, stating that HPE GreenLake change management strictly follows ITIL without customization is incorrect.

Q58: When preparing for a major update in an HPE GreenLake environment, which of the following elements is most critical to include in the change management documentation?

A) A list of all team members involved in the project.

B) A detailed rollback plan in case the update fails.

C) The cost analysis of the update.

D) A marketing plan for announcing the update.

E) A list of competitors' IT changes.

F) A schedule of team-building activities post-update.

Answer: B

Explanation: A detailed rollback plan is crucial in change management documentation for any major update in an HPE GreenLake environment. This plan outlines the steps necessary to revert to the previous stable state if the update encounters issues. It includes data backup procedures, resource allocation for the rollback, and a communication strategy to inform stakeholders of the rollback. Having a solid rollback plan mitigates risks and ensures business continuity, which is vital in maintaining operational stability and stakeholder trust.

Q59: During a change management review for a GreenLake environment, a team discovers that a recent update has led to unexpected downtimes. What is the best course of action to address this issue?

A) Ignore the issue and proceed with further updates.

B) Revert to the previous version of the environment immediately.

C) Investigate the root cause of the downtimes before making further changes.

D) Communicate the downtime to external customers without internal review.

E) Blame the issue on the third-party vendors involved.

F) Conduct a team meeting to discuss non-related future projects.

Answer: C

Explanation: Investigating the root cause of unexpected downtimes is the best course of action. This approach involves analyzing system logs, reviewing update procedures, and evaluating the specific conditions that led to the issue. Understanding the root cause helps in developing a targeted solution that prevents recurrence and ensures that future updates do not lead to similar problems. Immediate reversion or blaming external parties without understanding the cause can result in repeated issues and does not contribute to a learning culture necessary for continuous improvement in change management processes.

Q60: In the context of change management for HPE GreenLake, which best practice ensures minimal disruption during the implementation of changes?

A) Implement changes during high-traffic periods for maximum visibility.

B) Involve only senior management in the change approval process.

C) Schedule changes during planned maintenance windows.

D) Make changes without prior testing in a staging environment.

E) Communicate changes after implementation to avoid unnecessary delays.

F) Focus solely on cost reduction as the main objective of the change.

Answer: C

Explanation: Scheduling changes during planned maintenance windows is a best practice that ensures minimal disruption. Maintenance windows are pre-defined periods when planned changes can be implemented with minimal impact on users and business operations. This approach allows for thorough testing and validation of changes in a controlled environment, facilitating smoother transitions. Ensuring that changes are well-communicated and adequately tested before implementation further reduces the risk of unforeseen issues, aligning with organizational goals of maintaining service reliability and customer satisfaction.

Q61: Scenario-based question XYZ Corporation is a multinational company utilizing HPE GreenLake to manage its IT resources. The company recently embarked on a project to deploy a new customer relationship management (CRM) system, estimating a need for 200 virtual machines (VMs) and 500 TB of storage over the next year. The IT team has been monitoring the actual resource usage through the HPE GreenLake dashboard and noticed discrepancies between the planned and actual usage. While they planned for a gradual increase, actual usage has shown sporadic spikes and dips, likely due to unanticipated project timelines and fluctuating user demand. As the project lead, you're tasked with presenting these findings to senior management and recommending adjustments to the resource allocation strategy. What is the most appropriate initial step to take in analyzing and addressing the discrepancies in planned versus actual resource usage?

A) Conduct a detailed trend analysis of the resource usage data over the past year to identify patterns.

B) Immediately increase resource allocations to accommodate the sporadic spikes in usage.

C) Schedule a meeting with the CRM project team to discuss the unexpected usage patterns.

D) Implement automated scaling policies to dynamically adjust resources based on real-time usage.

E) Request additional funding to cover potential shortfalls in resource availability.

F) Ignore the discrepancies for now, as they are likely to stabilize over time.

Answer: A

Explanation: A detailed trend analysis of the resource usage data is crucial for understanding the nature of the discrepancies observed. By identifying patterns and correlating them with project timelines and user activities, the IT team can pinpoint the root causes of the sporadic spikes and dips in usage. This analysis will provide the necessary insights to develop a more accurate forecasting model, informing future resource planning and allocation strategies. Conducting this analysis as an initial step ensures that subsequent actions, such as adjusting resource allocations or implementing automated policies, are based on data-driven insights rather than reactive measures.

Q62: True/False Planned resource usage estimates in HPE GreenLake should always account for potential future growth to avoid resource shortfalls.
A) True

B) False

Answer: A

Explanation: True. When planning resource usage in HPE GreenLake, it's essential to account for potential future growth to avoid resource shortfalls, which can lead to performance issues and hinder project timelines. Anticipating future needs ensures that resources are provisioned adequately, providing a buffer for unexpected demands. This approach aligns with best practices in capacity planning, which advocate for a proactive strategy in managing IT infrastructure, especially in dynamic environments where demand can fluctuate.

Q63: Which of the following is NOT a typical consequence of failing to accurately compare planned versus actual resource usage in an HPE GreenLake environment?
A) Increased operational costs due to over-provisioning of resources.

B) Potential delays in project timelines due to resource shortages.

C) Enhanced efficiency in resource utilization with accurate planning.

D) Difficulty in justifying IT budget allocations to senior management.

E) Risk of service disruptions impacting business operations.

F) Improved predictive analytics for future resource planning.

Answer: F

Explanation: F is not a typical consequence of failing to accurately compare planned versus actual resource usage. Inaccurate comparisons can lead to increased operational costs, project delays, and difficulties in budget justifications, among other negative outcomes. Conversely, improved predictive analytics for future resource planning would typically result from an accurate comparison, as it allows the organization to refine its forecasting models based on past data. This refinement enables more efficient and effective resource management, preventing service disruptions and optimizing costs.

Q64: When analyzing planned versus actual resource usage in HPE GreenLake, which factor should be considered to ensure alignment with business objectives?

A) Historical resource consumption trends.

B) Current market conditions and competitor actions.

C) The personal preferences of the IT team.

D) Seasonal variations in business activity.

E) Regulatory compliance requirements.

F) The geographical location of the data center.

Answer: D

Explanation: Seasonal variations in business activity should be considered when analyzing planned versus actual resource usage to ensure alignment with business objectives. Many businesses experience fluctuations in demand at different times of the year, such as retail companies during holiday seasons or tax firms during tax season. Recognizing these patterns allows organizations to adjust their resource planning and allocations accordingly, ensuring that they can meet customer demands and maintain operational efficiency. While historical trends provide useful insights, aligning resource usage with anticipated seasonal peaks and troughs is critical for aligning with broader business goals.

Q65: In the context of HPE GreenLake, what is the primary benefit of using predictive analytics to compare planned versus actual resource usage?

A) It guarantees 100% accuracy in future resource forecasts.

B) It eliminates the need for manual monitoring of resource usage.

C) It provides insights that can enhance decision-making for capacity planning.

D) It allows for immediate adjustment of resources without human intervention.

E) It minimizes the need for financial investment in additional resources.

F) It ensures compliance with all industry regulations.

Answer: C

Explanation: Predictive analytics in HPE GreenLake provides insights that enhance decision-making for capacity planning. By analyzing historical and real-time data, predictive analytics tools can identify trends and patterns that help forecast future resource needs more accurately. This capability enables organizations to proactively adjust resource allocations, optimize costs, and support strategic business initiatives. While predictive analytics improves forecasting accuracy, it does not guarantee 100% accuracy, eliminate the need for human oversight, or automatically ensure regulatory compliance. It is a tool that supports informed decision-making and strategic planning.

Q66: Scenario-Based Question Your company, TechSolutions Inc., has recently implemented HPE GreenLake to manage its IT infrastructure. The company operates in a highly regulated industry and must adhere to stringent compliance requirements, including GDPR and HIPAA. The compliance team is concerned about ensuring that all audit logs are appropriately captured, stored securely, and reviewed regularly to meet these regulatory standards. As the HPE GreenLake Administrator, you have been tasked with configuring the compliance and audit logging features. The goal is to ensure that any non-compliance issues can be quickly identified and addressed. Which of the following actions should you prioritize to achieve this goal?

A) Enable automatic log archiving and set retention policies to meet regulatory requirements.

B) Configure alerting for any failed login attempts within the GreenLake environment.

C) Set up daily reports summarizing all user activities for compliance review.

D) Integrate GreenLake logs with a third-party SIEM tool for advanced threat detection.

E) Perform manual reviews of logs on a weekly basis to identify potential compliance breaches.

F) Ensure all logs are encrypted and stored in a secure, access-controlled environment.

Answer: A

Explanation: In a regulated industry, it is critical to ensure that audit logs are not only captured but also stored in a manner that complies with regulatory requirements. Automatic log archiving with defined retention policies ensures that logs are retained for the necessary period as dictated by regulations such as GDPR and HIPAA. This approach minimizes human error and ensures that logs are always available for review in case of an audit or investigation. While integrating logs with SIEM tools and configuring alerts are also important, the priority should be to establish a compliant log retention and archiving process first.

Q67: True/False Question HPE GreenLake provides native integration with third-party compliance management tools to enhance audit logging capabilities.

A) True

B) False

Answer: A

Explanation: HPE GreenLake offers native integration capabilities with various third-party compliance management tools. This integration allows organizations to enhance their audit logging capabilities by leveraging the advanced features of these third-party solutions, such as real-time monitoring, automated compliance checks, and detailed reporting. These capabilities are crucial for organizations aiming to maintain compliance with industry standards and regulations, providing a more comprehensive view of audit logs and potential compliance issues.

Q68: Standard Multiple-Choice Question Which of the following features in HPE GreenLake best supports the regular auditing of user access and activity within the platform?

A) User role management

B) Access control lists (ACLs)

C) Comprehensive audit trails

D) Automated compliance reporting

E) Multi-factor authentication

F) Real-time monitoring dashboards

Answer: C

Explanation: Comprehensive audit trails are vital for regularly auditing user access and activity within HPE GreenLake. These trails provide a detailed record of all user actions, including logins, configuration changes, and resource access. This level of detail is crucial for compliance audits, as it allows administrators to track user behavior and ensure that all actions are in line with organizational policies and regulatory requirements. While features like role management and multi-factor authentication enhance security, they do not provide the detailed historical records necessary for thorough audits.

Q69: Fill-in-the-Gap Question To ensure that your HPE GreenLake environment is compliant with data protection regulations, it is essential to _____.

A) Implement network segmentation

B) Regularly update system firmware

C) Conduct periodic security audits

D) Encrypt all stored and transmitted data

E) Use a dedicated compliance officer

F) Maintain an incident response plan

Answer: D

Explanation: Encrypting all stored and transmitted data is essential for compliance with data protection regulations such as GDPR and HIPAA. Encryption ensures that sensitive data remains confidential and protected from unauthorized access, both at rest and in transit. This practice is a fundamental component of many regulatory frameworks, which mandate the protection of personal and sensitive information. While other actions like conducting security audits and maintaining an incident response plan are important, encryption directly addresses data confidentiality and protection requirements.

Q70: Standard Multiple-Choice Question What is the primary benefit of integrating HPE GreenLake's audit logs with a Security Information and Event Management (SIEM) system?

A) Enhanced data storage efficiency

B) Improved user experience

C) Centralized log analysis and correlation

D) Reduced compliance costs

E) Simpler user access management

F) Automated firmware updates

Answer: C

Explanation: The primary benefit of integrating HPE GreenLake's audit logs with a SIEM system is centralized log analysis and correlation. SIEM systems are designed to aggregate logs from multiple sources, analyze them for patterns and anomalies, and correlate events to identify potential security threats or compliance issues. This centralized approach allows organizations to gain a comprehensive view of their security posture, quickly detect incidents, and respond effectively. While other benefits such as improved user experience or reduced costs may be secondary effects, the main advantage lies in the enhanced ability to monitor and manage compliance and security events.

Q71: Scenario-Based Question Your company, DataTech Solutions, is transitioning to a hybrid cloud model to improve flexibility and scalability. As part of this transition, you are tasked with configuring compute resources using HPE GreenLake to support a critical application that experiences variable demand throughout the year. The application requires burst capacity during peak times and minimal resources during off-peak periods. The CFO is particularly concerned about cost optimization while ensuring performance during peak demand. As the HPE GreenLake administrator, you need to configure the compute resources to align with these requirements. What configuration should you implement in HPE GreenLake to meet the company's needs?   ---

A) Configure auto-scaling rules to add resources during peak periods and remove them automatically during off-peak periods.

B) Allocate a fixed amount of compute resources to ensure consistent availability, regardless of demand.

C) Set up a pay-as-you-go model without any pre-provisioning to handle any demand fluctuations.

D) Pre-provision maximum resources for peak demand and manually adjust during off-peak periods.

E) Implement a resource quota system to limit usage during off-peak periods.

F) Schedule batch processing only during off-peak hours to save costs.

Answer: A

Explanation: In this scenario, the primary goal is to manage compute resources efficiently to handle fluctuating demand while optimizing costs. HPE GreenLake's auto-scaling capability is designed to address these challenges by dynamically allocating compute resources based on real-time demand. By configuring auto-scaling rules, you can ensure that additional resources are automatically provisioned during peak periods and de-provisioned during off-peak times, aligning resource availability with application needs. This approach ensures optimal performance when needed while minimizing costs during low-demand periods, addressing both the CFO's cost concerns and the operational requirements of the application.

Q72: True/False Question HPE GreenLake allows administrators to configure compute resources to automatically adjust based on real-time application performance metrics.   ---
A) True

B) False

Answer: A

Explanation: HPE GreenLake provides the capability to automatically adjust compute resources based on real-time application performance metrics. This feature is part of the platform's auto-scaling and resource management tools, which monitor application performance and resource utilization. When configured correctly, these tools can dynamically add or remove resources to maintain optimal performance levels, ensuring that applications receive the necessary resources when demand increases and conserving resources when demand is lower. This automation is key to maintaining efficiency and cost-effectiveness in a dynamic application environment.

Q73: When setting up compute resources in HPE GreenLake for a new application deployment, which feature allows you to manage and predict costs effectively?   ---

A) Manual resource allocation

B) Fixed subscription model

C) Capacity planning tools

D) Pay-as-you-go billing

E) Static resource provisioning

F) Dynamic workload balancing

Answer: C

Explanation: Capacity planning tools in HPE GreenLake are essential for effective cost management, especially in dynamic and scalable environments. These tools allow administrators to forecast future resource needs based on historical usage patterns and projected demand. By using capacity planning, you can predict costs and budget accordingly, avoiding over-provisioning or unexpected expenses. Manual resource allocation and static provisioning lack the flexibility and insight provided by capacity planning, while pay-as-you-go billing, although flexible, can lead to unpredictability in costs if not carefully monitored and managed.

Q74: Which HPE GreenLake feature should be utilized to ensure high availability and disaster recovery for compute resources?   ---

A) Resource tagging

B) Auto-scaling groups

C) Data replication across regions

D) Single-zone deployment

E) Manual backup scheduling

F) Cost allocation reports

Answer: C

Explanation: Data replication across regions is a critical feature in HPE GreenLake for ensuring high availability and disaster recovery. By replicating data across multiple geographical locations, you can protect against data loss and service interruptions caused by localized failures or disasters. This approach provides redundancy and resilience, ensuring that compute resources can be quickly restored or accessed from another region if necessary. While auto-scaling enhances performance and cost-efficiency, it does not inherently provide disaster recovery capabilities, which are crucial for maintaining business continuity.

Q75: Fill in the gap: To facilitate efficient resource allocation and minimize waste in HPE GreenLake, administrators should regularly perform _____ to review and adjust resource usage based on changing business needs.
A) Security audits

B) Performance tuning

C) Resource utilization assessments

D) Code reviews

E) Network latency tests

F) User access reviews

Answer: C

Explanation: Regular resource utilization assessments are vital for efficient resource allocation and minimizing waste in environments managed by HPE GreenLake. By performing these assessments, administrators can identify underutilized resources and adjust allocations to better match current business needs. This proactive approach helps in optimizing resource usage, ensuring that resources are not wasted and costs are kept under control. Performance tuning and security audits, while important, do not directly address the dynamic allocation of compute resources based on business demand changes.

Q76: Scenario-Based Question You are the IT manager of a mid-sized retail company that has recently migrated its infrastructure to the HPE GreenLake platform. The company is planning a major sales event in two months, which is expected to significantly increase the demand for compute and storage resources. As part of the preparation, you've been tasked with ensuring that there are adequate service quotas and limits in place to handle the anticipated load. The company has a history of underestimating resource needs during peak times, leading to customer dissatisfaction during past events. You need to prevent this by properly configuring the GreenLake quotas and limits, taking into consideration both historical data and projected demand increases.

A) Increase the compute resource limits by 50% and storage by 30%, based on historical peak usage.

B) Set the quotas to twice the historical peak usage to ensure there is ample overhead.

C) Use the HPE GreenLake AI-driven analytics to forecast demand and adjust quotas accordingly.

D) Contact HPE support to temporarily remove all quotas and limits during the event.

E) Double the quotas based on current usage, without considering historical data.

F) Maintain current quotas and rely on auto-scaling to manage increased demand.

Answer: C

Explanation: Using HPE GreenLake's AI-driven analytics to forecast demand and adjust quotas is the most strategic approach. This method allows you to base your configurations on data-driven insights, considering both historical usage patterns and projected future demand. Increasing resources arbitrarily (as suggested in A, B, and E) or relying solely on auto-scaling (as in F) could lead to either over-provisioning or resource shortages. Removing quotas altogether (as in D) could potentially lead to uncontrolled spending. Using analytics ensures a balanced and cost-effective strategy that aligns with your business needs.

Which of the following configurations would ensure that a specific department within an organization does not exceed its allocated storage quota in HPE GreenLake?

A) Assign a fixed storage quota and enable alert notifications when 80% of the quota is reached.

B) Allocate resources dynamically based on usage patterns and projections.

C) Set a flexible quota that adjusts automatically with usage spikes.

D) Disable quota limits and rely on departmental budget monitoring.

E) Set a fixed quota and provide training on efficient resource usage.

F) Use a third-party tool to manage and enforce storage quotas.

Answer: A

Explanation: Assigning a fixed storage quota and enabling alerts when a certain percentage (such as 80%) of the quota is reached allows you to manage resources proactively. This approach helps prevent overuse by notifying administrators before the limit is reached, allowing them to take corrective action. Options B, C, and D could lead to uncontrolled usage and potential cost overruns, while E and F do not provide an effective means of direct quota management within the GreenLake environment.

Q78: True/False Style True or False: In HPE GreenLake, service quotas can only be configured at the global organizational level.

A) True

B) False

Answer: B

Explanation: This statement is false. HPE GreenLake allows for the configuration of service quotas at multiple levels within the organization, not just at the global level. Quotas can be set for specific departments, projects, or even individual users, providing flexibility and control over resource allocation. This granularity is essential for effectively managing resources and ensuring that different parts of the organization adhere to their designated limits.

Q79: Fill-in-the-Gap When configuring service quotas in HPE GreenLake, which of the following is NOT a best practice?

A) Regularly reviewing and adjusting quotas based on changes in business needs.

B) Setting quotas based on current usage only, ignoring future growth projections.

C) Implementing automated alerts to warn when usage approaches quota limits.

D) Engaging stakeholders in quota planning to align with business objectives.

E) Utilizing analytics tools to predict future resource requirements.

F) Establishing a process for requesting additional resources when needed.

Answer: B

Explanation: Setting quotas based on current usage only, without considering future growth projections, is not a best practice. It fails to account for potential increases in demand, which can lead to resource shortages and negatively impact business operations. Best practices involve a proactive approach that includes reviewing historical data, consulting with stakeholders, and using analytics to forecast future needs. This ensures that quotas are aligned with both current and future business objectives, allowing for smooth operational scalability.

A) Setting CPU quotas at the maximum possible value to avoid any performance issues.

B) Configuring quotas based solely on average usage metrics.

C) Understanding the application's performance requirements and historical peak usage patterns.

D) Applying the same CPU quotas across all applications for consistency.

E) Choosing quotas lower than current usage to encourage efficiency.

F) Setting quotas based on industry standards without customization.

Answer: C

Explanation: Understanding the application's performance requirements and historical peak usage patterns is critical when setting CPU quotas. This knowledge allows administrators to configure quotas that provide sufficient resources during peak times, ensuring the application performs optimally. Setting quotas at the maximum (as in A) may lead to unnecessary costs, while options B, D, E, and F ignore the specific needs and variability of different applications. A tailored approach based on data and performance requirements is key to balancing resource allocation and cost efficiency.

Q81: Scenario-Based Question A mid-sized retail company, RetailCo, has recently adopted HPE GreenLake to manage its IT resources more effectively. The CFO is concerned about increasing operational costs and has asked the IT department to provide a detailed cost analysis report. The IT manager, responsible for this task, needs to utilize HPE GreenLake's cost analysis and reporting features to present a comprehensive report that highlights cost savings and potential areas of optimization. Which feature should the IT manager primarily utilize to meet the CFO's request for detailed insights into cost distribution and potential savings?

A) HPE GreenLake Central Dashboard

B) Cost Explorer Tool

C) Usage Analytics Reports

D) Budget and Forecasting Module

E) Resource Performance Optimizer

F) Service Level Agreement (SLA) Tracker

Answer: B

Explanation: The Cost Explorer Tool in HPE GreenLake is designed to provide detailed insights into cost distribution and identify potential savings. It allows users to analyze costs by different dimensions such as service type, department, or project, making it ideal for generating comprehensive cost analysis reports. The tool also helps in visualizing spending patterns over time, which is crucial for presenting to the CFO in understanding operational costs and identifying optimization opportunities. While the central dashboard gives a broad overview, it is the Cost Explorer that provides the granularity required for detailed reporting and analysis.

Q82: True/False Question The HPE GreenLake platform automatically generates monthly cost reports that are emailed to all users in the organization.
A) True

B) False

Answer: B

Explanation: HPE GreenLake does not automatically email cost reports to all users. Instead, it provides tools and features within the platform that allow users with appropriate permissions to generate and customize cost reports as needed. This approach ensures that sensitive financial data is only accessed by authorized personnel and that reports are tailored to the specific needs and structure of the organization. It also allows organizations to align reporting with their internal financial and operational review cycles.

Q83: Which HPE GreenLake feature should a user leverage to project future costs based on historical usage data?

A) Cost Explorer Tool

B) Resource Performance Optimizer

C) Budget and Forecasting Module

D) Usage Analytics Reports

E) Trend Analysis Toolkit

F) Predictive Billing Interface

Answer: C

Explanation: The Budget and Forecasting Module in HPE GreenLake is specifically designed to project future costs based on historical usage data. This feature uses past consumption trends to help organizations predict future spending, allowing for more accurate budgeting and financial planning. By leveraging historical data, this module can provide insights into expected costs, making it an essential tool for financial strategists and planners within an organization. While other tools like Usage Analytics Reports can provide historical data, the Budget and Forecasting Module is specifically tailored for future cost projection.

An IT administrator wants to understand the distribution of costs across different departments within their organization using HPE GreenLake. Which feature would best provide this information?

A) SLA Tracker

B) Resource Performance Optimizer

C) Cost Allocation Module

D) Usage Analytics Reports

E) Budget and Forecasting Module

F) Central Dashboard

Answer: C

Explanation: The Cost Allocation Module is the most suitable feature for understanding the distribution of costs across different departments. This module allows administrators to attribute costs to specific departments or projects, providing transparency and accountability. It enables detailed tracking and analysis of how resources are consumed across the organization, facilitating more informed decision-making and financial management. While the Central Dashboard and Usage Analytics Reports may offer some of this information, the Cost Allocation Module is specifically designed for detailed departmental cost distribution analysis.

Q85: A financial analyst at a large enterprise is tasked with identifying trends in IT spending over the past year using HPE GreenLake. Which feature would be most effective for this analysis?

A) Trend Analysis Toolkit

B) SLA Tracker

C) Central Dashboard

D) Cost Explorer Tool

E) Usage Analytics Reports

F) Predictive Billing Interface

Answer: E

Explanation: Usage Analytics Reports are designed to provide detailed historical usage and spending data, making them ideal for identifying trends in IT spending. These reports can be customized to show various metrics over selected time periods, enabling analysts to discern patterns and trends in resource consumption and associated costs. The ability to analyze changes in usage and spending over time helps organizations understand their financial trajectory and make data-driven decisions. While the Trend Analysis Toolkit sounds relevant, it is the Usage Analytics Reports that offer the comprehensive historical data needed for such analysis.

Q86: Imagine you are the IT administrator for a mid-sized financial services company that has recently adopted HPE GreenLake. The company wants to streamline its IT service delivery by offering a user-friendly service catalog accessible via a new user portal. The goal is to improve internal customer satisfaction and reduce the time spent by IT staff on repetitive service requests. You are tasked with creating a service catalog that includes virtual machine provisioning, data storage services, and software deployment. As part of your planning, you need to ensure that the portal is intuitive and aligns with the company's business processes. Which initial step should you prioritize to ensure the successful creation of a service catalog that meets the company's needs?

A) Immediately start configuring the HPE GreenLake platform with default templates.

B) Conduct a survey of all employees to gather their personal IT preferences.

C) Perform a detailed analysis of the most frequent service requests received by the IT department.

D) Implement a trial version of the service catalog and gather feedback from a small user group.

E) Focus on creating a visually appealing user interface for the portal first.

F) Consult with other departments to understand their unique IT requirements.

Answer: C

Explanation: The first step in creating an effective service catalog should be to understand the current demand for IT services within the organization. By performing a detailed analysis of the most frequent service requests received by the IT department, you can identify which services are most critical to the business operations and should be prioritized in the catalog. This approach ensures that the catalog is relevant and addresses actual user needs, leading to increased satisfaction and efficiency. While consulting with other departments and gathering feedback are also important steps, they typically follow the initial analysis to validate and refine the service offerings. Starting with default templates or focusing on aesthetics without understanding the core requirements can lead to a misaligned service catalog that does not effectively serve its purpose.

Q87: True or False: In the HPE GreenLake platform, a service catalog can only include infrastructure services, such as compute and storage, and cannot be extended to include application-level services.
A) True

B) False

Answer: B

Explanation: False. The HPE GreenLake platform is designed to be flexible and adaptable to various business needs, allowing organizations to create service catalogs that include both infrastructure and application-level services. This flexibility enables businesses to offer a comprehensive range of IT services through a single portal, enhancing user experience and operational efficiency. By integrating application-level services, such as software deployment, alongside infrastructure services, organizations can provide a more complete service offering that aligns with their strategic IT goals.

Q88: When designing a user portal for the HPE GreenLake service catalog, which feature is most critical to enhance user experience and ensure ease of access to services?

A) Integration with social media platforms for easier sharing.

B) A customizable dashboard that users can personalize.

C) A sophisticated approval workflow for each service request.

D) A detailed user manual accessible within the portal.

E) A chatbot for real-time support and troubleshooting.

F) High-level encryption to secure user data and service requests.

Answer: B

Explanation: A customizable dashboard is a crucial feature for enhancing user experience in a service catalog portal. It allows users to personalize their view, prioritize the services they access most frequently, and receive relevant notifications or updates. This personalization makes the portal more intuitive and user-friendly, leading to higher user satisfaction and adoption rates. While other features like real-time support and security are important, the ability to customize the dashboard directly impacts how users interact with the portal on a daily basis, thereby improving their overall experience.

Q89: During the testing phase of the new HPE GreenLake user portal, you notice that service request completion times are longer than anticipated. Which action should you take first to diagnose and resolve this issue?

A) Increase server capacity to handle more simultaneous requests.

B) Review the service request approval workflows for potential bottlenecks.

C) Conduct a survey to gather user feedback on portal performance.

D) Implement a caching mechanism to store frequently accessed data.

E) Analyze network traffic to identify any latency issues.

F) Consult with HPE support for troubleshooting advice.

Answer: B

Explanation: Reviewing the service request approval workflows is a logical first step when faced with longer than expected completion times. Approval processes often introduce delays, especially if they involve multiple steps or require input from different departments. By identifying and addressing any bottlenecks or unnecessary steps in the workflow, you can streamline the process, reducing the time taken to complete service requests. While other actions like increasing server capacity or analyzing network traffic may be necessary later, understanding and optimizing workflows should be prioritized to improve efficiency.

Q90: Fill in the gap: To ensure that the HPE GreenLake service catalog remains relevant and effective, it is important to continuously _____.

A) implement new technologies without testing.

B) expand the list of services regardless of user demand.

C) gather and analyze user feedback and usage data.

D) update the portal design to match current trends.

E) hire more IT staff to manage the catalog.

F) reduce the number of available services to simplify choices.

Answer: C

Explanation: Continuously gathering and analyzing user feedback and usage data is essential to maintaining a relevant and effective service catalog. By understanding how users interact with the portal and which services are most utilized, IT administrators can make informed decisions about which services to enhance, retire, or introduce. This approach ensures that the catalog evolves in alignment with user needs and business objectives, leading to sustained engagement and satisfaction. Simply expanding the list of services or updating the design without understanding user needs can lead to inefficiencies and decreased satisfaction.

Q91: Scenario-Based Question Your company, TechInnovate, is planning to deploy a new cloud-native application that requires high availability and scalability. The application will be deployed on a Kubernetes cluster managed through HPE GreenLake. The application consists of multiple microservices that communicate with each other. The development team has expressed concerns about ensuring the application can handle high traffic loads and maintain performance. Additionally, they need a method to roll out updates with minimal downtime. As the HPE GreenLake Administrator, you need to configure the Kubernetes cluster to meet these requirements.   ---

A) Configure a single-node cluster with auto-scaling enabled.

B) Deploy a multi-node cluster with horizontal pod autoscaling.

C) Use a single large node and implement vertical pod autoscaling.

D) Deploy multiple clusters in different geographic regions.

E) Utilize a managed Kubernetes service without configuring autoscaling.

F) Implement a canary deployment strategy for rolling updates.

Answer: B

Explanation: Deploying a multi-node cluster with horizontal pod autoscaling is crucial for handling high traffic loads and maintaining application performance. Horizontal pod autoscaling adjusts the number of pod replicas based on current demand, providing scalability. This approach ensures the application can handle varying traffic without manual intervention. A single-node cluster doesn't offer redundancy or scalability, while vertical autoscaling may not address traffic spikes effectively. Deploying clusters in different regions can aid in disaster recovery but doesn't inherently solve scalability issues. Managed services can simplify management but still require proper configuration for autoscaling. Implementing a canary deployment strategy is beneficial for updates but does not directly address scalability concerns.

A) ConfigMap

B) Secret

C) Service

D) Deployment

E) PersistentVolume

F) Ingress

Answer: F

Explanation: An Ingress resource in Kubernetes is used to expose HTTP and HTTPS routes from outside the cluster to services within the cluster. It provides load balancing, SSL termination, and name-based virtual hosting. While Services can also expose applications, they typically do so at the cluster level or through a cloud provider's load balancer. Ingress provides a more sophisticated method of directing external traffic to specific services based on URL paths or hostnames. ConfigMaps, Secrets, Deployments, and PersistentVolumes are not used for exposing applications to external users.

Q93: Fill-in-the-Gap Multiple-Choice Question To ensure that your Kubernetes cluster can recover from node failures and maintain high availability, you should implement a(n) _____. ---

A) StatefulSet

B) DaemonSet

C) Horizontal Pod Autoscaler

D) Multi-zone cluster setup

E) ConfigMap

F) Custom Resource Definition

Answer: D

Explanation: A multi-zone cluster setup ensures high availability and fault tolerance by distributing nodes across multiple availability zones. This configuration allows the cluster to withstand failures of individual zones, as workloads can be rescheduled to nodes in other zones. StatefulSets and DaemonSets are specific to pod management within the cluster but do not inherently provide high availability. Horizontal Pod Autoscalers adjust the number of pods, but without multiple zones, node failures can still cause outages. ConfigMaps and Custom Resource Definitions (CRDs) are unrelated to node failure recovery and high availability.

Q94: True/False Question True or False: In HPE GreenLake, Kubernetes cluster upgrades are fully automated and require no administrator intervention.   ---
A) True

B) False

Answer: B

Explanation: While HPE GreenLake provides tools and services to simplify infrastructure management, Kubernetes cluster upgrades typically require some level of administrator intervention. Administrators must plan and execute upgrades to ensure compatibility and minimal disruption to running applications. Automation can assist with certain aspects, but careful planning and monitoring are essential to address potential issues that arise during the upgrade process. Therefore, claiming that upgrades are fully automated without any need for administrator intervention is inaccurate.

Q95: Standard Multiple-Choice Question Which Kubernetes object should be used to store sensitive information, such as passwords and API keys, ensuring they are available to applications in the cluster?
A) ConfigMap

B) Secret

C) PersistentVolumeClaim

D) ServiceAccount

E) PodSecurityPolicy

F) RoleBinding

Answer: B

Explanation: Kubernetes Secrets are specifically designed to store sensitive information like passwords, API keys, and tokens. Unlike ConfigMaps, which store non-sensitive configuration data, Secrets are encoded and can be accessed by applications running in the cluster. PersistentVolumeClaims, ServiceAccounts, PodSecurityPolicies, and RoleBindings serve different purposes related to storage, identity, security, and access control, respectively, and are not intended for storing sensitive data. Storing such information in Secrets helps protect it from being exposed inadvertently.

Q96: Scenario-based Question Your company, a leading financial services provider, is migrating its data infrastructure to HPE GreenLake to leverage its cloud-native capabilities. Given the sensitive nature of financial data and compliance requirements, ensuring robust encryption and data protection practices is paramount. The IT security team mandates that all data must be encrypted at rest and in transit, and they are particularly concerned about the potential for data breaches during the initial migration phase. Additionally, the company has operations in multiple countries, each with its own data protection regulations. As the HPE GreenLake Administrator, which approach should you prioritize to align with these requirements?

A) Implement HPE GreenLake's default encryption settings without additional configuration.

B) Use HPE GreenLake's built-in encryption for data at rest and configure TLS for data in transit.

C) Rely on third-party encryption solutions to supplement HPE GreenLake's capabilities.

D) Configure encryption keys manually for each country to comply with local regulations.

E) Focus on encrypting only the most sensitive data categories to optimize performance.

F) Deploy a multi-layered security strategy with user access controls as the primary focus.

Answer: B

Explanation: Encryption in HPE GreenLake is crucial for protecting sensitive financial data, especially when complying with different international regulations. The correct approach involves using HPE GreenLake's built-in encryption capabilities for data at rest, ensuring that all stored data is protected. For data in transit, configuring TLS (Transport Layer Security) is essential to safeguard data as it moves between systems and locations. This method effectively addresses the compliance and protection concerns without introducing unnecessary complexity by relying on third-party solutions or manual encryption key configurations. Encrypting only the most sensitive data could leave other critical information vulnerable, and focusing solely on access controls does not address the encryption requirement.

Q97: True/False Question In the context of HPE GreenLake, enabling encryption at rest ensures that data is protected from unauthorized access during both storage and transmission.
A) True

B) False

Answer: B

Explanation: Encryption at rest specifically refers to the protection of data when it is stored on disk, ensuring that even if the storage media is compromised, the data remains inaccessible without the proper decryption keys. However, encryption at rest does not cover the protection of data during transmission; for that, encryption in transit, such as TLS, is required. In HPE GreenLake, both encryption at rest and in transit must be configured to ensure comprehensive data protection.

Q98: What is a key advantage of using HPE GreenLake's integrated data protection solutions over third-party alternatives?

A) Better integration with existing IT infrastructure.

B) Lower cost compared to all third-party solutions.

C) More extensive encryption algorithms are available.

D) Faster deployment times due to pre-configured settings.

E) Enhanced scalability for future expansion needs.

F) Higher user satisfaction based on industry surveys.

Answer: D

Explanation: HPE GreenLake's integrated data protection solutions are designed to work seamlessly within the platform, providing pre-configured settings that facilitate rapid deployment. This advantage is particularly significant in environments where time-to-market is critical, and IT teams need to minimize setup complexity. While third-party solutions might offer comparable encryption algorithms or scalability, the built-in integration and ease of deployment with HPE GreenLake present a distinct advantage in terms of operational efficiency.

Q99: In the context of data protection best practices within HPE GreenLake, what is the primary purpose of configuring role-based access control (RBAC)?

A) To encrypt user credentials during login.

B) To prevent unauthorized users from accessing encryption keys.

C) To assign encryption algorithms based on user roles.

D) To manage data replication settings effectively.

E) To define and enforce permissions for data access.

F) To monitor encryption performance metrics.

Answer: E

Explanation: Role-based access control (RBAC) is a critical component of data protection strategies, including those implemented in HPE GreenLake. The primary purpose of RBAC is to define and enforce permissions for data access, ensuring that users can only access the information necessary for their roles. This minimizes the risk of data breaches by limiting exposure and preventing unauthorized access to sensitive data. While other options may relate to security, RBAC specifically focuses on access permissions rather than encryption or performance monitoring.

Q100: When setting up data encryption in HPE GreenLake, what should be the first step to ensure compliance with international data protection regulations?

A) Conduct a security audit to identify vulnerabilities.

B) Choose the strongest available encryption algorithm.

C) Assess data residency requirements for each region.

D) Implement a comprehensive backup and recovery plan.

E) Train staff on encryption management and compliance.

F) Integrate with a global third-party compliance tool.

Answer: C

Explanation: The first step in ensuring compliance with international data protection regulations when setting up data encryption in HPE GreenLake is to assess data residency requirements for each region where the company operates. Different countries have specific laws and regulations concerning where data can be stored and how it must be protected. Understanding these requirements is crucial for configuring encryption settings that meet legal obligations and avoid potential fines or legal issues. While other steps are also important in a comprehensive data protection strategy, assessing residency requirements is foundational for compliance.

Q101: Scenario-based Question You are the IT administrator for a large retail company that uses HPE GreenLake for its hybrid cloud solutions. Recently, your company experienced a significant drop in online sales due to a system outage. Subsequent analysis revealed that the outage was caused by multiple simultaneous failures across different infrastructure components. The CEO has requested a detailed report on how such incidents can be avoided in the future. Your task is to use HPE GreenLake's event correlation and log analysis capabilities to identify and address the root cause of system failures efficiently. Which feature or approach should you prioritize to enhance your system's resilience against similar issues?

A) Implement predictive analytics to forecast potential failures.

B) Prioritize real-time monitoring dashboards.

C) Focus on service level agreement (SLA) optimization.

D) Enhance manual log analysis procedures.

E) Invest in additional hardware redundancy.

F) Concentrate on improving user access controls.

Answer: A

Explanation: Predictive analytics in HPE GreenLake can proactively identify potential system failures before they occur by analyzing historical data and identifying patterns that precede outages. This approach is more effective than reactive solutions like manual log analysis or hardware redundancy, which address issues only after they manifest. Real-time monitoring is helpful, but without predictive capabilities, it may not prevent simultaneous failures. Focusing on SLAs or user access controls does not directly address the underlying technical causes of system outages. By implementing predictive analytics, you can preemptively mitigate risks, thereby preventing system downtime and ensuring business continuity.

Q102: Multiple-Choice Question In the context of event correlation within HPE GreenLake, what is the primary benefit of utilizing machine learning algorithms?

A) Reducing the need for human oversight in log management.

B) Automatically generating new hardware requirements.

C) Enabling quicker updates to the software environment.

D) Enhancing the ability to detect complex patterns across multiple logs.

E) Simplifying the user interface for easier access by non-technical staff.

F) Increasing the speed of network traffic.

Answer: D

Explanation: Machine learning algorithms are instrumental in detecting complex patterns across multiple logs, which may not be easily identified by human analysis alone. This enhances the system's ability to correlate seemingly unrelated events and uncover underlying issues that could lead to system failures. While machine learning can reduce some human oversight, its primary advantage in event correlation is its pattern recognition capability. It does not directly handle hardware requirements, software updates, or network speed. The user interface might benefit from machine learning insights but simplifying it is not the primary benefit in the context of event correlation.

Q103: True/False Question True or False: In HPE GreenLake's log analysis, correlation rules must be manually defined to detect all types of anomalies.

A) True

B) False

Answer: B

Explanation: False. HPE GreenLake incorporates advanced algorithms, including machine learning, that can autonomously detect anomalies without the need for manually defined correlation rules. These algorithms can learn from historical data and automatically adjust to recognize patterns that deviate from the norm, thereby identifying potential issues proactively. Manual rule definition can still be used for specific, known issues, but it is not necessary for detecting all types of anomalies.

Q104: Multiple-Choice Question Which of the following is a key advantage of using event correlation in HPE GreenLake for managing hybrid cloud environments?

A) Reducing the cost of cloud services.

B) Improving the accuracy of capacity planning.

C) Minimizing the time to resolve incidents.

D) Enhancing physical security measures.

E) Increasing the number of supported users.

F) Streamlining regulatory compliance processes.

Answer: C

Explanation: One of the primary advantages of event correlation is its ability to minimize the time required to resolve incidents. By effectively linking related events and logs, administrators can quickly identify the root cause of an issue and implement solutions faster. This reduces downtime and improves system reliability. While event correlation might indirectly aid in capacity planning or compliance, its direct impact is on incident resolution speed. It does not directly reduce cloud service costs, enhance physical security, or increase user support capacity.

Q105: Fill-in-the-Gap Question To maximize the effectiveness of log analysis in HPE GreenLake, it is crucial to integrate _____ to filter and prioritize critical events automatically.
A) advanced encryption protocols

B) a multi-factor authentication system

C) an AI-driven analytics platform

D) additional storage solutions

E) manual review processes

F) decentralized data centers

Answer: C

Explanation: Integrating an AI-driven analytics platform is essential for filtering and prioritizing critical events in HPE GreenLake's log analysis. AI can process vast amounts of log data in real-time, recognizing patterns and anomalies that might indicate potential issues. This not only enhances the speed and accuracy of root cause identification but also ensures that critical events are prioritized for immediate attention. While encryption, authentication, and storage solutions are important for security and capacity, they do not directly impact log analysis effectiveness. Manual reviews are time-consuming and less efficient than AI-based approaches, and decentralized data centers pertain to infrastructure design rather than log management.

Q106: A mid-sized retail company, RetailPro, uses HPE GreenLake for their machine learning and analytics workloads. They aim to optimize customer experience by predicting shopping trends and personalizing product recommendations. The data science team has built multiple models, but they realize the need for real-time analytics to enhance decision-making. They are considering implementing HPE GreenLake's analytics services to support this initiative. What is the primary service within HPE GreenLake that RetailPro should leverage to achieve real-time analytics?

A) HPE GreenLake Central

B) HPE Ezmeral Data Fabric

C) HPE InfoSight

D) HPE GreenLake for SAP HANA

E) HPE Nimble Storage

F) HPE Synergy

Answer: B

Explanation: HPE Ezmeral Data Fabric is designed to support real-time analytics by providing a robust, scalable data platform that integrates with various data sources. It offers capabilities such as streaming analytics, which are crucial for processing data in real-time and deriving insights that can drive immediate actions. RetailPro's requirement for real-time decision-making aligns well with the functionalities provided by HPE Ezmeral Data Fabric, which can handle large data volumes and deliver insights at the speed necessary for improving customer experience through predictive analytics and personalized recommendations.

Q107: True or False: HPE GreenLake offers a pay-per-use model for its machine learning and analytics services, allowing organizations to scale resources based on demand without upfront capital expenditure.
A) True

B) False

Answer: A

Explanation: The statement is true. HPE GreenLake's offering is specifically designed around a pay-per-use model, which provides flexibility and financial efficiency to organizations. This model allows businesses to scale their IT resources according to current needs and only pay for what they use. This approach reduces the burden of significant upfront capital investments and aligns costs with business growth, making it ideal for dynamic environments like machine learning and analytics, where demand can fluctuate significantly.

Q108: When considering the deployment of HPE GreenLake for machine learning workloads, which of the following factors should be prioritized to ensure an effective implementation?

A) The availability of a trained in-house IT team

B) The current data center's cooling efficiency

C) The integration capability with existing data pipelines

D) The geographical location of the organization's headquarters

E) The number of competitors using similar solutions

F) The color scheme of the user interface

Answer: C

Explanation: The integration capability with existing data pipelines is crucial when deploying HPE GreenLake for machine learning workloads. Effective implementation depends on seamless data flow and compatibility with current systems to ensure that the machine learning models can access, process, and analyze data efficiently. Organizations must ensure their data infrastructure can support new technologies without creating bottlenecks or data silos. This approach enables smooth transitions and enhances the overall effectiveness of the machine learning initiatives.

Q109: A leading financial services firm, FinBank, is using HPE GreenLake to enhance its analytics capabilities. They have sensitive customer data that needs to be protected while performing large-scale analytics. Which feature of HPE GreenLake would best address FinBank's concerns regarding data security?

A) Multi-cloud connectivity

B) Automated provisioning

C) Data encryption at rest and in transit

D) High-performance computing

E) Flexible resource allocation

F) Built-in business intelligence tools

Answer: C

Explanation: Data encryption at rest and in transit is a critical feature for addressing data security concerns. For FinBank, which handles sensitive customer data, ensuring that data is encrypted both when stored and during transmission is essential to protecting against unauthorized access and data breaches. HPE GreenLake offers robust security measures, including encryption, to safeguard data, which is particularly vital in industries like financial services where regulatory compliance and data protection are paramount.

Q110: During a strategic review, a tech startup, InnovateAI, decides to leverage HPE GreenLake's analytics services to gain a competitive edge through artificial intelligence. They need to ensure their infrastructure can handle sudden spikes in data processing demand without compromising on performance. What feature of HPE GreenLake is most critical for InnovateAI to meet this requirement?

A) Predefined analytics templates

B) On-demand scalability

C) Built-in machine learning algorithms

D) Dedicated customer support

E) Comprehensive training resources

F) Enhanced graphical user interface

Answer: B

Explanation: On-demand scalability is crucial for handling sudden spikes in data processing demand. HPE GreenLake's ability to scale resources dynamically in response to workload changes ensures that InnovateAI can maintain high performance levels even during peak times. This capability allows the startup to adapt quickly to changing demands without the need for over-provisioning resources, thereby optimizing both performance and cost-efficiency. By leveraging scalable infrastructure, InnovateAI can focus on innovation and growth, confident that their analytics capabilities will meet the demands of their business.

Q111: Scenario-Based Question A multinational corporation, XYZ Inc., has recently partnered with HPE to transition their IT infrastructure to a more flexible consumption-based model using HPE GreenLake. The company has data centers in North America, Europe, and Asia, and they aim to optimize resource utilization while ensuring compliance with regional regulatory requirements. As they begin this transition, they need to establish a clear understanding of the lifecycle services provided by HPE GreenLake to ensure seamless delivery and operation. Which GreenLake lifecycle service is essential for XYZ Inc. to focus on to ensure a smooth transition and continuous compliance with local regulations?

A) Asset Management Services

B) Capacity Planning and Management Services

C) Compliance and Risk Management Services

D) Data Migration Services

E) IT Support Services

F) Installation and Deployment Services

Answer: C

Explanation: Compliance and Risk Management Services are crucial for a multinational corporation like XYZ Inc., operating in multiple regulatory environments. These services ensure that all data handling and IT operations comply with local laws, such as GDPR in Europe or data sovereignty laws in Asia. HPE GreenLake provides compliance and risk management frameworks that help businesses navigate complex regulatory landscapes by continuously monitoring and adjusting processes to meet legal requirements. This proactive approach minimizes the risk of non-compliance, which could otherwise lead to significant fines or operational disruptions.

Q112: True/False Question True or False: The HPE GreenLake lifecycle includes a specific phase dedicated to sustainability assessments and recommendations for reducing carbon footprint.

A) True

B) False

Answer: A

Explanation: True. HPE GreenLake incorporates sustainability assessments as part of its lifecycle services. This phase focuses on evaluating the environmental impact of IT operations and provides recommendations to reduce energy consumption and carbon footprint. By integrating sustainability into the lifecycle, HPE GreenLake helps organizations align their IT infrastructure with broader environmental goals, such as reducing greenhouse gas emissions and improving energy efficiency.

Q113: During the delivery phase of HPE GreenLake lifecycle services, which of the following activities is critical to ensure that IT resources are aligned with the business's evolving needs?

A) Regular software updates

B) Infrastructure health monitoring

C) Continuous capacity management

D) User training and support

E) Vendor contract negotiations

F) Network security audits

Answer: C

Explanation: Continuous capacity management is vital during the delivery phase of HPE GreenLake lifecycle services. This activity involves monitoring and adjusting the allocation of IT resources to align with the organization's changing demands. As business needs evolve, capacity management ensures that there is always sufficient compute, storage, and network resources available, preventing overprovisioning or underutilization. This not only optimizes costs but also ensures optimal performance and scalability in response to business fluctuations.

Q114: Which of the following tasks is NOT typically part of the HPE GreenLake installation and deployment services?

A) Configuring IT infrastructure

B) Customizing software applications

C) On-site hardware setup

D) Establishing network connectivity

E) Creating user access policies

F) Developing data analytics strategies

Answer: F

Explanation: Developing data analytics strategies is not typically part of the installation and deployment services provided by HPE GreenLake. This service phase focuses on setting up the physical and virtual infrastructure, ensuring that hardware is correctly installed, configured, and connected to networks. Tasks like configuring IT systems, establishing network connectivity, and creating user access policies are standard, whereas data analytics strategy development is a separate strategic activity that involves higher-level planning and decision-making beyond the scope of initial deployment.

Q115: In the context of HPE GreenLake lifecycle services, what is the primary purpose of ongoing IT support services?

A) To provide financial management assistance

B) To ensure continuous availability and reliability of IT resources

C) To develop custom software applications

D) To facilitate quarterly business reviews

E) To conduct market research for technology trends

F) To assist with employee onboarding processes

Answer: B

Explanation: The primary purpose of ongoing IT support services within HPE GreenLake lifecycle services is to ensure the continuous availability and reliability of IT resources. This includes troubleshooting, maintenance, and performance optimization to prevent downtime and address issues promptly. Effective IT support services are crucial for business continuity and operational efficiency, providing organizations with the reassurance that their IT infrastructure is consistently monitored and maintained, allowing them to focus on core business activities without IT disruptions.

Q116: Scenario-Based Question XYZ Corporation, a global retail company, has recently transitioned its IT infrastructure to HPE GreenLake to streamline operations and improve resource management. The IT team, led by Maria, aims to enhance the overall efficiency of their GreenLake environment by implementing operational best practices. Maria's team notices fluctuating performance metrics on their analytics dashboard. They suspect this is due to inconsistent resource allocation during peak sales periods. To address these challenges, they are considering several strategies, including revisiting their current configuration and implementing more robust monitoring tools. Which operational best practice should Maria prioritize to ensure optimal resource utilization and consistent performance?   ---

A) Increase the total provisioned capacity by 20% to handle peak loads.

B) Schedule regular maintenance windows during peak sales periods.

C) Implement predictive analytics tools for proactive resource management.

D) Reduce the number of users accessing the system during peak times.

E) Migrate critical workloads to a public cloud for better scalability.

F) Disable non-essential services during peak operating hours.

Answer: C

Explanation: In this scenario, implementing predictive analytics tools for proactive resource management is the most effective operational best practice. Predictive analytics can help the IT team anticipate resource needs and adjust allocations before performance issues arise, thus ensuring that the system runs smoothly during peak sales periods. Increasing provisioned capacity (option A) may not be cost-effective or necessary, and scheduling maintenance during peak times (option B) could exacerbate performance issues. Reducing the number of users (option D) and migrating workloads to a public cloud (option E) might not align with the company's objectives or budget. Disabling services (option F) might hinder essential operations. Therefore, employing predictive analytics aligns with GreenLake's capabilities in providing dynamic and adaptive resource management.

Q117: True/False Question True or False: An HPE GreenLake administrator should regularly review usage data to ensure that the organization's current configuration aligns with its operational goals and cost management strategies.

A) True

B) False

Answer: A

Explanation: Regularly reviewing usage data is a critical operational best practice for HPE GreenLake administrators. This practice ensures that IT resources are aligned with organizational goals and that cost management strategies are effective. By analyzing usage data, administrators can identify trends, inefficiencies, or unnecessary expenditures, allowing them to make informed decisions that optimize resource allocation and cost-effectiveness. This proactive approach helps maintain alignment with business objectives and maximizes the value derived from the GreenLake infrastructure.

Q118: Which of the following actions is considered a best practice for maintaining security within an HPE GreenLake environment?   ---

A) Disabling all user authentication requirements.

B) Implementing multi-factor authentication for all users.

C) Allowing unrestricted access to all data by default.

D) Regularly updating only the hardware components.

E) Sharing administrator credentials among team members.

F) Ignoring security patches for non-critical systems.

Answer: B

Explanation: Implementing multi-factor authentication (MFA) for all users is a best practice for maintaining security within an HPE GreenLake environment. MFA adds an additional layer of security beyond simple password protection, making it harder for unauthorized users to gain access. Options A, C, E, and F compromise security by either reducing access controls or neglecting important updates. While hardware updates (option D) are important, they must be part of a comprehensive security strategy that includes software updates and access controls. Ensuring strong authentication practices such as MFA is essential for protecting sensitive data and maintaining system integrity in a cloud-based service environment like GreenLake.

Q119: To ensure efficient cost management in an HPE GreenLake environment, which practice should an administrator focus on?   ---

A) Provisioning resources based on peak demand at all times.

B) Regularly evaluating service level agreements (SLAs) for compliance.

C) Utilizing fixed resource allocations regardless of usage trends.

D) Conducting quarterly audits of resource usage and costs.

E) Encouraging unlimited resource usage to maximize productivity.

F) Disabling cost tracking features to simplify management.

Answer: D

Explanation: Conducting quarterly audits of resource usage and costs is an essential practice for efficient cost management in an HPE GreenLake environment. These audits allow administrators to assess how resources are being utilized, identify inefficiencies, and make necessary adjustments to align with budgetary constraints. Provisioning for peak demand at all times (option A) and using fixed allocations (option C) can lead to wasted resources and increased costs. While SLAs (option B) are important, they typically focus on performance rather than cost management. Unlimited usage (option E) and disabling cost tracking (option F) undermine the goal of cost efficiency. Regular audits provide the data-driven insights necessary for optimizing spending and ensuring that resources are used effectively.

Q120: When managing workloads in an HPE GreenLake environment, what is a recommended best practice to enhance performance and reliability?

A) Consolidate all workloads onto a single server to simplify management.

B) Regularly rebalance workloads across available resources based on performance metrics.

C) Use the default settings for all workload configurations to maintain consistency.

D) Segregate workloads based on departmental divisions without regard to resource demands.

E) Limit workload distribution to only the newest hardware to ensure peak performance.

F) Schedule all workloads to run simultaneously during off-peak hours.

Answer: B

Explanation: Regularly rebalancing workloads across available resources based on performance metrics is a recommended best practice for enhancing performance and reliability in an HPE GreenLake environment. This practice ensures that workloads are optimally distributed according to current resource availability and demands, preventing bottlenecks and maximizing system efficiency. Consolidating workloads onto a single server (option A) can create a single point of failure, while using default settings (option C) may not be optimized for specific workloads. Segregating workloads without regard to resource demands (option D) and limiting distribution to only the newest hardware (option E) ignore the benefits of a balanced and flexible environment. Scheduling all workloads at the same time (option F) could lead to resource contention and decreased performance. By regularly rebalancing workloads, administrators can maintain a dynamic and resilient operational environment.

Q121: Scenario-Based Question: A leading e-commerce company, QuickShopOnline, is experiencing rapid growth and needs to manage its IT infrastructure more effectively. The CTO is considering HPE GreenLake to manage workloads for their online platform, analytics, and customer relationship management systems. The team is particularly interested in the flexibility of workload templates and blueprints to quickly deploy new services and scale existing ones. As the newly appointed HPE GreenLake administrator, you are tasked with planning the deployment strategy. Which consideration is MOST important when selecting a blueprint for launching a new analytics service?

A) The blueprint must support multiple cloud service providers to ensure flexibility.

B) It should be pre-configured with analytics-specific optimizations to reduce deployment time.

C) The cost-effectiveness of the blueprint compared to traditional infrastructure.

D) The blueprint must have in-built security features to protect sensitive customer data.

E) The compatibility of the blueprint with existing on-premises hardware.

F) The availability of technical support and documentation for the chosen blueprint.

Answer: B

Explanation: When deploying a new analytics service, using a blueprint pre-configured with analytics-specific optimizations is crucial as it reduces deployment time and ensures the service is fine-tuned for performance. This is especially important for a rapidly growing e-commerce company like QuickShopOnline, where time-to-market is critical. While flexibility, cost, security, compatibility, and support are all important considerations, the primary goal in this scenario is rapid and efficient deployment tailored to the specific needs of analytics workloads.

Q122: In the context of HPE GreenLake workload templates, which feature allows administrators to easily replicate a configuration across multiple environments?

A) Template Cloning

B) Configuration Synchronization

C) Deployment Automation

D) Environment Duplication

E) Scalability Features

F) Blueprint Replication

Answer: A

Explanation: Template Cloning is a feature in HPE GreenLake that allows administrators to replicate configurations across multiple environments efficiently. This is particularly useful in scenarios where similar configurations are needed across different departments or geographic locations. By cloning a template, administrators save time and reduce the risk of configuration errors, ensuring consistency and reliability across deployments.

Q123: True/False: HPE GreenLake workload blueprints require manual configuration for each deployment, as they are not pre-configured with any settings.

A) True

B) False

Answer: B

Explanation: False. HPE GreenLake workload blueprints are designed to be pre-configured with specific settings, allowing for streamlined and efficient deployment. They provide a framework with pre-set configurations tailored to specific types of workloads, which reduces the need for manual configuration and accelerates deployment processes.

Q124: When assessing the suitability of a workload template in HPE GreenLake for a hybrid cloud deployment, which factor is LEAST critical?

A) Integration capability with existing public cloud services.

B) Pre-configured compliance with industry regulations.

C) The number of users supported by the template.

D) The ability to customize the template for future scalability.

E) The template's support for multi-tenancy.

F) The initial deployment speed offered by the template.

Answer: C

Explanation: The number of users supported by the template is the least critical factor when assessing a workload template for hybrid cloud deployment. Hybrid cloud environments are typically designed to scale with demand, and user numbers can often be adjusted post-deployment. Other factors, such as integration with existing services, compliance, customization, multi-tenancy, and deployment speed, are more influential in determining the success and efficiency of the initial setup and ongoing operations.

Q125: Fill-in-the-Gap: In the HPE GreenLake platform, _____ are used to automate the workflow of deploying a complete stack, including compute, storage, and networking resources.

A) Service Chains

B) Blueprint Schedules

C) Stack Automators

D) Deployment Scripts

E) Infrastructure Pipelines

F) Resource Orchestrators

Answer: E

Explanation: Infrastructure Pipelines in the HPE GreenLake platform are designed to automate the workflow of deploying a complete stack of resources, including compute, storage, and networking. These pipelines help streamline the process by managing dependencies and automating repetitive tasks, which can significantly reduce setup time and minimize the potential for human error. This automation is critical for organizations looking to scale their IT infrastructure efficiently and reliably.

Q126: Scenario-Based Question A rapidly growing tech company, TechWave Inc., has recently adopted HPE GreenLake for their infrastructure needs to handle their increased data processing demands. They have a mix of on-premises and cloud-based resources. The IT team is tasked with ensuring that hardware lifecycle management is optimized to meet the company's dynamic requirements. The team must ensure minimal downtime, efficient resource utilization, and proactive hardware maintenance. They need to decide on the best practices for managing the hardware lifecycle to align with their business goals. Which strategy should they implement for optimal hardware lifecycle management?   ---

A) Implement regular firmware updates and hardware monitoring to preemptively address potential failures.

B) Focus solely on extending the lifetime of existing hardware to reduce costs.

C) Use a reactive maintenance model, addressing issues as they arise.

D) Outsource all hardware management tasks to a third-party vendor.

E) Invest heavily in new hardware every year to always have the latest technology.

F) Rely on warranties and service agreements without additional monitoring.

Answer: A

Explanation: Implementing regular firmware updates and hardware monitoring is crucial for preemptive hardware lifecycle management. This approach allows the IT team to anticipate and address potential hardware issues before they lead to failures, thereby minimizing downtime and ensuring efficient resource utilization. By proactively managing hardware, TechWave Inc. can maintain optimal performance levels and extend the lifecycle of their equipment. This strategy aligns with their business goals of minimizing downtime and ensuring efficient resource utilization. In contrast, options B, C, D, E, and F either focus too narrowly, lack proactive measures, or significantly increase costs without corresponding benefits.

Q127: True/False Question A hardware lifecycle management strategy should prioritize the extension of hardware warranties to ensure long-term cost savings and avoid unexpected expenses.   ---
A) True

B) False

Answer: B

Explanation: While extending warranties can be a component of hardware lifecycle management, it should not be the sole focus. A comprehensive strategy should include proactive maintenance, regular updates, and monitoring to prevent issues before they occur. Solely relying on warranties may lead to higher costs in the long run due to potential downtime and inefficiencies. Effective lifecycle management involves a balanced approach that includes predictive maintenance and resource optimization, ensuring overall cost savings and reliability.

Q128: When planning for hardware lifecycle management within HPE GreenLake, which of the following is the most effective practice to ensure scalability and flexibility in resource allocation?   ---
A) Implementing a fixed refresh cycle for all hardware components.

B) Regularly evaluating and optimizing the allocation of resources based on current and future workloads.

C) Keeping a static inventory of hardware and avoiding changes.

D) Using a single vendor for all hardware needs to simplify management.

E) Focusing on maximizing the use of existing hardware without upgrades.

F) Allocating resources based solely on historical data.

Answer: B

Explanation: Regularly evaluating and optimizing resource allocation is vital for ensuring scalability and flexibility in hardware lifecycle management. This practice allows organizations to adjust their resources based on both current demands and anticipated future needs, thus supporting growth and adaptability. Options A and F may result in inefficiencies due to rigidity or outdated data reliance, while C and E limit the ability to adapt to changing requirements. Option D might reduce complexity but could also limit flexibility and innovation, as it ties the organization to a single vendor's product lifecycle.

Q129: In the context of HPE GreenLake, which of the following is the best indicator that a piece of hardware is nearing the end of its lifecycle and should be considered for replacement?   ---
A) The hardware is over three years old.

B) The hardware frequently requires maintenance and incurs unexpected downtime.

C) The hardware no longer supports the latest software updates.

D) The warranty period has expired.

E) The hardware costs have depreciated significantly.

F) The hardware was purchased during a company expansion.

Answer: B

Explanation: Frequent maintenance and unexpected downtime are clear indicators that hardware may be nearing the end of its lifecycle. This suggests that the hardware is not performing reliably, which can lead to increased operational costs and decreased productivity. While the other factors such as age, warranty, and depreciation may contribute to lifecycle considerations, they do not directly impact performance and reliability. Thus, prioritizing performance metrics and downtime over arbitrary timelines or financial depreciation gives a more accurate assessment of hardware health.

Q130: Which of the following actions should a GreenLake administrator take to effectively manage hardware lifecycle and ensure alignment with changing business objectives?

A) Create a rigid five-year hardware replacement plan and adhere strictly to it.

B) Conduct annual reviews of hardware performance and adjust plans based on business needs.

C) Limit hardware upgrades to major system overhauls.

D) Focus resources on maintaining legacy systems to avoid transition risks.

E) Exclusively use predictive analytics to manage hardware lifecycle.

F) Prioritize aesthetic upgrades to maintain modern appearance.

Answer: B

Explanation: Conducting annual reviews of hardware performance allows administrators to align lifecycle management with evolving business objectives. This approach provides flexibility, enabling the organization to adapt to changes in technology and business requirements. A rigid plan (option A) may not accommodate unexpected changes, while options C, D, and F either limit innovation or focus on non-essential aspects. Although predictive analytics (option E) can be useful, relying solely on it may overlook qualitative factors such as strategic business directions. A balanced, responsive approach ensures hardware resources support both current operations and future growth.

Q131: Scenario-Based Question XYZ Corporation is a global financial services company relying heavily on its HPE GreenLake infrastructure to support critical applications in various regions. Recently, the company experienced a significant outage in its primary data center due to a natural disaster, impacting its services in the Asia-Pacific region. The IT team has been tasked with implementing a high availability and failover strategy to prevent similar disruptions in the future. They need to ensure minimal downtime and data loss, considering both cost and performance. Given these requirements, which strategy should the IT team prioritize to enhance their infrastructure's resilience?

A) Implement a single-site clustering solution with data replication to a local backup.

B) Establish an active-passive failover strategy across multiple global data centers.

C) Upgrade to a higher tier of HPE GreenLake service without changing the current setup.

D) Develop a redundant load balancing system within the primary data center.

E) Deploy an active-active configuration across two geographically dispersed sites.

F) Use local backups and disaster recovery procedures without real-time failover capabilities.

Answer: E

Explanation: In this scenario, XYZ Corporation needs a robust solution that minimizes both downtime and data loss. An active-active configuration across geographically dispersed sites ensures that applications remain available even if one site fails, as the other site continues to operate. This strategy provides real-time data synchronization and load balancing between sites, offering the highest availability and resilience. Options like a single-site solution or local backups do not provide sufficient failover capabilities during a site-wide disaster. Upgrading service tiers or using local-only strategies do not address global failover needs, and an active-passive strategy may involve more downtime during failover transitions.

Q132: True/False High availability configurations in HPE GreenLake always require active-active clustering to ensure zero downtime.

A) True

B) False

Answer: B

Explanation: High availability in HPE GreenLake can be achieved through various configurations, not just active-active clustering. While active-active setups provide maximum uptime by having multiple nodes actively handling requests, active-passive configurations can also offer high availability by having a standby node ready to take over in case of a failure. The choice between these setups depends on the specific requirements, budget, and acceptable levels of downtime. Therefore, it is not true that zero downtime always requires active-active clustering, as active-passive can also meet high availability needs with potentially less complexity and cost.

Q133: When designing a failover strategy for HPE GreenLake, which factor is the most crucial to consider to ensure data integrity during a failover event?

A) Network latency between data centers

B) Storage capacity of the backup site

C) Real-time data synchronization mechanisms

D) Number of active users on the system

E) Geographic location of data centers

F) Type of applications hosted

Answer: C

Explanation: Ensuring data integrity during a failover event is critical, and real-time data synchronization mechanisms are crucial for this purpose. These mechanisms ensure that data is continuously replicated between the primary and secondary sites, minimizing the risk of data loss and providing the most up-to-date information in the event of a failover. While other factors like network latency and storage capacity are important, they mainly affect performance and storage capability rather than directly impacting data integrity. Geographic location and application types influence overall strategy but are secondary to ensuring data consistency through real-time synchronization.

Q134: Which of the following is the least effective approach for minimizing downtime in an HPE GreenLake environment during a planned maintenance event?

A) Scheduling maintenance during off-peak hours

B) Implementing automated failover processes

C) Increasing the redundancy of critical components

D) Utilizing a rolling update strategy

E) Deploying a dedicated maintenance mode

F) Relying solely on manual intervention for failover

Answer: F

Explanation: Relying solely on manual intervention for failover is the least effective approach for minimizing downtime during planned maintenance. Manual processes are typically slower and more prone to human error, leading to increased downtime. Automated failover and redundancy mechanisms ensure a more seamless transition during maintenance events, while scheduling during off-peak hours and using rolling updates can further reduce impact. A dedicated maintenance mode and automated processes together ensure that any necessary transitions or updates happen smoothly and efficiently without significant service interruptions.

Q135: In the context of disaster recovery for HPE GreenLake, which approach provides the best balance of cost and effectiveness for a midsize enterprise?

A) Complete duplication of all infrastructure components on a secondary site

B) Implementing a cloud-based disaster recovery solution

C) Utilizing local tape backups with monthly offsite storage

D) Deploying a hybrid approach with cloud backups and a smaller secondary site

E) Relying solely on high availability within a single data center

F) Contracting a third-party disaster recovery service for emergency use

Answer: D

Explanation: For a midsize enterprise seeking a cost-effective and efficient disaster recovery solution, a hybrid approach with cloud backups and a smaller secondary site offers the best balance. This strategy leverages the scalability and flexibility of cloud services while maintaining a physical secondary site for critical applications that require faster recovery times. Complete duplication of infrastructure is often prohibitively expensive, while local tape backups and single data center solutions do not provide sufficient reliability or speed. Contracting third-party services can be cost-effective but may not offer the same level of control or immediacy as a dedicated hybrid solution.

Q136: A mid-sized retail company is in the process of digital transformation and is evaluating the use of container platforms to enhance its application deployment strategy. The company already utilizes HPE GreenLake for its infrastructure needs and is considering integrating HPE Ezmeral Container Platform to manage its containerized applications. The IT team is concerned about the complexity of integration and wants to ensure seamless monitoring and management of applications across on-premises and cloud environments. What key feature of the HPE Ezmeral Container Platform could address these concerns by enabling centralized management and observability?

A) Multi-tenant isolation

B) Auto-scaling capabilities

C) Unified control plane

D) Integrated AI/ML support

E) Cost optimization tools

F) DevOps toolchain integration

Answer: C

Explanation: The HPE Ezmeral Container Platform's unified control plane is a critical feature that provides centralized management for containerized applications across distributed environments, including on-premises and public cloud. This unified approach allows IT teams to manage, monitor, and secure applications consistently, addressing concerns about complexity and ensuring seamless integration into existing infrastructure. It provides comprehensive observability tools that help in monitoring application performance and resource utilization, which is crucial for effective management in a hybrid cloud setting.

Q137: True or False: HPE Ezmeral Container Platform requires a separate, dedicated hardware stack independent of HPE GreenLake for deployment.
A) True

B) False

Answer: B

Explanation: HPE Ezmeral Container Platform is designed to work seamlessly with HPE GreenLake, leveraging its flexible and scalable infrastructure. It does not require a dedicated hardware stack; instead, it can be deployed on existing GreenLake resources, providing a cohesive environment for managing containerized applications. This integration simplifies deployment and reduces the need for additional hardware investments, aligning with the GreenLake model of delivering on-demand services.

Q138: When integrating HPE Ezmeral Container Platform with HPE GreenLake, which component is essential for enabling data persistence for stateful applications?

A) Virtual network interface

B) Persistent storage interface

C) Load balancing service

D) Identity and access management

E) Logging and monitoring service

F) Container registry

Answer: B

Explanation: The persistent storage interface is crucial for enabling data persistence in stateful applications running on the HPE Ezmeral Container Platform. This component allows applications to maintain data across container restarts and failures, which is essential for applications that require data retention beyond the lifecycle of a container instance. In the context of HPE GreenLake, leveraging existing storage solutions ensures efficient use of resources and aligns with the hybrid cloud model.

Q139: In a scenario where a company is utilizing HPE Ezmeral Container Platform for AI/ML workloads, which feature would most effectively optimize resource allocation and improve workload performance?

A) Horizontal pod autoscaling

B) Machine learning pipelines

C) GPU acceleration support

D) Multi-cloud deployment

E) Role-based access control

F) Network policy management

Answer: C

Explanation: GPU acceleration support is the feature that optimizes resource allocation and enhances performance for AI/ML workloads on the HPE Ezmeral Container Platform. By leveraging GPU resources, the platform can significantly speed up processing times for machine learning and deep learning tasks, which are computationally intensive. This feature is critical for organizations aiming to maximize the efficiency and performance of their AI/ML workflows in production environments.

Q140: Fill in the gap: To ensure secure access and operations within the HPE Ezmeral Container Platform, the integration with HPE GreenLake should prioritize _____ to manage user permissions and enforce security policies.

A) Network security policies

B) Application firewalls

C) Data encryption standards

D) Role-based access control

E) Continuous integration pipelines

F) Automated compliance checks

Answer: D

Explanation: Role-based access control (RBAC) is essential for managing user permissions and enforcing security policies within the HPE Ezmeral Container Platform. By implementing RBAC, administrators can define roles and assign specific permissions to users or groups, ensuring that only authorized personnel can access sensitive resources and perform critical operations. This is particularly important in a hybrid cloud environment, where security and compliance are top priorities. Integration with HPE GreenLake allows for consistent application of these controls across the infrastructure.

Q141: A multinational retail company is planning to revamp its IT infrastructure to enhance scalability and flexibility while maintaining cost-efficiency. They have operations across North America, Europe, and Asia, each with varying data privacy regulations and network requirements. The company is considering HPE GreenLake's edge-to-cloud deployment models to meet these regional demands without redundant infrastructure investments. They need a solution that allows for centralized management but enables localized compliance and performance optimizations. Which HPE GreenLake deployment model should they adopt to best meet their needs?

A) Public Cloud Deployment

B) On-Premises Deployment

C) Multi-Cloud Deployment

D) Hybrid Cloud Deployment

E) Private Cloud Deployment

F) Edge-to-Edge Deployment

Answer: D

Explanation: HPE GreenLake's Hybrid Cloud Deployment is ideal for organizations like the multinational retail company described, as it combines both on-premises and cloud-based resources, offering centralized management while maintaining compliance with local regulations. It allows for optimization of workloads based on regional requirements and provides the flexibility to scale resources as needed across different geographies. This model ensures robust data sovereignty controls and offers the ability to leverage both local and remote resources cost-effectively.

Q142: Which component is NOT essential for deploying an HPE GreenLake edge-to-cloud solution?

A) HPE GreenLake Central

B) HPE Ezmeral Container Platform

C) HPE Synergy

D) HPE Moonshot

E) HPE OneView

F) HPE Nimble Storage

Answer: D

Explanation: While HPE Moonshot can be beneficial for specific high-density compute scenarios, it is not an essential component of a typical HPE GreenLake edge-to-cloud deployment. HPE GreenLake Central provides the management interface, HPE Ezmeral Container Platform supports containerized workloads, HPE Synergy offers composable infrastructure, HPE OneView provides infrastructure management, and HPE Nimble Storage ensures efficient data storage. The foundational components listed are critical for the deployment and management of resources in an edge-to-cloud environment.

Q143: True or False: HPE GreenLake deployment models support both pay-per-use and reserved capacity billing options.

A) True

B) False

Answer: A

Explanation: True. HPE GreenLake offers flexible billing options that include both pay-per-use and reserved capacity models. This flexibility allows businesses to align their IT expenditures more closely with actual usage, providing cost predictability for reserved capacities and the ability to scale dynamically with pay-per-use as demand fluctuates.

Q144: In a scenario where a company is constrained by limited IT staff but requires rapid deployment of new edge services, which HPE GreenLake feature would most adequately address this challenge?

A) HPE GreenLake Quick Quote Tool

B) HPE GreenLake Management Services

C) HPE GreenLake AI Operations

D) HPE GreenLake Flex Capacity

E) HPE GreenLake Marketplace

F) HPE GreenLake Virtual Private Cloud

Answer: B

Explanation: HPE GreenLake Management Services are designed to support companies with limited IT staff by providing comprehensive management and operational support for deployed services. This feature helps organizations deploy edge services rapidly and efficiently without the need for extensive in-house expertise. It includes monitoring, management, and optimization of the customer's environment, allowing the internal team to focus on strategic initiatives.

Q145: Fill in the gap: HPE GreenLake's _____ feature enables businesses to enhance security and compliance by offering centralized policy management and automated updates across all deployment models.

A) HPE GreenLake Central

B) HPE GreenLake Edge

C) HPE GreenLake Flex Capacity

D) HPE GreenLake AI Operations

E) HPE GreenLake Compliance Manager

F) HPE GreenLake Data Fabric

Answer: A

Explanation: HPE GreenLake Central is the feature that provides centralized management capabilities, enhancing security and compliance across deployment models. It allows businesses to manage policies and automate updates efficiently, ensuring all resources adhere to established security protocols and regulatory requirements. This centralized approach simplifies the administration of diverse environments, contributing to a streamlined and compliant IT operation.

Q146: Scenario-Based Question XYZ Corporation, a multinational company, is planning to migrate its SAP HANA workloads to the cloud. The company is considering HPE GreenLake as a potential solution due to its flexible consumption model. They need to ensure that the solution can handle fluctuating workloads and provide real-time analytics capabilities. Additionally, XYZ Corporation has strict compliance requirements and needs to maintain data sovereignty within certain geographic regions. Which feature of HPE GreenLake is most beneficial for addressing these specific needs?

A) HPE GreenLake's pay-per-use model for cost management

B) Built-in AI operations for automated performance tuning

C) Global compliance and data sovereignty features

D) Multi-cloud integration capabilities

E) Support for hybrid cloud environments

F) On-premises infrastructure with cloud-like flexibility

Answer: C

Explanation: HPE GreenLake's global compliance and data sovereignty features are crucial for organizations like XYZ Corporation, which has specific compliance requirements and needs to maintain data within certain regions. While the pay-per-use model, AI operations, and multi-cloud capabilities are valuable, the ability to manage data in compliance with regional laws is essential for regulatory adherence. This feature ensures that data residency and integrity are maintained according to local regulations, which is a primary concern for industries with stringent data governance requirements.

Q147: True/False Style Question HPE GreenLake for SAP and SAP HANA allows businesses to deploy SAP HANA workloads solely in the public cloud environment without any on-premises infrastructure.
A) True

B) False

Answer: B

Explanation: HPE GreenLake enables businesses to deploy SAP HANA workloads in a hybrid environment, which includes on-premises infrastructure with cloud-like flexibility. This approach allows businesses to maintain control over their data and operations while benefiting from the scalability and elasticity of cloud resources. It is not limited to solely public cloud deployment, providing a flexible solution that can adapt to the specific needs and constraints of the business.

Q148: Standard Multiple-Choice Question When configuring HPE GreenLake for SAP HANA, which of the following is a critical component to ensure high availability and disaster recovery?

A) Load balancing across multiple regions

B) Use of HPE Synergy frames

C) Implementation of HPE Primera storage arrays

D) Deployment across multiple availability zones

E) Integration with HPE OneView

F) Configuration of SAP HANA System Replication

Answer: F

Explanation: Configuring SAP HANA System Replication is a critical component for ensuring high availability and disaster recovery. This feature allows for continuous synchronization of data between primary and secondary systems, providing a robust mechanism to protect against system failures and data loss. While other options like load balancing and multi-zone deployment contribute to availability, SAP HANA System Replication specifically addresses the need for real-time data protection and system failover in the event of a disaster.

Q149: Fill-in-the-Gap Style Question In the context of HPE GreenLake for SAP, which component is responsible for providing real-time analytics and insights to optimize SAP workloads?

A) HPE InfoSight

B) SAP Data Services

C) HPE CloudPhysics

D) SAP BusinessObjects

E) HPE Nimble Storage

F) SAP Leonardo

Answer: A

Explanation: HPE InfoSight is the component that provides real-time analytics and insights to optimize SAP workloads. It leverages AI and machine learning to predict and prevent issues before they impact operations, thereby improving performance and availability. By analyzing data from across the infrastructure, HPE InfoSight enables proactive management and optimization of SAP environments, ensuring efficient resource utilization and minimizing downtime.

Q150: Standard Multiple-Choice Question Which HPE GreenLake feature specifically enhances the integration of SAP HANA with existing IT infrastructure to streamline data management processes?

A) HPE Ezmeral Data Fabric

B) HPE GreenLake Central

C) HPE ProLiant for Microsoft Azure Stack

D) HPE Composable Cloud

E) HPE OneSphere

F) HPE SimpliVity

Answer: A

Explanation: HPE Ezmeral Data Fabric enhances the integration of SAP HANA with existing IT infrastructure by providing a unified data platform that simplifies data management processes. It enables seamless data access and movement across different environments, ensuring efficient data integration and management. This capability is particularly important for organizations looking to streamline operations and improve data agility within their SAP HANA deployments.

Q151: Scenario-Based Question: A mid-sized tech company, TechVantage Solutions, is planning to transition from their existing on-premises infrastructure to a hybrid cloud model using HPE GreenLake for VMs and Containers. They have a mix of legacy applications and modern microservices and need to ensure seamless integration and management across both environments. The IT team is concerned about the complexity of managing workloads and ensuring optimal performance without disrupting their current operations. Which feature of HPE GreenLake enables TechVantage Solutions to efficiently manage their hybrid environment and optimize resource utilization?

A) HPE OneView for Automation

B) HPE InfoSight for predictive analytics

C) HPE Synergy for composable infrastructure

D) HPE CloudPhysics for cost management

E) HPE GreenLake Central for unified management

F) HPE SimpliVity for hyperconvergence

Answer: E

Explanation: HPE GreenLake Central provides a unified management interface that allows businesses like TechVantage Solutions to manage both their on-premises and cloud resources efficiently. This feature is crucial for hybrid environments as it enables seamless integration and optimization of resources across various platforms. The ability to manage applications, data, and resources from a single dashboard helps in reducing complexity and improving operational efficiency, which addresses the concerns of TechVantage's IT team about potential disruptions and performance issues.

Q152: True/False Question: HPE GreenLake can only be used for managing virtual machines (VMs) and does not support containerized workloads.

A) True

B) False

Answer: B

Explanation: HPE GreenLake is designed to support a wide range of workloads, including both virtual machines and containerized applications. The platform provides the flexibility and tools necessary to manage modern application architectures, such as those using Kubernetes for containers, alongside traditional virtualized environments. This capability allows businesses to leverage the benefits of containerization, such as scalability and efficiency, while still managing legacy applications through VMs.

Q153: Which HPE GreenLake feature specifically aids in the proactive identification and resolution of issues in VM and container environments by utilizing AI and machine learning?

A) HPE OneView

B) HPE InfoSight

C) HPE Synergy

D) HPE CloudPhysics

E) HPE GreenLake Central

F) HPE SimpliVity

Answer: B

Explanation: HPE InfoSight is an AI-driven tool that provides predictive analytics and proactive insights to identify and resolve potential issues before they impact the environment. It uses machine learning to analyze data from across the infrastructure to predict problems and recommend solutions, thereby optimizing performance and availability for both VMs and containerized environments. This proactive approach is crucial for maintaining high levels of service in complex, hybrid IT setups.

Q154: Fill-in-the-Gap Question: By using _____, organizations can allocate resources dynamically to meet the changing demands of applications in real-time, which is essential for managing containerized workloads efficiently within HPE GreenLake.

A) HPE OneView

B) HPE InfoSight

C) HPE Synergy

D) HPE CloudPhysics

E) HPE GreenLake Central

F) HPE SimpliVity

Answer: C

Explanation: HPE Synergy provides a composable infrastructure that allows for dynamic resource allocation, which is particularly beneficial for managing containerized workloads that require flexibility and scalability. This feature enables organizations to configure compute, storage, and networking resources on-demand, helping to meet the fluctuating resource demands of modern applications and ensuring efficient workload management within the HPE GreenLake model.

Q155: Which aspect of HPE GreenLake helps businesses optimize their cloud spending and resource utilization by providing detailed insights into usage patterns and cost allocation?

A) HPE OneView

B) HPE InfoSight

C) HPE Synergy

D) HPE CloudPhysics

E) HPE GreenLake Central

F) HPE SimpliVity

Answer: D

Explanation: HPE CloudPhysics provides comprehensive insights into cloud usage and cost management. This tool is designed to help businesses optimize their cloud spending by analyzing usage patterns and identifying areas for cost savings. By using CloudPhysics, organizations can make informed decisions about resource allocation and utilization, ensuring that they are getting the most value from their HPE GreenLake investment. This capability is particularly important in a hybrid cloud environment where cost management can become complex due to the mix of on-premises and cloud resources.

Q156: A medium-sized enterprise, TechSolutions Inc., is planning to transition their IT infrastructure to a hybrid cloud environment. They are considering using HPE GreenLake to manage workloads across on-premises and cloud resources. The CTO is particularly concerned about scalability and cost predictability as the company anticipates rapid growth in the coming years. Additionally, they require a solution that integrates seamlessly with their existing VMware environment. Which feature of the HPE GreenLake platform best addresses the company's need for scalability and cost management?

A) Pay-per-use pricing model

B) Dedicated HPE support team

C) HPE OneView integration

D) Built-in data analytics tool

E) Multi-cloud compatibility

F) HPE Ezmeral software suite

Answer: A

Explanation: The pay-per-use pricing model in HPE GreenLake is designed to provide scalability and cost predictability. It allows companies like TechSolutions Inc. to scale their

IT resources up or down based on demand without incurring unnecessary costs. This model aligns costs with actual usage, offering financial flexibility and operational efficiency. It eliminates the need for large upfront investments and ensures that the organization only pays for the resources it consumes. This is particularly beneficial for companies anticipating rapid growth, as it allows them to scale seamlessly without financial strain. The integration with VMware is also supported by GreenLake, but the key concern here was scalability and cost management, making the pay-per-use model the most relevant feature.

Q157: True or False: HPE GreenLake's architecture requires all data to be transferred to public cloud environments for processing.
A) True

B) False

Answer: B

Explanation: The statement is false. HPE GreenLake's architecture is designed to provide a cloud-like experience on-premises or in a co-location facility, allowing data to be processed where it resides. This means that organizations can keep their data on-premises for security, compliance, or latency reasons while still benefiting from the cloud's scalability and flexibility. GreenLake offers the ability to run workloads locally, which helps in managing sensitive data without transferring it to a public cloud environment. This approach is particularly valuable for companies with strict regulatory requirements or those concerned about data sovereignty.

Q158: Which component of HPE GreenLake is responsible for providing a unified view and management of both on-premises and cloud-based resources?
A) HPE OneView

B) HPE GreenLake Central

C) HPE Synergy Composer

D) HPE Cloud Volumes

E) HPE Ezmeral Container Platform

F) HPE InfoSight

Answer: B

Explanation: HPE GreenLake Central is the component that provides a unified view and management interface for both on-premises and cloud-based resources. It acts as a centralized control plane where users can monitor, manage, and optimize their entire IT environment. This includes capabilities such as usage analytics, capacity planning, and cost management. GreenLake Central integrates with various tools and platforms, offering a seamless experience for IT administrators to manage hybrid environments effectively. Its comprehensive dashboard allows for easy tracking of resource utilization, ensuring that organizations can make informed decisions and optimize their IT operations.

Q159: In the context of HPE GreenLake, what is the primary benefit of using HPE InfoSight within the platform?

A) Provides backup and recovery solutions

B) Integrates with third-party cloud providers

C) Offers predictive analytics and AI-driven insights

D) Facilitates workload containerization

E) Manages network traffic efficiently

F) Automates compliance reporting

Answer: C

Explanation: The primary benefit of using HPE InfoSight within the HPE GreenLake platform is its ability to offer predictive analytics and AI-driven insights. HPE InfoSight is a cloud-based AI platform that predicts and prevents issues across the IT environment. It provides deep insights into the performance and health of IT infrastructure, helping to optimize resources and improve operational efficiency. By leveraging machine learning algorithms, InfoSight can identify patterns and anomalies, offering proactive recommendations and solutions. This reduces downtime and enhances the overall reliability of IT operations, making it a valuable tool for organizations looking to maximize their infrastructure's performance and availability.

Q160: Fill in the gap: HPE GreenLake offers a _____ that allows businesses to manage and deploy containerized applications across their hybrid cloud environments.

A) Virtualization platform

B) Cloud-native security solution

C) Software-defined storage solution

D) Container orchestration platform

E) Continuous integration tool

F) Network optimization tool

Answer: D

Explanation: HPE GreenLake offers a container orchestration platform, specifically through the HPE Ezmeral Container Platform. This platform enables businesses to manage and deploy containerized applications seamlessly across their hybrid cloud environments. By using Kubernetes as a base for container orchestration, the Ezmeral platform provides scalability, flexibility, and efficiency in running containerized workloads. It supports both stateful and stateless applications, offering a robust solution for modern application development and deployment. This capability is crucial for organizations aiming to accelerate their digital transformation and enhance their agility in a rapidly changing market.

Q161: Scenario-Based Question A multinational corporation, TechGlobal Inc., is planning to implement HPE GreenLake Private Cloud for Business to enhance their IT infrastructure's responsiveness and scalability. Their main objectives include reducing capital expenditure, increasing operational efficiency, and ensuring data sovereignty across various regions. The company has data centers in North America, Europe, and Asia, each with distinct compliance requirements and varying workloads. As an HPE GreenLake Administrator, you are tasked with designing a solution that meets these regional needs while optimizing overall resource allocation and cost. What is the most important initial step in developing the GreenLake solution for TechGlobal Inc.?

A) Conduct a workload analysis to determine resource needs across data centers.

B) Develop a unified compliance framework for all regions.

C) Negotiate service level agreements with HPE.

D) Deploy a pilot solution in the North American data center.

E) Design a custom billing model for each region.

F) Create a hybrid cloud integration plan.

Answer: A

Explanation: The initial and most critical step in developing a GreenLake solution for TechGlobal Inc. is conducting a comprehensive workload analysis. This analysis will help identify the specific resource requirements, usage patterns, and potential bottlenecks across the data centers in different regions. Understanding these factors is crucial for tailoring the HPE GreenLake solution to meet TechGlobal's objectives, such as optimizing cost and efficiency while maintaining compliance. The workload analysis provides the foundation upon which other decisions, such as compliance frameworks and billing models, can be effectively built. Without this step, the risk of over-provisioning or under-provisioning resources increases, potentially leading to inefficiencies and increased costs.

Q162: Fill-in-the-Gap Question In the context of the HPE GreenLake Private Cloud for Business, the _____ feature allows businesses to manage and monitor their cloud resources in real-time, providing insights into cost, usage, and performance metrics.

A) HPE OneView

B) HPE InfoSight

C) HPE CloudPhysics

D) HPE Right Mix Advisor

E) HPE Operations Bridge

F) HPE GreenLake Central

Answer: F

Explanation: HPE GreenLake Central is the platform that provides a comprehensive suite of tools for managing and monitoring cloud resources in real-time. It offers businesses transparency and insights into their cloud infrastructure, including cost, usage, and performance metrics. This visibility is essential for optimizing resource allocation, controlling costs, and ensuring that the cloud environment aligns with business objectives. HPE GreenLake Central's dashboards and reporting features empower administrators to make informed decisions, enhancing operational efficiency and strategic planning.

Q163: True/False Question In HPE GreenLake Private Cloud for Business, the billing model is entirely fixed, with no flexibility to adjust based on actual usage.

A) True

B) False

Answer: B

Explanation: The statement is false. One of the key advantages of the HPE GreenLake Private Cloud for Business is its flexible billing model, which is based on actual usage rather than fixed costs. This consumption-based model allows businesses to pay only for the resources they use, providing greater financial flexibility and the ability to scale according to demand. This approach helps in reducing capital expenditures and aligning IT spending with business growth, ensuring that resources are efficiently utilized and costs are controlled.

Q164: Standard Multiple-Choice Question Which of the following is a primary benefit of using HPE GreenLake Private Cloud for Business in a hybrid cloud strategy?

A) Guaranteed data residency in all global regions

B) Unlimited capacity for data storage

C) On-premises deployment with cloud-like flexibility

D) Integration with third-party cloud providers

E) Pre-configured network security settings

F) Access to HPE's proprietary hardware only

Answer: C

Explanation: HPE GreenLake Private Cloud for Business provides on-premises deployment with cloud-like flexibility, which is a major benefit in a hybrid cloud strategy. This allows businesses to enjoy the agility and scalability of the cloud while maintaining control over their data and infrastructure within their own data centers. Such flexibility is crucial for organizations that require the security and compliance of on-premises solutions but also want to benefit from the dynamic resource allocation and cost efficiencies typically associated with public clouds. By integrating with existing IT environments, HPE GreenLake enables seamless expansion and retraction of resources based on real-time needs.

A) Selecting the right hardware configurations

B) Implementing multi-factor authentication for all users

C) Ensuring data encryption both at rest and in transit

D) Limiting the number of virtual machines per host

E) Establishing a disaster recovery plan

F) Configuring automated patch management

Answer: C

Explanation: Ensuring data encryption both at rest and in transit is a critical consideration for compliance with industry regulations when deploying HPE GreenLake Private Cloud for Business. Regulations like GDPR, HIPAA, and others often mandate stringent data protection measures, and encryption is a fundamental component of safeguarding sensitive information against unauthorized access. By implementing robust encryption protocols, businesses can mitigate the risk of data breaches and demonstrate compliance with legal and regulatory requirements. This approach not only protects the organization's reputation but also builds trust with customers and stakeholders, essential for maintaining business operations and avoiding legal penalties.

Q166: A mid-sized enterprise, XYZ Corp, has recently transitioned its IT infrastructure to the HPE GreenLake platform to better manage its growing data storage needs. The IT manager is tasked with optimizing storage utilization across multiple departments while ensuring data security and compliance with regional data protection laws. The company has diverse storage requirements ranging from high-performance storage for transactional databases to archival storage for compliance records. What is the most appropriate approach for the IT manager to effectively allocate storage resources to meet these diverse needs within HPE GreenLake?

A) Use a single storage pool for all departments to simplify management and monitoring.

B) Allocate dedicated storage resources for each department based on their individual requirements.

C) Implement a tiered storage model, assigning high-performance storage to critical applications and archival storage to compliance records.

D) Enable automated storage provisioning to dynamically allocate resources based on real-time usage patterns.

E) Focus on compliance requirements first, then allocate remaining resources based on performance needs.

F) Integrate third-party storage solutions to supplement HPE GreenLake's capabilities.

Answer: C

Explanation: The most efficient approach for XYZ Corp is to implement a tiered storage model, which aligns with varying performance and compliance needs. HPE GreenLake's flexibility allows for the assignment of high-performance storage to applications that demand quick access and processing speed, such as transactional databases. Conversely, compliance records, which are typically accessed less frequently, can be stored on archival storage tiers, optimizing cost and performance. This strategy not only ensures that critical applications receive the resources they need but also maintains compliance by using appropriate storage types for different data categories. This approach also allows for better cost management by matching storage resources to their specific workload requirements.

Q167: When configuring storage in HPE GreenLake, which feature allows administrators to automate the scaling of storage resources based on predictive analytics?

A) Manual scaling

B) Predictive scaling

C) Policy-based scaling

D) Dynamic scaling

E) Reactive scaling

F) Automated scaling

Answer: B

Explanation: Predictive scaling is a feature that leverages analytics to forecast future storage requirements and automatically adjust resources accordingly. This allows administrators to proactively manage storage capacities, ensuring that there is always sufficient resource availability to meet demand without manual intervention. This feature is crucial for maintaining performance and cost efficiency in environments with fluctuating workloads. By using predictive analytics, HPE GreenLake can anticipate needs based on historical data trends, which helps prevent resource over-allocation or shortages, ensuring optimized storage management.

Q168: True or False: HPE GreenLake supports the integration of third-party storage solutions.

A) True

B) False

Answer: A

Explanation: True. HPE GreenLake is designed to be a versatile cloud service platform that supports integration with third-party storage solutions. This interoperability is crucial for organizations that want to leverage existing investments in other storage technologies while benefiting from the scalability and flexibility of the GreenLake model. By supporting third-party integrations, HPE GreenLake provides a cohesive storage management framework that can accommodate diverse infrastructure landscapes, enabling businesses to maintain operational continuity and achieve their storage objectives.

Q169: In HPE GreenLake, what is the primary benefit of utilizing a multi-tenant architecture for storage management?

A) Simplified billing for individual departments

B) Enhanced data security through isolation

C) Reduced storage costs by sharing resources

D) Increased complexity in management

E) Improved performance through dedicated resources

F) Better tracking of individual user activities

Answer: C

Explanation: The primary benefit of a multi-tenant architecture in HPE GreenLake is the reduction of storage costs by sharing resources among different users or departments within an organization. This architecture allows multiple tenants to use the same physical infrastructure while maintaining logical isolation of data, which maximizes resource utilization and reduces overall expenses. By pooling resources, organizations can achieve economies of scale, leading to cost savings. Additionally, multi-tenancy simplifies management by centralizing control while still providing isolated environments for different users, thus maintaining a balance between cost-efficiency and data security.

Q170: During a quarterly review, it was identified that the storage utilization in HPE GreenLake has significantly increased. The IT team must identify the application responsible for the surge and implement measures to manage resource usage effectively. Which HPE GreenLake feature should they use to analyze storage consumption by application?

A) Usage reporting dashboard

B) Application profiling tool

C) Resource allocation monitor

D) Storage analytics platform

E) Performance assessment module

F) Capacity planning toolkit

Answer: A

Explanation: The usage reporting dashboard in HPE GreenLake is the appropriate feature for analyzing storage consumption by application. This tool provides detailed insights into how resources are being utilized across different applications and departments. By examining these reports, the IT team can identify which applications are driving increased storage usage and take appropriate actions to optimize resource allocation. This might include adjusting storage tiers, implementing data deduplication techniques, or setting usage policies to ensure efficient storage management. The dashboard's comprehensive analytics facilitate data-driven decision-making, allowing for better resource optimization and cost management.

Q171: You are the IT manager at a mid-sized manufacturing company that recently adopted HPE GreenLake to optimize IT resources and costs. Your team is responsible for managing the infrastructure and ensuring seamless operations. During a routine check, you realize that your team needs additional training on using the HPE GreenLake support portal effectively. You want to ensure that the team can navigate the portal to access technical support, view usage reports, and manage subscriptions efficiently. Which feature of the HPE GreenLake support portal will be most beneficial for providing your team with the necessary training resources?

A) Direct access to HPE technical support engineers

B) Comprehensive training modules and documentation

C) Real-time monitoring dashboard

D) Advanced subscription management tools

E) Interactive community forums

F) Personalized account management

Answer: B

Explanation: The HPE GreenLake support portal offers a range of features designed to assist users in managing their IT infrastructure effectively. For a team needing training, the availability of comprehensive training modules and documentation is crucial. These resources provide step-by-step guidance on using the portal, accessing technical support, and understanding various functionalities. While direct access to HPE technical support engineers and real-time monitoring dashboards are important for operational support, they do not cater directly to training needs. Interactive community forums and personalized account management are helpful for user engagement and customization, respectively, but do not focus on structured learning. Thus, comprehensive training modules and documentation are the most beneficial for equipping your team with the knowledge to navigate the portal proficiently.

Q172: The HPE GreenLake support portal provides a feature that allows users to track their IT resource consumption in real-time. Which of the following best describes this feature?

A) Subscription Management

B) Technical Support Dashboard

C) Real-Time Usage Reporting

D) Billing and Invoicing System

E) Security Alerts and Notifications

F) Resource Allocation Wizard

Answer: C

Explanation: Real-time usage reporting is a critical feature of the HPE GreenLake support portal that allows users to monitor their IT resource consumption continuously. This functionality is essential for organizations to track usage patterns, optimize resource allocation, and manage costs effectively. Subscription management, billing systems, and security alerts serve different purposes such as handling contract details, financial transactions, and security monitoring, respectively. The technical support dashboard and resource allocation wizard are geared towards operational support and planning rather than real-time tracking. Therefore, real-time usage reporting is the feature that directly addresses the need for monitoring IT resource consumption.

Q173: True or False: The HPE GreenLake support portal allows administrators to customize alert notifications based on specific usage thresholds.

A) True

B) False

Answer: A

Explanation: The HPE GreenLake support portal is designed to provide flexible and proactive management of IT resources. One of its features includes the ability to customize alert notifications based on predefined usage thresholds. This capability enables administrators to receive timely alerts when resource consumption approaches or exceeds specified limits, allowing them to take corrective actions promptly. This feature is part of the portal's commitment to optimizing resource utilization and preventing unexpected overuse, contributing to effective cost management and operational efficiency. Thus, the statement is true, as the portal indeed allows for such customization.

Q174: A large retail organization is using the HPE GreenLake support portal to manage its global IT operations. The organization needs to ensure high availability and minimize downtime across its multiple data centers. Which feature of the portal should the organization leverage to monitor and maintain optimal performance?

A) Advanced Troubleshooting Tools

B) Real-Time Usage Reporting

C) Security and Compliance Dashboard

D) Proactive Health Monitoring

E) Customizable Alert System

F) Subscription Management Interface

Answer: D

Explanation: For an organization focused on ensuring high availability and minimizing downtime, proactive health monitoring is a critical feature of the HPE GreenLake support portal. This functionality continuously assesses the health of IT infrastructure components, enabling early detection of potential issues that could lead to downtime. By leveraging this feature, the organization can take preventative measures to address problems before they impact operations. While advanced troubleshooting tools and customizable alert systems are valuable for issue resolution and notifications, respectively, proactive health monitoring provides a more comprehensive approach to maintaining optimal performance and uptime. Real-time usage reporting, security and compliance dashboards, and subscription management interfaces serve different operational needs that do not directly address availability and downtime concerns.

Q175: While managing the HPE GreenLake support portal, an administrator notices that the portal's interface seems cluttered, making it difficult to find specific tools quickly. To enhance user experience, which feature should the administrator use to streamline the portal's interface?

A) Simplified Navigation Menu

B) Customizable Dashboard Layout

C) Integrated Search Functionality

D) User Activity Log

E) Default View Settings

F) Role-Based Access Control

Answer: B

Explanation: The HPE GreenLake support portal offers a customizable dashboard layout that allows administrators to streamline the interface according to their preferences. By using this feature, an administrator can organize tools and information in a way that enhances visibility and accessibility, reducing clutter and improving user experience. While a simplified navigation menu and integrated search functionality aid in locating specific tools, they do not reduce interface clutter. User activity logs, default view settings, and role-based access control are more focused on security and operational management rather than interface customization. Therefore, customizing the dashboard layout is the most effective way to enhance the user experience by organizing the portal's interface according to user needs.

Q176: A mid-sized retail company has been experiencing rapid growth, leading to increased demands on its IT infrastructure. The company is struggling with scaling its on-premises data center to meet seasonal spikes in customer demand, which is impacting customer experience during peak shopping periods. They are considering moving to a hybrid cloud solution to ensure that they have the flexibility to scale resources as needed. The company is particularly interested in optimizing costs and ensuring data security. How can HPE GreenLake address these challenges?

A) By providing a fixed-cost, long-term contract that simplifies budgeting, but offers limited scalability.

B) By offering a pay-per-use model that aligns costs with actual usage, allowing for scalability during peak periods.

C) By requiring full upfront payment for anticipated peak capacity, ensuring resources are always available.

D) By offering a public cloud solution that replaces all on-premises infrastructure, reducing security concerns.

E) By providing a rigid infrastructure that requires manual intervention to scale resources.

F) By offering guaranteed uptime without any customization options for specific business needs.

Answer: B

Explanation: HPE GreenLake's pay-per-use model is designed to align costs with actual resource usage, making it ideal for businesses experiencing fluctuating demands, like the mid-sized retail company in this scenario. This model enables businesses to scale resources dynamically, ensuring they meet peak demands without over-provisioning during off-peak times. Additionally, HPE GreenLake offers a hybrid cloud environment that can help optimize costs and enhance data security by maintaining critical workloads on-premises while leveraging cloud resources as needed. This flexible approach ensures the company can effectively manage costs while also safeguarding customer data, addressing both of their primary business concerns.

Q177: Which of the following is a key business driver for organizations to adopt HPE GreenLake?

A) The need for fixed, predictable IT expenses.

B) The ability to rapidly scale IT resources without upfront capital investment.

C) The requirement for entirely on-premises IT solutions.

D) The desire to eliminate all IT management and maintenance responsibilities.

E) The preference for a one-time payment model for IT infrastructure.

F) The need for a public cloud-only strategy.

Answer: B

Explanation: A significant business driver for organizations adopting HPE GreenLake is the ability to rapidly scale IT resources without the need for upfront capital investment. This is particularly valuable for businesses with variable workloads or those experiencing growth, as it allows them to align costs with actual usage and avoid the substantial upfront costs associated with traditional IT infrastructure. HPE GreenLake's consumption-based model provides flexibility and financial predictability, which are critical for businesses seeking to optimize their IT spending while maintaining the agility to respond to changing demands.

Q178: True/False: HPE GreenLake can only be used for cloud-native applications and is not suitable for traditional workloads.

A) True

B) False

Answer: B

Explanation: False. HPE GreenLake is designed to support a wide range of workloads, including both cloud-native and traditional applications. Its flexible architecture allows businesses to deploy hybrid cloud solutions that can host traditional workloads on-premises while also providing cloud-like scalability and management. This versatility makes

HPE GreenLake suitable for enterprises looking to modernize their IT infrastructure while still supporting legacy applications, ensuring a seamless transition to a more flexible, consumption-based model.

Q179: In what way does HPE GreenLake help businesses achieve better data security compared to traditional public cloud solutions?

A) By storing all data in a single, centralized public cloud location.

B) By requiring customers to manage their own security protocols independently.

C) By offering on-premises deployment options, keeping sensitive data within the customer's own data center.

D) By providing standardized security solutions with no customization options.

E) By utilizing a shared infrastructure with multiple tenants to reduce costs.

F) By limiting access to data through a single, static security protocol.

Answer: C

Explanation: HPE GreenLake helps businesses achieve better data security by offering on-premises deployment options, which allow organizations to keep sensitive data within their own data centers. This approach provides businesses with greater control over their data security protocols and compliance requirements, reducing the risks associated with data breaches and unauthorized access that can occur in public cloud environments. By maintaining critical workloads and sensitive data on-premises, businesses can leverage HPE GreenLake's hybrid cloud capabilities while ensuring robust data protection and meeting regulatory standards.

Q180: A large financial institution is evaluating its IT infrastructure strategy to better support its digital transformation goals. They aim to improve operational efficiency, reduce costs, and enhance customer experiences through advanced analytics and personalized services. Given their regulatory requirements, data privacy, and need for real-time processing, they are considering a hybrid cloud solution. How does HPE GreenLake align with the institution's IT strategy?

A) By providing a fully public cloud environment to minimize on-premises management.

B) By offering a pay-per-use model that scales with the institution's analytics and processing needs.

C) By enforcing a one-size-fits-all solution that may not align with regulatory requirements.

D) By restricting the deployment of advanced analytics to pre-defined templates.

E) By providing a subscription model with substantial upfront costs to ensure infrastructure availability.

F) By offering limited support for personalized services and customer engagement tools.

Answer: B

Explanation: HPE GreenLake's pay-per-use model is particularly well-suited for a large financial institution seeking to enhance operational efficiency and reduce costs while supporting advanced analytics and personalized services. This model enables the institution to scale its IT resources in line with analytics and processing demands, ensuring it can process real-time data efficiently without unnecessary expenditures. Additionally, HPE GreenLake's hybrid cloud capabilities allow the institution to keep sensitive data on-premises, addressing regulatory compliance and data privacy concerns. This aligns with the institution's digital transformation goals by providing the flexibility, security, and scalability needed to deliver improved customer experiences through innovative services.

Q181: Scenario-Based Question XYZ Corporation has recently expanded its operations to multiple regions and aims to streamline user management by integrating their existing identity management system with HPE GreenLake. The IT department is tasked with implementing identity federation to allow seamless Single Sign-On (SSO) for employees accessing HPE GreenLake services. This integration needs to accommodate a diverse workforce while maintaining high security and compliance with regional data protection laws. What initial step should the IT department take to ensure a successful identity federation integration with HPE GreenLake?   ---

A) Configure SSO settings directly in the HPE GreenLake portal without consulting any external resources.

B) Assess and document the current identity management system to understand its compatibility with SAML or OAuth protocols.

C) Immediately deploy a third-party identity provider without reviewing existing policies.

D) Enable multi-factor authentication (MFA) for all users before proceeding with federation.

E) Create individual user accounts manually within HPE GreenLake to test SSO integration.

F) Bypass identity federation and use a VPN for secure access to HPE GreenLake.

Answer: B

Explanation: Integrating identity federation with HPE GreenLake involves using protocols like SAML or OAuth to enable SSO. The first essential step is to assess and document the current identity management system to ensure compatibility with these protocols. This helps identify necessary configurations and potential challenges in the integration process. Skipping this assessment could lead to integration failures or security vulnerabilities. Therefore, understanding the system's capabilities is crucial before proceeding with any configuration changes or deployments.

Q182: True/False Style Question The integration of identity federation with HPE GreenLake requires that the identity provider must support the OAuth protocol.   ---

A) True

B) False

Answer: B

Explanation: While OAuth is a widely used protocol for authorization, identity federation with HPE GreenLake can also be achieved using the SAML protocol. SAML is often preferred for enterprise-level SSO integrations due to its robust support for authentication assertions. Therefore, stating that OAuth is a requirement is incorrect; the integration could leverage either protocol, depending on the existing infrastructure and specific needs.

Q183: Multiple-Choice Question Which of the following best describes the role of a Security Assertion Markup Language (SAML) assertion in HPE GreenLake's identity federation?   ---

A) It stores user passwords and encryption keys for secure authentication.

B) It provides a single point of failure for the authentication process.

C) It delivers authentication and attribute information from the identity provider to the service provider.

D) It encrypts the data transferred between the client and server during login.

E) It provides a backup authentication method in case the primary fails.

F) It manages user access rights within the HPE GreenLake platform.

Answer: C

Explanation: In the context of identity federation, a SAML assertion is a critical component that carries authentication and attribute information from the identity provider to the service provider, like HPE GreenLake. This allows the service provider to authenticate the user based on the trusted assertion, facilitating SSO. SAML assertions do not store passwords or encryption keys; instead, they serve as secure tokens that convey information necessary for authentication and authorization processes.

Q184: Multiple-Choice Question During the integration of HPE GreenLake with an existing identity provider for SSO, which aspect is most crucial to ensure compliance with data protection regulations like GDPR?   ---

A) Ensuring OAuth tokens are stored securely.

B) Limiting authentication attempts to prevent brute force attacks.

C) Configuring consent mechanisms to inform users about data sharing.

D) Implementing robust password policies for all users.

E) Utilizing firewalls to protect SSO communication channels.

F) Creating a detailed log of all user access attempts.

Answer: C

Explanation: Compliance with data protection regulations such as GDPR requires transparency regarding how user data is handled and shared. Configuring consent mechanisms is crucial in informing users about what data will be shared with HPE GreenLake during the SSO process. This ensures that users are aware of and consent to the data exchange, aligning with GDPR's principles of informed consent and data minimization. While other options are important for security, consent mechanisms directly address compliance requirements.

Q185: Multiple-Choice Question When configuring identity federation for HPE GreenLake, which type of metadata is typically exchanged between the identity provider and the service provider?

A) User demographic information.

B) Security questions and answers.

C) Public key certificates and service endpoints.

D) Password hashes and salt values.

E) VPN configuration settings.

F) Network bandwidth requirements.

Answer: C

Explanation: In identity federation, metadata exchange between the identity provider and the service provider, such as HPE GreenLake, typically includes public key certificates and service endpoints. This information is vital for establishing trust and facilitating the secure exchange of authentication assertions. The public key certificates are used to verify signatures on SAML assertions, while service endpoints define the URLs where authentication requests and responses should be sent. This metadata ensures that both parties can communicate securely and effectively.

Q186: A mid-sized enterprise, TechNova, is shifting its infrastructure management to a more automated model to reduce manual overhead and increase service delivery speed. The company has chosen HPE GreenLake as their hybrid cloud solution and is looking to integrate it with Ansible to automate infrastructure provisioning and management tasks. The IT team at TechNova is relatively new to automation tools and is seeking a method that allows them to effectively manage HPE GreenLake resources using Ansible. They require a solution that not only supports basic operations but also provides robust error handling and reporting capabilities. Which of the following approaches should TechNova adopt to achieve seamless integration of HPE GreenLake with Ansible?

A) Use the Ansible playbooks provided by the HPE GitHub community repository to manage GreenLake resources.

B) Develop custom Python scripts to interface between Ansible and HPE GreenLake API for more control.

C) Utilize the Ansible modules specifically designed for HPE GreenLake that are available in the Ansible Galaxy library.

D) Implement a continuous integration pipeline with Jenkins to manage Ansible playbooks for HPE GreenLake.

E) Leverage HPE OneView Ansible modules, applying them directly to HPE GreenLake management.

F) Use Terraform alongside Ansible to enhance the provisioning capabilities of GreenLake resources.

Answer: C

Explanation: Ansible Galaxy is a community repository that provides pre-built Ansible modules for various platforms, including HPE GreenLake. Utilizing these specific Ansible modules allows TechNova to manage their GreenLake resources effectively, offering an out-of-the-box solution that reduces the need for custom development. These modules are designed to support a wide range of operations on HPE GreenLake, including provisioning, configuration, and management tasks. Additionally, they include error handling and reporting capabilities, which are essential for robust automation solutions. This approach is ideal for teams new to automation, as it provides a standardized, community-supported method for integrating Ansible with HPE GreenLake, ensuring compatibility and reducing the risk of errors.

Q187: True or False: The integration of HPE GreenLake with Ansible requires the installation of additional software components on the GreenLake management console.
A) True

B) False

Answer: B

Explanation: HPE GreenLake's integration with Ansible does not require the installation of additional software components on the GreenLake management console itself. The integration is typically achieved through the use of Ansible modules and playbooks that interact with the GreenLake API. These modules are executed on a server where Ansible is installed, which communicates with the GreenLake environment remotely. This approach maintains the integrity and security of the GreenLake management console while leveraging Ansible's automation capabilities externally.

Q188: When setting up Ansible to manage HPE GreenLake resources, which authentication method is recommended to ensure secure and reliable API access?

A) Basic Authentication with username and password stored in the playbook

B) OAuth2 tokens stored in Ansible Vault

C) API keys hardcoded within the Ansible configuration files

D) SSH key-based authentication

E) LDAP-based authentication

F) Kerberos authentication

Answer: B

Explanation: OAuth2 tokens stored in Ansible Vault are the recommended method for authenticating with HPE GreenLake APIs securely. OAuth2 provides a secure token-based authentication mechanism that is more secure than basic authentication, which can expose credentials. Storing these tokens in Ansible Vault ensures they are encrypted and protected from unauthorized access, maintaining the security of the integration. This approach minimizes the risk of credential leakage and aligns with best practices for managing sensitive information within automation scripts.

During a scheduled maintenance window, the IT team at a large corporation plans to automate the expansion of storage resources in their HPE GreenLake environment using Ansible. However, they encounter an error due to insufficient permissions while attempting to execute the playbook. To resolve this issue, which step should the team take to ensure the playbook runs successfully?

A) Modify the playbook to include root-level access for all operations.

B) Update the Ansible configuration to run in 'sudo' mode by default.

C) Ensure the API credentials used have the necessary permissions to modify storage resources.

D) Restart the Ansible control node to refresh the environment variables.

E) Execute the playbook as a different user with administrative privileges.

F) Adjust the inventory file to include the correct host definition for the storage resource.

Answer: C

Explanation: The error encountered is due to the API credentials used lacking the necessary permissions to modify storage resources within the HPE GreenLake environment. Ensuring that the API credentials have the appropriate permissions is crucial for the successful execution of the Ansible playbook. This involves verifying and updating the user roles and permissions associated with the credentials to include operations on storage resources. This approach addresses the root cause of the error without resorting to potentially risky practices like using root access or altering default configurations that could lead to security vulnerabilities.

Q190: To optimize the performance of Ansible when managing a large-scale HPE GreenLake deployment, which strategy should be implemented?

A) Increase the number of forks used by Ansible to execute tasks in parallel.

B) Reduce the verbosity level in Ansible to minimize logging overhead.

C) Utilize Ansible Tower to distribute workloads across multiple nodes.

D) Limit the number of tasks per playbook to streamline execution.

E) Implement a callback plugin to monitor task execution time.

F) Use inventory scripts to dynamically generate host lists based on GreenLake resource tags.

Answer: A

Explanation: Increasing the number of forks used by Ansible allows for the execution of tasks in parallel, which can significantly enhance performance when managing large-scale deployments like an HPE GreenLake environment. Ansible defaults to a limited number of forks, and raising this number enables more simultaneous connections to target nodes, reducing the overall time required for playbook execution. This strategy is particularly beneficial in environments with numerous resources to manage, ensuring efficient use of available system resources while maintaining performance and scalability. However, care should be taken to adjust the number of forks based on the capabilities of the system running Ansible to avoid overloading it.

Q191: Scenario-Based Question: A mid-sized company, TechFusion Inc., has recently adopted HPE GreenLake to manage its hybrid IT infrastructure. As part of their digital transformation strategy, they plan to leverage HPE InfoSight for advanced analytics. The IT team is tasked with ensuring that InfoSight's predictive analytics are effectively integrated to enhance performance and preemptively address potential issues. However, they are concerned about the complexity of integrating their existing legacy systems with InfoSight. They need a solution that minimizes disruption while maximizing the insights gained from their infrastructure. What initial step should the IT team take to ensure a seamless integration of HPE InfoSight with their current systems?

A) Conduct a full audit of existing IT systems to identify integration points.

B) Directly integrate HPE InfoSight with all legacy systems without modifications.

C) Perform a pilot test on a non-critical segment of the infrastructure.

D) Hire a third-party consultant to manage the integration process.

E) Upgrade all legacy systems to the latest version before integration.

F) Deploy HPE InfoSight only on new systems and gradually phase out legacy systems.

Answer: A

Explanation: The first step in integrating HPE InfoSight with existing systems is to conduct a comprehensive audit of the current IT infrastructure. This audit helps to identify potential integration points, compatibility issues, and areas where predictive analytics can provide the most value. By understanding the existing environment, the IT team can develop a strategic integration plan that minimizes disruption, leverages the full capabilities of InfoSight, and ensures legacy systems can be supported effectively. Skipping this step could lead to unforeseen challenges and suboptimal performance of the analytics platform.

Q192: True/False Question: HPE InfoSight can automatically integrate with all legacy systems without any additional configuration or adjustments.
A) True

B) False

Answer: B

Explanation: HPE InfoSight requires configuration and possibly adjustments to integrate effectively with legacy systems. Legacy systems often have unique architectures and may not natively support modern analytics tools. Therefore, additional configuration or middleware may be necessary to enable seamless integration. Assuming automatic integration without any setup can lead to inaccurate analytics and missed insights.

Q193: Standard Multiple-Choice Question: Which feature of HPE InfoSight significantly enhances its predictive analytics capabilities when integrated with HPE GreenLake?

A) Real-time data visualization

B) Automated ticket generation

C) Cross-stack telemetry

D) Manual performance tuning

E) Static reporting templates

F) Local storage analytics

Answer: C

Explanation: Cross-stack telemetry is a key feature that enhances predictive analytics by collecting data from across the entire IT stack, including servers, storage, and network components. This comprehensive data collection allows InfoSight to provide deep insights into system performance, potential bottlenecks, and failure predictions. Without cross-stack telemetry, the analytics would be less comprehensive and potentially miss critical interdependencies that affect system performance.

Q194: Fill-in-the-Gap Multiple-Choice Question: In the context of HPE InfoSight integration, _____ is crucial for ensuring that the analytics platform can accurately predict and preemptively solve issues across diverse IT environments.

A) Manual configuration

B) Data normalization

C) Third-party software

D) On-site support

E) Custom hardware

F) User training

Answer: B

Explanation: Data normalization is crucial for ensuring that the analytics platform can accurately interpret and predict issues across diverse IT environments. By standardizing data formats and structures, InfoSight can more effectively analyze information from various sources, leading to accurate predictions and actionable insights. Without normalization, data discrepancies can lead to incorrect analysis and ineffective problem-solving.

Q195: Advanced Multiple-Choice Question: When integrating HPE InfoSight with HPE GreenLake, which of the following is a primary benefit of using InfoSight's machine learning algorithms?

A) Reduced need for IT staff

B) Elimination of all hardware failures

C) Immediate resolution of software bugs

D) Enhanced predictive maintenance

E) Increased power consumption

F) Decreased network latency

Answer: D

Explanation: The primary benefit of using InfoSight's machine learning algorithms is enhanced predictive maintenance. These algorithms analyze vast amounts of telemetry data to identify patterns and trends that could indicate future issues. By predicting potential problems before they occur, InfoSight helps organizations proactively maintain their infrastructure, reducing downtime and improving system reliability. While other benefits may occur, predictive maintenance is a core advantage of machine learning in this context.

Q196: A mid-sized retail company, RetailCo, is planning to enhance its IT infrastructure by integrating HPE GreenLake with its existing HPE OneView and InfoSight solutions. The primary goal is to improve resource management and predictive analytics capabilities. RetailCo's IT team is concerned about potential integration challenges, especially regarding data flow and system compatibility. As the HPE GreenLake Administrator, you are tasked with ensuring a seamless integration process that maximizes the value of both HPE OneView and InfoSight. Which initial step should you prioritize to address their concerns and ensure a successful integration?

A) Upgrade HPE OneView to the latest version to ensure compatibility with HPE GreenLake.

B) Conduct a comprehensive assessment of RetailCo's existing network architecture.

C) Train the IT team on the functionalities and benefits of HPE GreenLake.

D) Develop a customized API to facilitate data exchange between systems.

E) Schedule a pilot test to evaluate integration performance.

F) Review the compatibility matrix for HPE GreenLake, HPE OneView, and InfoSight.

Answer: F

Explanation: Before initiating any technical changes or upgrades, it's critical to assess the compatibility between the systems involved. Reviewing the compatibility matrix for HPE GreenLake, HPE OneView, and InfoSight allows the administrator to identify any potential mismatches or prerequisites needed for integration. This step will help in planning the integration process more effectively, ensuring that all systems can work together seamlessly. While upgrading systems and training the team are important steps, they should follow the compatibility assessment to avoid unnecessary changes or confusion.

Q197: True or False: HPE InfoSight can predict and automatically resolve issues in the HPE GreenLake environment without any manual intervention.

A) True

B) False

Answer: B

Explanation: HPE InfoSight is a powerful predictive analytics tool that can forecast potential issues and provide recommendations for resolution. However, it does not automatically resolve issues without manual intervention. The insights and recommendations provided by InfoSight require action from IT administrators to implement changes or rectify issues. This collaborative approach ensures a balance between automation and human oversight, allowing for more informed decision-making.

Q198: Which of the following is NOT a benefit of integrating HPE GreenLake with HPE OneView?

A) Enhanced visibility into infrastructure performance.

B) Automated provisioning of applications.

C) Real-time analytics and insights into resource usage.

D) Simplified management through a unified dashboard.

E) Increased manual intervention for routine tasks.

F) Improved scalability and flexibility of IT resources.

Answer: E

Explanation: One of the key advantages of integrating HPE GreenLake with HPE OneView is the reduction of manual intervention for routine tasks. This integration offers enhanced automation and management capabilities, allowing IT administrators to focus on strategic initiatives rather than mundane tasks. Options A, C, D, and F highlight the core benefits of this integration, such as improved visibility, analytics, and scalability. Option E is incorrect as the integration aims to decrease, not increase, manual intervention.

Q199: When configuring HPE InfoSight to work with HPE GreenLake, which of the following is a crucial step to ensure successful data integration and accurate analytics?

A) Enable multi-factor authentication for all administrators.

B) Regularly update the firmware of all connected devices.

C) Establish a secure connection between HPE InfoSight and HPE GreenLake.

D) Configure alert notifications for all possible issues.

E) Schedule regular downtime for system maintenance.

F) Set up a dedicated team to manually monitor data flow.

Answer: C

Explanation: Establishing a secure connection between HPE InfoSight and HPE GreenLake is critical for ensuring data integrity and security during integration. This secure connection facilitates the flow of data, allowing InfoSight to collect and analyze information accurately. Other steps, such as enabling authentication and updating firmware, are essential for general system security and performance but are not directly related to the data integration process. By prioritizing a secure connection, organizations can trust the insights derived from InfoSight and make informed decisions.

Q200: To maximize the predictive capabilities of HPE InfoSight when integrated with HPE GreenLake, what should be prioritized in the initial setup?

A) Configuring user access levels for security compliance.

B) Ensuring all devices are enrolled in the InfoSight portal.

C) Customizing dashboards for personalized insights.

D) Activating all available alerts for comprehensive monitoring.

E) Implementing a robust change management process.

F) Defining clear roles and responsibilities within the IT team.

Answer: B

Explanation: Ensuring all devices are enrolled in the InfoSight portal is crucial for maximizing the predictive capabilities of HPE InfoSight. This step allows InfoSight to gather comprehensive data across the entire infrastructure, which is essential for accurate analysis and predictive insights. While configuring user access, customizing dashboards, and defining roles are important for overall system management, they do not directly impact the predictive analytics capabilities of InfoSight as much as comprehensive device enrollment does. By focusing on this aspect, organizations can leverage the full potential of InfoSight's analytics and predictive features.

Q201: True or False: HPE GreenLake can directly integrate with AWS CloudFormation templates to automate the deployment of resources in an AWS environment.

A) True

B) False

Answer: B

Explanation: HPE GreenLake does not natively support direct integration with AWS CloudFormation templates. Instead, GreenLake provides its own set of APIs and tools for infrastructure management and provisioning. While AWS CloudFormation is a powerful tool for automating resource deployment within AWS, integrating it directly with HPE GreenLake requires custom workflows or intermediary tools that can translate GreenLake's infrastructure management capabilities to AWS-specific deployments. This distinction is crucial for administrators planning automation strategies across hybrid environments.

Q202: When integrating HPE GreenLake with Microsoft Azure, which service should be configured to ensure that billing data is accurately reflected and reconciled across both platforms?

A) Azure Cost Management and Billing

B) HPE GreenLake Central

C) AWS Billing and Cost Management

D) Azure Data Factory

E) HPE OneView

F) Microsoft Power Automate

Answer: A

Explanation: Azure Cost Management and Billing is the appropriate service for managing and reconciling billing data when integrating Microsoft Azure with HPE GreenLake. This service provides tools to analyze cloud spending and optimize costs across Azure and HPE GreenLake environments. While HPE GreenLake Central (option B) is essential for unified management, it does not directly handle detailed billing reconciliation. Options C, D, E, and F are either irrelevant to billing or pertain to other functionalities like data integration, infrastructure monitoring, or workflow automation.

Q203: Which AWS service can be leveraged to facilitate secure and efficient data transfer from an on-premises HPE GreenLake environment to AWS for hybrid cloud applications?

A) AWS Direct Connect

B) Amazon S3 Transfer Acceleration

C) AWS Snowball

D) AWS DataSync

E) AWS VPN

F) Amazon CloudFront

Answer: D

Explanation: AWS DataSync is designed for secure and efficient data transfer between on-premises environments and AWS, making it ideal for scenarios involving hybrid cloud applications with HPE GreenLake. DataSync automates and accelerates the process of transferring large amounts of data, with built-in encryption and error handling. While AWS Direct Connect (option A) provides a dedicated network connection, it does not specifically handle the data transfer process. Options B, C, E, and F either focus on different aspects of data movement, like content delivery or physical data transport, or provide connectivity solutions without addressing the transfer process itself.

Q204: To enable HPE GreenLake's integration with an AWS environment for monitoring and analytics, which approach should be adopted to ensure minimal latency and maximum efficiency?

A) Deploy HPE GreenLake instances within the same AWS region as your primary workloads.

B) Use AWS Global Accelerator to improve data transfer speeds between GreenLake and AWS services.

C) Set up HPE GreenLake in a separate region to balance load and enhance redundancy.

D) Implement AWS CloudFront to cache HPE GreenLake data for faster access.

E) Utilize AWS Transit Gateway to connect GreenLake with multiple VPCs for better analytics.

F) Configure AWS Lambda functions to process HPE GreenLake monitoring data in real-time.

Answer: A

Explanation: Deploying HPE GreenLake instances within the same AWS region as the primary workloads minimizes latency and enhances efficiency by reducing the distance data needs to travel. This approach ensures that monitoring and analytics operations are performed quickly and accurately. While options B, D, and F offer performance improvements for specific scenarios, they do not address the fundamental issue of regional proximity. Option C unnecessarily complicates the setup by introducing additional latency, and option E focuses on VPC connectivity rather than optimizing GreenLake integration specifically.

Q205: Scenario-Based Question Your company, TechCorp, has been using HPE GreenLake to manage its IT infrastructure. Recently, the finance department requested a detailed report on resource utilization and costs for the past six months to prepare for the annual budget review. The IT department has been experiencing challenges with tracking real-time usage and accurately forecasting future resource needs. The CIO emphasizes the importance of optimizing resource allocation and avoiding over-provisioning. You are tasked with ensuring the inventory management system is robust enough to provide the required data efficiently. What is the most effective way to address the CIO's concerns and provide the finance department with the necessary reports using HPE GreenLake?

A) Manually track resource usage using spreadsheets and generate reports every quarter.

B) Utilize HPE GreenLake's built-in analytics to automate the generation of detailed usage reports.

C) Implement third-party software to monitor resource utilization and generate custom reports.

D) Schedule monthly meetings with department heads to gather resource usage data.

E) Use HPE GreenLake's API to integrate with existing ERP systems for seamless data transfer.

F) Allocate a dedicated team to manually audit and verify resource usage data continuously.

Answer: B

Explanation: Utilizing HPE GreenLake's built-in analytics is the most effective way to address the CIO's concerns. HPE GreenLake provides comprehensive analytics capabilities that can automate the generation of detailed usage reports, which are essential for financial planning and resource optimization. This approach minimizes human error, reduces the administrative burden, and ensures that data is accurate and up-to-date. Manual tracking or relying on third-party software could lead to delays and inaccuracies, while meetings and manual audits are inefficient and prone to oversight. Integrating with ERP systems via API is beneficial but may not directly address the immediate need for built-in analytics and automated reporting capabilities.

Q206: True/False Question The HPE GreenLake platform allows administrators to dynamically adjust resource allocations based on real-time usage data.
A) True

B) False

Answer: A

Explanation: The statement is true. HPE GreenLake is designed to provide flexibility and scalability, allowing administrators to dynamically adjust resource allocations based on real-time usage data. This capability is crucial for optimizing resource utilization and ensuring that businesses only pay for the resources they actually use. By monitoring real-time data, administrators can make informed decisions about scaling resources up or down, which helps in managing costs effectively and ensuring the system adapts to changing business needs.

Q207: When managing inventory of deployed resources in HPE GreenLake, what is a critical first step for ensuring accurate tracking and reporting?
A) Conducting regular manual inventory audits.

B) Setting up automated alerts for resource usage thresholds.

C) Implementing a consistent naming convention for all resources.

D) Using third-party software to complement HPE GreenLake's tracking.

E) Training all staff on the resource management processes.

F) Hiring a dedicated inventory manager to oversee resources.

Answer: C

Explanation: Implementing a consistent naming convention for all resources is a critical first step in ensuring accurate tracking and reporting within HPE GreenLake. A clear and standardized naming convention allows for easy identification and categorization of resources, which is essential for efficient resource management and reporting. This practice reduces confusion, minimizes errors, and enhances the ability to quickly generate reports and analyze data. While automated alerts and training are important, they rely on a well-organized system to be effective. Manual audits and third-party software may support the process but are not foundational like a naming convention.

Q208: In HPE GreenLake, which feature is instrumental in predicting future resource needs and preventing over-provisioning?

A) Real-time usage monitoring.

B) Historical usage trend analysis.

C) Manual resource allocation adjustments.

D) Automated billing alerts.

E) Predictive analytics.

F) Scheduled downtime for resource evaluation.

Answer: E

Explanation: Predictive analytics in HPE GreenLake is instrumental in predicting future resource needs and preventing over-provisioning. This feature analyzes historical usage patterns and applies algorithms to forecast future demand, allowing administrators to make informed decisions about scaling resources. By leveraging predictive analytics, businesses can optimize their resource allocation, reduce costs associated with over-provisioning, and ensure they have the capacity to meet future demands. Real-time monitoring and historical analysis provide useful insights, but predictive analytics specifically focuses on future trends and needs.

Q209: Which of the following practices can lead to inefficiencies and increased costs in the management of deployed resources in HPE GreenLake?

A) Regularly reviewing and optimizing resource allocations.

B) Allowing individual departments to manage their own resources independently.

C) Using automated tools for tracking and reporting resource usage.

D) Establishing clear policies for resource requests and approvals.

E) Consolidating resources to reduce redundancy.

F) Implementing a centralized management system for all resources.

Answer: B

Explanation: Allowing individual departments to manage their own resources independently can lead to inefficiencies and increased costs. This practice can result in a lack of coordination and oversight, leading to resource duplication, underutilization, and inconsistent application of best practices. It also complicates the ability to maintain a holistic view of resource usage and costs, making it difficult to optimize allocations and reduce expenses. Centralized management, clear policies, and regular optimization reviews are essential for ensuring efficient resource management and cost control within HPE GreenLake.

Q210: Scenario-Based As the IT Director of a rapidly expanding retail company, you are exploring options to better manage your hybrid cloud infrastructure. Your current setup involves multiple public cloud services and on-premises data centers. You face challenges with unpredictable costs, complex management, and slow deployment times for new services. After consulting with your team, you've decided to evaluate HPE GreenLake to address these issues. Your main objectives are to gain better cost control, streamline operations, and accelerate time-to-market for new services. Considering your business context, which key benefit of HPE GreenLake is most aligned with your objectives?   ---
A) Simplified billing with a single monthly invoice for all services.

B) Enhanced security through advanced encryption protocols.

C) Predictable costs with a pay-per-use model that aligns with consumption.

D) Integrated AI-driven analytics for improved decision-making.

E) Seamless integration with existing on-premises systems.

F) Access to a wide range of open-source software tools.

Answer: C

Explanation: HPE GreenLake is particularly effective for businesses looking to gain better cost control and streamline operations. Its pay-per-use model allows businesses to only pay for the resources they consume, which can lead to more predictable IT spending and help avoid over-provisioning. This model also supports the rapid scaling of resources, which accelerates time-to-market for new services. The ability to align costs directly with usage is especially beneficial in hybrid environments where demand can fluctuate significantly, making cost predictability a critical factor for planning and budgeting. Unlike traditional capital expenditure models, HPE GreenLake's approach reduces upfront costs and financial risk, aligning IT spending more closely with actual business needs.

Q211: True/False Adopting HPE GreenLake for hybrid cloud environments can significantly reduce the time it takes to deploy IT resources compared to traditional on-premises deployments.   ---
A) True

B) False

Answer: A

Explanation: One of the primary benefits of HPE GreenLake is its ability to accelerate the deployment of IT resources. In traditional on-premises environments, deploying new infrastructure often requires significant lead time for procurement, setup, and configuration. HPE GreenLake, however, offers pre-configured solutions that can be rapidly deployed and scaled as needed. This reduction in deployment time is crucial for businesses that need to quickly respond to changing market demands and technological advancements.

The platform's ability to deliver ready-to-use infrastructure significantly shortens the time from concept to implementation, allowing businesses to innovate faster.

Q212: Multiple Choice Which of the following benefits does HPE GreenLake offer that particularly enhances operational efficiency in a hybrid cloud setup?

A) Comprehensive training programs for IT staff.

B) Unified management platform for both cloud and on-premises resources.

C) Built-in firewall and network security features.

D) Customizable dashboards for monitoring energy efficiency.

E) Integration with third-party CRM software.

F) Support for legacy systems without modifications.

Answer: B

Explanation: HPE GreenLake provides a unified management platform that significantly enhances operational efficiency in hybrid cloud environments. This platform allows IT teams to manage both on-premises and cloud resources from a single interface, reducing the complexity associated with managing disparate systems. This centralization of management reduces the administrative overhead and allows IT staff to focus on higher-value tasks, such as optimizing workloads and improving performance. Additionally, the unified platform supports automation and orchestration, further streamlining operations and improving resource utilization. The ability to manage resources seamlessly across a hybrid environment is a key advantage of adopting HPE GreenLake.

Q213: Multiple Choice What is a primary advantage of HPE GreenLake's consumption-based pricing model for businesses with fluctuating workloads?

A) Lower upfront capital investment requirements.

B) Access to the latest technological advancements.

C) Increased employee satisfaction and retention.

D) Enhanced brand reputation and market position.

E) Improved energy efficiency and sustainability.

F) Greater flexibility in choosing service providers.

Answer: A

Explanation: One of the primary advantages of HPE GreenLake's consumption-based pricing model is the reduced need for upfront capital investments. Businesses only pay for the resources they use, which allows them to scale up or down according to their workload demands without the financial burden of over-provisioning. This flexibility is particularly beneficial for businesses with fluctuating workloads, as it aligns IT costs with actual usage, ensuring that resources are available when needed without unnecessary expense. Additionally, this model enables organizations to preserve capital for other strategic initiatives or investments, enhancing overall business agility and financial health.

Q214: Multiple Choice In what way does HPE GreenLake's service model contribute to quicker innovation cycles for companies operating in competitive markets?

A) By providing exclusive access to proprietary applications.

B) Through partnerships with leading technology universities.

C) By offering pre-configured, rapidly deployable IT solutions.

D) Via exclusive collaboration with industry-specific consultants.

E) Through comprehensive market analysis tools.

F) By maintaining a global network of customer support centers.

Answer: C

Explanation: HPE GreenLake's service model contributes to quicker innovation cycles by offering pre-configured, rapidly deployable IT solutions. This approach allows companies to quickly implement and scale new technologies without the lengthy processes typically associated with traditional infrastructure deployments. By reducing the time required to bring new services and solutions to market, businesses can stay competitive and respond swiftly to industry trends and customer demands. The ability to innovate rapidly is essential in today's fast-paced business environment, and HPE GreenLake's model supports this by providing the necessary infrastructure quickly and efficiently, enabling companies to focus on developing and delivering innovative solutions.

Q215: Scenario-Based Question A multinational retail company, RetailCorp, has recently implemented HPE GreenLake to optimize its IT infrastructure across multiple global data centers. The company intends to leverage AI-driven operations to enhance predictive maintenance and reduce downtime. RetailCorp's IT team has noticed varying performance metrics across different regions and wants to ensure consistent service quality. They plan to use AI-driven insights to identify and address these discrepancies proactively. Which AI-driven feature should RetailCorp prioritize to achieve consistent service quality across regions?

A) Anomaly detection to spot deviations in performance metrics

B) Automated workload balancing to distribute resources effectively

C) Predictive analytics for disk failure prevention

D) AI-driven security threat detection

E) Dynamic pricing models based on usage patterns

F) AI-based customer support escalation prediction

Answer: A

Explanation: In the context of RetailCorp's scenario, anomaly detection is the most relevant AI-driven feature for ensuring consistent service quality across different regions. Anomaly detection can identify deviations in performance metrics that could indicate potential issues before they impact service quality. By addressing these anomalies proactively, RetailCorp can maintain a consistent level of service across its global operations. Automated workload balancing, while useful, is more about resource distribution rather than identifying underlying performance issues. Predictive analytics for disk failure is specific to hardware maintenance, and AI-driven security threat detection focuses on security rather than performance consistency. Dynamic pricing models and AI-based customer support escalation prediction do not directly relate to the IT infrastructure's performance metrics.

Q216: True/False Question In HPE GreenLake, AI-driven operations can automatically adjust resource allocations in real-time based on predictive analytics to optimize performance and cost-efficiency.

A) True

B) False

Answer: A

Explanation: True. HPE GreenLake's AI-driven operations include capabilities for automatic real-time adjustments in resource allocations. By leveraging predictive analytics, GreenLake can optimize both performance and cost-efficiency, ensuring that resources are used effectively and that performance metrics are met without unnecessary expenditures. This autonomous adjustment is a key advantage of using AI in managing cloud resources, as it allows for both operational efficiency and cost savings.

Q217: Which component of HPE GreenLake's AI operations is primarily responsible for providing insights into potential future infrastructure needs based on current usage patterns?

A) Predictive analytics module

B) Capacity planning dashboard

C) Anomaly detection system

D) Real-time monitoring tool

E) AI-driven support ticket system

F) Automated workload scheduler

Answer: A

Explanation: The predictive analytics module in HPE GreenLake is specifically designed to analyze current usage patterns and provide insights into future infrastructure needs. This component uses machine learning algorithms to forecast demand, allowing IT administrators to make informed decisions about scaling resources up or down. The capacity planning dashboard may display these insights, but it is not responsible for generating them. Anomaly detection focuses on identifying irregularities, while real-time monitoring provides current data rather than future predictions. The AI-driven support ticket system and automated workload scheduler serve different operational roles.

Q218: In the context of HPE GreenLake's AI-driven operations, what is the primary benefit of using machine learning algorithms for workload management?

A) Enhanced security threat detection

B) Improved user interface customization

C) Real-time analytics and reporting

D) Optimized resource allocation and efficiency

E) Automated software patch management

F) Predictive maintenance alerts

Answer: D

Explanation: The primary benefit of using machine learning algorithms for workload management in HPE GreenLake is optimized resource allocation and efficiency. Machine learning models can analyze patterns in workload demands and adjust resources accordingly, ensuring that workloads are handled efficiently without over-provisioning or under-utilizing resources. This leads to cost savings and better performance. While security,

UI customization, real-time analytics, and other options are important, they are not the direct benefits of workload management using machine learning.

Q219: Fill in the gap: In HPE GreenLake, the use of AI-driven operations helps organizations move towards a _____ model, allowing for more strategic decision-making and resource management.

A) Reactive

B) Predictive

C) Static

D) Manual

E) Costly

F) Decentralized

Answer: B

Explanation: In HPE GreenLake, the use of AI-driven operations helps organizations move towards a predictive model, allowing for more strategic decision-making and resource management. By predicting future trends and potential issues, organizations can plan proactively rather than reacting to problems as they arise. This shift from a reactive to a predictive model enables businesses to optimize their operations, reduce downtime, and allocate resources more effectively. The other options do not align with the strategic benefits of AI-driven operations in GreenLake.

Q220: Scenario-Based As the IT manager of a mid-sized retail company, you've been tasked with ensuring that your infrastructure can handle peak shopping times, such as Black Friday and holiday seasons. Your company has recently adopted HPE GreenLake to manage its IT resources efficiently. You have access to HPE's predictive analytics tools, which provide insights into capacity trends. With the upcoming holiday season, you need to ensure that you have adequate compute and storage resources without overspending. You've noticed a 20% increase in online traffic over the past quarter, which is expected to double during peak times. How should you leverage HPE GreenLake's predictive analytics to plan for this surge?

A) Use predictive analytics to simulate various traffic scenarios and adjust capacity in real-time as demand increases.

B) Rely on historical data alone to forecast future trends and purchase additional resources based on last year's usage.

C) Set up automatic scaling policies based on predictive analytics to ensure resources match the demand peaks.

D) Manually monitor resource usage and request additional capacity as soon as you notice a peak.

E) Schedule a fixed increase in resources for the holiday season without using predictive insights.

F) Use predictive analytics to decrease capacity during non-peak times to save costs.

Answer: C

Explanation: HPE GreenLake's predictive analytics tools are designed to provide insights into future demand by analyzing historical data and current trends. By setting up automatic scaling policies based on these analytics, you can ensure that your infrastructure dynamically adjusts to meet the demand peaks without manual intervention. This approach not only helps in maintaining optimal performance but also prevents over-provisioning and unnecessary spending. Simply relying on past data may not capture current trends accurately, and manual monitoring may lead to delayed responses. Scheduling fixed increases or decreasing capacity without predictive insights doesn't leverage the full capabilities of predictive analytics.

Q221: True/False Predictive analytics in HPE GreenLake can automatically adjust resource allocations without user intervention to meet anticipated demand changes.

A) True

B) False

Answer: A

Explanation: The statement is true. HPE GreenLake's predictive analytics can be configured to automatically adjust resource allocations in response to anticipated demand changes. This functionality allows for real-time scaling and optimization, ensuring that resources are allocated efficiently based on forecasted needs. By automating this process, businesses can maintain optimal performance levels without manual oversight, reducing the risk of human error and ensuring cost-effective resource management.

Q222: Standard Multiple-Choice Which of the following is the primary advantage of using predictive analytics within HPE GreenLake to manage capacity?

A) It eliminates the need for IT staff to monitor resource usage.

B) It allows for precise, data-driven capacity planning to prevent under-provisioning and over-provisioning.

C) It provides fixed capacity recommendations based on industry standards.

D) It automatically purchases additional hardware as needed.

E) It eliminates the need for historical data in forecasting.

F) It offers real-time alerts for system failures.

Answer: B

Explanation: The primary advantage of using predictive analytics in HPE GreenLake is that it enables precise, data-driven capacity planning. By analyzing historical data and current trends, predictive analytics helps in forecasting future demand with high accuracy. This prevents both under-provisioning, which can lead to performance issues, and over-provisioning, which can result in unnecessary costs. While predictive analytics can provide recommendations, it does not automatically purchase hardware or eliminate the need for IT staff; instead, it aids them in making informed decisions.

Q223: Fill-in-the-Gap Multiple-Choice When managing capacity with predictive analytics in HPE GreenLake, which factor is most crucial to ensuring accurate demand forecasts?

A) The use of real-time monitoring tools.

B) The frequency of capacity reviews.

C) The quality and completeness of historical data.

D) The number of users accessing the system.

E) The speed of the network connection.

F) The geographical location of data centers.

Answer: C

Explanation: The quality and completeness of historical data are crucial for accurate demand forecasts in predictive analytics. Reliable and comprehensive historical data allows predictive models to identify patterns and trends accurately, leading to more precise predictions about future demand. While real-time monitoring and capacity reviews are important for ongoing management, they do not directly impact the accuracy of demand forecasts. Other factors like user count, network speed, and geographical location may influence performance but are not directly tied to forecast accuracy.

Q224: Standard Multiple-Choice What is a potential risk of not using predictive analytics for capacity management in HPE GreenLake?

A) Increased complexity in managing multi-cloud environments.

B) Difficulty in integrating third-party applications.

C) The potential for unexpected resource shortages during peak times.

D) Reduced ability to automate routine maintenance tasks.

E) Limited options for data backup and recovery.

F) Increased manual intervention in security configurations.

Answer: C

Explanation: A potential risk of not using predictive analytics for capacity management is the possibility of unexpected resource shortages during peak times. Without predictive insights, businesses may not accurately anticipate demand spikes, leading to insufficient resources and potential performance issues. Predictive analytics helps ensure that capacity matches demand, minimizing the risk of such shortages. While predictive analytics can support automation and integration, its primary role in capacity management is to optimize resource allocation and prevent shortages.

Q225: Scenario-based Question Your organization, a multinational corporation, has recently adopted HPE GreenLake to better manage its cloud resources across multiple regions. The IT team is tasked with ensuring compliance with data governance policies that vary significantly between regions, especially with strict regulations in Europe compared to more lenient policies in North America. The company has been facing challenges in maintaining compliance due to the varying data residency requirements and security standards. The IT team must implement a solution that not only tracks compliance but also enforces governance policies without hindering operational efficiency. Which strategy would best address these challenges using HPE GreenLake capabilities?

A) Implement a centralized policy management system in North America to oversee compliance for all regions.

B) Utilize HPE GreenLake's built-in compliance tools to create region-specific policies and automate their enforcement.

C) Deploy separate HPE GreenLake instances for each region to manage compliance independently.

D) Use third-party compliance software integrated with HPE GreenLake to monitor global compliance.

E) Appoint regional compliance officers to manually track and report compliance using HPE GreenLake dashboards.

F) Conduct quarterly manual audits using HPE GreenLake reports to ensure compliance.

Answer: B

Explanation: HPE GreenLake offers built-in compliance tools that allow for the creation and automation of region-specific governance policies. This is particularly useful for multinational corporations that must adhere to varying regulations across different regions. By utilizing these tools, the IT team can automate the enforcement of compliance measures, ensuring that each region meets its specific requirements without manual intervention, which can be error-prone and time-consuming. This approach also maintains operational efficiency, as it minimizes the administrative overhead involved in tracking and enforcing compliance manually. A centralized system would not be effective due to the diverse policy requirements, and deploying separate instances or relying solely on manual audits could lead to inconsistencies and inefficiencies.

Q226: True/False Question HPE GreenLake allows administrators to configure governance policies that automatically adjust based on real-time compliance monitoring.
A) True

B) False

Answer: A

Explanation: HPE GreenLake is designed with advanced capabilities that include real-time monitoring and automated adjustment of governance policies. This feature is integral to maintaining compliance across diverse environments and adapting to changing regulatory landscapes. By automating these adjustments, HPE GreenLake ensures that organizations remain compliant without manual intervention, reducing the risk of non-compliance and associated penalties. This capability is particularly beneficial for businesses operating in multiple jurisdictions with varying regulations.

Q227: Which feature of HPE GreenLake provides the ability to continuously monitor and report on compliance status to ensure adherence to governance policies?

A) HPE GreenLake Central

B) HPE InfoSight

C) HPE OneView

D) HPE Data Services Cloud Console

E) HPE CloudPhysics

F) HPE Nimble Storage

Answer: A

Explanation: HPE GreenLake Central is the platform's main control hub, providing a comprehensive view of all resources and their compliance status. It offers tools for monitoring, managing, and reporting on compliance, making it an invaluable feature for ensuring that governance policies are adhered to consistently. This centralized oversight allows administrators to quickly identify and address any compliance issues, thereby maintaining adherence to external regulations and internal policies. The other options, while part of the HPE portfolio, do not specifically focus on comprehensive compliance monitoring and reporting.

To ensure compliance with industry standards, which HPE GreenLake feature should be utilized to automate the enforcement of data governance policies?

A) HPE Synergy Composer

B) HPE GreenLake Compliance Manager

C) HPE Aruba ClearPass

D) HPE GreenLake Workload Analytics

E) HPE Security Manager

F) HPE GreenLake Cloud Console

Answer: B

Explanation: HPE GreenLake Compliance Manager is specifically designed to automate the enforcement of data governance policies. This tool allows organizations to set rules and controls that automatically ensure compliance with industry standards and regulations. By using Compliance Manager, businesses can reduce the risk of human error and ensure that all data handling and processing activities are in line with regulatory requirements. The other options provide valuable functionality but do not focus directly on automating governance policy enforcement.

Q229: Fill-in-the-gap Question When managing compliance within HPE GreenLake, the process of _____ involves the identification and classification of sensitive data to ensure that it is handled according to regulatory requirements.

A) Data Masking

B) Data Encryption

C) Data Discovery

D) Data Loss Prevention

E) Data Governance

F) Data Auditing

Answer: C

Explanation: Data Discovery is the process of identifying and classifying sensitive data to ensure it is managed in compliance with regulatory requirements. In the context of HPE GreenLake, this involves utilizing tools that can scan and categorize data based on sensitivity and relevance to compliance standards. By effectively implementing data discovery, organizations can ensure that sensitive information is handled appropriately, reducing the risk of data breaches and non-compliance. This process is a fundamental part of any robust compliance strategy, as it provides the necessary insights to apply correct governance policies.

Q230: Scenario-Based Question A multinational corporation, with data centers across North America, Europe, and Asia, is using HPE GreenLake to manage its hybrid cloud infrastructure. The company is facing challenges with inconsistent firmware versions across its servers, leading to compatibility issues with some of their applications. The IT team, led by a GreenLake administrator, is tasked with ensuring all servers are at the optimal firmware level while minimizing downtime. The administrator plans to use HPE GreenLake's update management tools to streamline this process. Which approach should the administrator take to address the firmware inconsistency while adhering to business requirements?   Explanation: HPE GreenLake provides centralized tools for managing firmware updates, which can help ensure consistency across all servers. The best approach is to use the compliance feature to identify which servers are not up-to-date and employ a staged update process. This method minimizes downtime by updating servers incrementally and allows for testing and validation after each stage. Option A would be too labor-intensive, while B and C might lead to unnecessary downtime or issues due to lack of testing. Option E could be expensive and might not align with the company's in-house capabilities. Option F focuses only on one region, ignoring the global consistency requirement.

A) Manually check each server's firmware version and update them individually during off-peak hours.

B) Utilize HPE GreenLake's centralized update management to schedule updates across all regions simultaneously.

C) Configure automated updates in HPE GreenLake to apply the latest firmware as soon as they are released by HPE.

D) Use HPE GreenLake's compliance feature to identify outdated firmware and update them in a staged manner.

E) Outsource the firmware update process to a third-party vendor with expertise in HPE products.

F) Prioritize updating servers in the North American region first, as it has the largest user base.

Answer: D

Explanation: nan

Q231: Standard Multiple-Choice Question What is the primary benefit of using HPE GreenLake for managing firmware updates across a global enterprise infrastructure?   Explanation: The primary benefit of using HPE GreenLake for managing firmware updates is the centralized monitoring and management it offers. With a single dashboard, administrators can ensure compliance and efficiently manage updates across all devices globally. This centralized approach simplifies the update process and helps ensure consistency. Options A and D are incorrect because human oversight is typically needed to manage exceptions and validate updates. Option B is unrealistic due to the need for testing and validation. Option E is not feasible, as some downtime might be necessary depending on the update. Option F is incorrect as the main advantage is the native integration within GreenLake, not third-party tools.

A) Provides a fully automated update cycle without any need for human intervention.

B) Ensures all devices are updated to the latest firmware within minutes of release.

C) Offers a single dashboard for monitoring and managing firmware compliance across all devices.

D) Eliminates the need for IT staff to be involved in the update process.

E) Guarantees zero downtime during firmware updates across the entire infrastructure.

F) Allows direct integration with third-party update management tools.

Answer: C

Explanation: nan

Q232: True/False Question HPE GreenLake allows for immediate rollback of firmware updates in case of an update failure. Explanation: HPE GreenLake does not provide an immediate rollback feature for firmware updates. Instead, administrators need to perform manual intervention to roll back updates if necessary. This involves reverting to previous firmware versions using backup processes or reapplying earlier versions manually. While GreenLake offers robust update management features, immediate rollback is not typically available due to the complexities involved in firmware updates, which require careful testing and validation.

A) True

B) False

Answer: B

Explanation: nan

Q233: Fill-in-the-Gap Multiple-Choice Question When planning firmware updates in HPE GreenLake, which factor is most critical to minimizing impact on business operations? Explanation: The most critical factor in minimizing business impact during firmware updates is the downtime required. Each update can impact availability, so scheduling updates during off-peak hours or in a staged manner is crucial to maintaining business continuity. While other factors like cost and server numbers are important, they do not directly affect the immediate operational impact. Ensuring minimal downtime helps maintain service levels and reduces disruptions to business operations.

A) The cost of the update

B) The size of the update file

C) The release date of the update

D) The downtime required for the update

E) The number of servers to be updated

F) The geographic location of the data centers

Answer: D

Explanation: nan

Q234: Standard Multiple-Choice Question In the context of HPE GreenLake, which feature is essential for identifying and rectifying security vulnerabilities through firmware updates?   Explanation: Firmware compliance reporting is essential for identifying and rectifying security vulnerabilities. This feature allows administrators to quickly assess which devices are running outdated or vulnerable firmware versions and prioritize updates accordingly. By maintaining compliance, organizations can better protect against security threats. Options A and B relate to performance and resource management rather than security. Options D and E focus on integration and performance but do not address firmware vulnerabilities. Option F is unrelated to security concerns within firmware management.

A) Predictive analytics for hardware failures

B) Automated resource scaling

C) Firmware compliance reporting

D) Hypervisor integration

E) Network performance monitoring

F) Cloud cost analysis

Answer: C

Explanation: nan

Q235: Scenario-Based Question As a newly appointed IT manager at a mid-sized financial organization, you are tasked with overseeing the digital transformation initiative. The company has decided to move its on-premises storage infrastructure to a more flexible, cloud-like model using HPE GreenLake and HPE Alletra. Currently, the organization's IT team is familiar with traditional SAN and NAS systems but lacks experience with cloud-native solutions. Your goal is to ensure seamless integration and management of HPE Alletra through GreenLake, while minimizing disruption to ongoing operations. Given the importance of data compliance and the need for high availability, you must decide on the best approach to configure and manage the new setup. Which of the following actions should you prioritize to ensure a successful integration of HPE Alletra through GreenLake?   ---

A) Conduct a comprehensive training program for the IT team focused on GreenLake management and cloud-native storage concepts.

B) Immediately migrate all data to HPE Alletra to test the system's capabilities and performance.

C) Set up a dedicated on-premises data center to act as a backup for HPE Alletra.

D) Develop a phased migration plan that starts with non-critical data and gradually includes more sensitive information.

E) Focus on configuring advanced security protocols on HPE Alletra to ensure compliance from the start.

F) Hire an external consultant to manage the initial setup and integration process.

Answer: D

Explanation: When integrating HPE Alletra through GreenLake, especially in a financial organization with specific compliance and availability needs, a phased migration plan is crucial. This approach minimizes risks by allowing the IT team to test and familiarize themselves with the new system using non-critical data first. Gradual inclusion of more sensitive information ensures that any issues can be addressed without impacting critical operations. While training, security, and external expertise are important, they should complement, not replace, a structured and strategic migration plan.

Q236: True/False Question True or False: HPE GreenLake automatically manages all firmware updates for HPE Alletra, requiring no intervention from the IT administrator.   ---

A) True

B) False

Answer: B

Explanation: While HPE GreenLake provides streamlined management capabilities for HPE Alletra, including some automated processes, firmware updates often require administrator oversight. Administrators must ensure that updates do not disrupt operations and comply with internal policies and schedules. Moreover, they need to verify the compatibility of updates with existing configurations and applications. Therefore, IT administrators still play a critical role in managing firmware updates, even in a GreenLake environment.

Q237: When configuring HPE Alletra through GreenLake for a company that processes large volumes of sensitive customer data, which key feature should be prioritized to enhance data protection and compliance?   ---

A) Global deduplication

B) Multi-site replication

C) Data encryption at rest and in transit

D) Automated tiering

E) High-performance caching

F) Predictive analytics for performance tuning

Answer: C

Explanation: In environments where sensitive customer data is handled, data protection is paramount. Data encryption at rest and in transit ensures that information is secure both when stored and during transmission. This is essential for compliance with data protection regulations such as GDPR or HIPAA. While other features like replication and deduplication can enhance performance and efficiency, encryption directly addresses the core need for data security and compliance.

Q238: To optimize the cost efficiency of HPE Alletra under the GreenLake model, which strategy should an IT administrator employ when planning resource allocation?   ---

A) Allocate maximum resources upfront to avoid under-provisioning.

B) Use historical data to forecast and allocate resources dynamically.

C) Opt for minimum allocation and manually adjust as needed.

D) Focus solely on CPU and memory resources, ignoring storage needs.

E) Prefer fixed resource allocation to maintain predictable billing.

F) Conduct quarterly reviews to adjust resource allocation based on projections.

Answer: B

Explanation: Using historical data to forecast and allocate resources dynamically allows for flexible and cost-effective management under the GreenLake model. This approach helps in adjusting to real-time demands without over-provisioning, which can lead to unnecessary expenses. It also prevents under-provisioning, which can hinder performance. Dynamic resource allocation maximizes efficiency by scaling resources based on actual usage patterns and future projections, aligning costs with business needs.

Q239: Which monitoring tool within HPE GreenLake can specifically help an administrator ensure optimal performance and health of HPE Alletra systems?
A) HPE InfoSight

B) HPE OneView

C) HPE SimpliVity

D) HPE Synergy

E) HPE CloudPhysics

F) HPE Nimble Storage Toolkit

Answer: A

Explanation: HPE InfoSight is a powerful predictive analytics platform designed to monitor and optimize the performance and health of HPE Alletra systems within GreenLake. It uses AI and machine learning to predict potential issues before they occur, providing administrators with actionable insights and recommendations. This proactive management capability helps ensure high availability, optimal performance, and efficient resource utilization. Other tools like HPE OneView or CloudPhysics may offer some management functions but are not specifically tailored for predictive analytics in the context of HPE Alletra.

Q240: Scenario-Based Question A mid-sized company, TechSolutions, has recently adopted HPE GreenLake to manage its IT infrastructure, including HPE Nimble Storage. The company has been experiencing rapid growth and expects its data storage needs to increase by 50% in the next year. The IT department is tasked with ensuring that storage expansion can be managed seamlessly without disrupting business operations. Additionally, TechSolutions needs to ensure efficient cost management and optimal performance as they scale. The IT manager is considering automatic scaling features and wants to integrate these with their existing monitoring tools to anticipate storage needs better. What should the IT manager prioritize to ensure seamless integration and efficient scaling?

A) Enable predictive analytics to automatically adjust storage capacity based on trends.

B) Increase the current storage capacity by 50% immediately.

C) Schedule weekly manual reviews of storage usage and manually adjust capacity.

D) Integrate HPE GreenLake with existing monitoring tools and enable real-time alerts.

E) Focus on cost management by reducing storage performance levels.

F) Outsource storage management to a third-party vendor to ensure scalability.

Answer: A

Explanation: Predictive analytics in HPE GreenLake can anticipate future storage requirements based on historical data and trends, providing a seamless method to manage scaling without manual intervention. This not only ensures that TechSolutions remains ahead of their growing storage demands but also optimizes performance and cost by automatically adjusting resources as needed. Immediate storage capacity increases or manual adjustments are not sustainable long-term solutions. Integrating monitoring tools is beneficial but secondary to the proactive approach of predictive analytics. Outsourcing might lead to loss of control and potentially higher costs.

Q241: True/False Question HPE GreenLake provides an integrated dashboard for managing HPE Nimble Storage, which includes features for real-time performance monitoring and capacity planning.
A) True

B) False

Answer: A

Explanation: HPE GreenLake offers a comprehensive dashboard that integrates various management features for HPE Nimble Storage. This includes real-time performance monitoring and capacity planning, which are crucial for administrators to maintain optimal storage performance and anticipate future needs. These features allow for efficient management of resources and ensure that storage systems are aligned with business demands.

Q242: Standard Multiple-Choice Question What is the primary benefit of using HPE GreenLake for managing HPE Nimble Storage in a cloud-like environment?

A) It eliminates the need for any on-premise hardware.

B) It provides a pay-as-you-go model that aligns costs with usage.

C) It requires less technical expertise to manage storage infrastructure.

D) It offers the highest performance levels regardless of cost.

E) It guarantees data security through off-site backups.

F) It simplifies the user interface for non-technical users.

Answer: B

Explanation: The primary benefit of HPE GreenLake is its consumption-based model, which allows businesses to align their costs with actual usage. This is particularly advantageous for companies looking to manage finances more predictively while scaling their operations. Unlike traditional purchase models, GreenLake's pay-as-you-go structure helps avoid over-provisioning and reduces upfront capital expenses. While it provides flexible infrastructure management, the other options either do not reflect GreenLake's primary benefits or are not unique to the platform.

Q243: Fill-in-the-Gap Multiple-Choice Question When configuring HPE Nimble Storage through HPE GreenLake, which feature allows administrators to ensure optimal and automated response to storage demands?

A) Manual capacity upgrades

B) Predictive data analytics

C) Scheduled maintenance windows

D) Static resource allocation

E) User access control lists

F) Integrated billing reports

Answer: B

Explanation: Predictive data analytics is a feature within HPE GreenLake that analyzes usage patterns and trends to anticipate and automatically respond to changing storage demands. This ensures that the storage infrastructure can adapt dynamically to business needs without requiring manual intervention. Options like manual upgrades and static allocation do not provide the automation and optimization that predictive analytics offers.

Q244: Standard Multiple-Choice Question Which tool should be used to integrate HPE Nimble Storage monitoring with HPE GreenLake for enhanced visibility and management?

A) HPE OneView

B) HPE InfoSight

C) HPE Synergy

D) HPE StoreOnce

E) HPE 3PAR Service Processor

F) HPE Virtual Connect

Answer: B

Explanation: HPE InfoSight is the recommended tool for integrating HPE Nimble Storage with HPE GreenLake, providing enhanced visibility and analytics. InfoSight offers predictive analytics and machine learning capabilities that help in proactive monitoring and management. This integration allows administrators to gain insights into storage performance, predict issues before they occur, and optimize resource allocation. Other tools listed either do not offer the same level of integration with Nimble Storage or are not focused on predictive analytics.

Q245: A mid-sized financial services company, FinServe Inc., has recently transitioned to using HPE GreenLake for their on-premise infrastructure needs, focusing on HPE Primera storage solutions. They want to ensure that their data storage is efficiently managed, and performance is optimized as their customer base grows. The IT manager is tasked with setting up monitoring alerts and reporting capabilities to proactively manage the storage environment. The manager needs to decide on the best approach to integrate these capabilities within HPE GreenLake to maintain high performance and avoid any potential downtime.

A) Utilize HPE InfoSight for proactive management and insights.

B) Rely on manual monitoring through the HPE Primera GUI.

C) Set up email alerts directly from HPE Primera.

D) Use third-party monitoring tools for better integration.

E) Implement custom scripts for monitoring.

F) Depend on HPE GreenLake's default settings without customization.

Answer: A

Explanation: HPE InfoSight is an AI-driven management tool that provides predictive analytics and recommendations for proactive management of HPE storage solutions, including Primera. By leveraging InfoSight, FinServe Inc. can gain deep insights into performance trends, potential bottlenecks, and capacity planning, thus optimizing their storage environment. Unlike manual monitoring or third-party tools, InfoSight is integrated with HPE GreenLake, providing seamless management and reducing the overhead of maintaining additional systems. Custom scripts or default settings may not offer the same level of intelligence and predictive capabilities as InfoSight.

Q246: True or False: HPE GreenLake allows for direct integration with HPE Primera storage solutions, enabling users to manage storage infrastructure without the need for additional HPE software.
A) True

B) False

Answer: B

Explanation: While HPE GreenLake provides a flexible consumption model and management capabilities for on-premise infrastructure, it typically leverages additional HPE software like InfoSight for comprehensive management and optimization of storage solutions like HPE Primera. Direct integration requires these additional tools to provide full functionality and to leverage advanced features such as AI-driven insights and automated management.

Q247: When configuring data protection for HPE Primera through GreenLake, which feature would be most effective in ensuring critical business data is not lost in case of a storage failure?

A) HPE Primera's built-in RAID protection

B) HPE StoreOnce for backup and recovery

C) HPE Cloud Volumes Backup

D) Snapshot and replication features of HPE Primera

E) Manual backup to external drives

F) Third-party cloud-based backup solutions

Answer: D

Explanation: The snapshot and replication features of HPE Primera are designed to provide efficient data protection and disaster recovery capabilities. Snapshots allow for quick point-in-time copies of data, while replication ensures that data is continuously and automatically copied to another location, providing robust protection against data loss. While RAID offers basic protection against drive failures, and StoreOnce and Cloud Volumes provide backup options, integrated snapshot and replication features within Primera provide the most seamless and efficient protection for critical business data.

Q248: In the context of performance optimization for HPE Primera managed through GreenLake, which practice would best enhance storage efficiency and reduce latency?

A) Increasing the storage capacity beyond current needs

B) Utilizing thin provisioning to optimize resource utilization

C) Regularly updating the firmware of HPE Primera

D) Implementing deduplication and compression features

E) Conducting frequent manual performance audits

F) Segregating workloads based on data types

Answer: D

Explanation: Implementing deduplication and compression features directly enhances storage efficiency by reducing the amount of physical storage needed, which in turn can reduce latency by freeing up resources. Thin provisioning also helps in optimizing resources, but deduplication and compression have a more direct impact on reducing the data footprint, leading to improved performance. Regular firmware updates ensure the system is running optimally, but they do not directly enhance storage efficiency like deduplication and compression do. Segregating workloads and manual audits can help in management but do not inherently reduce latency.

Q249: A retail company using HPE GreenLake and Primera is experiencing unpredictable spikes in data traffic during promotional sales. To ensure consistent performance during these peak times, which strategy should the IT team prioritize?

A) Implementing a dedicated high-performance storage tier

B) Increasing the overall storage capacity

C) Utilizing HPE Primera's Quality of Service (QoS) settings

D) Manually adjusting resource allocations during sales

E) Outsourcing peak demand management to a third-party provider

F) Utilizing HPE GreenLake's built-in load balancing features

Answer: C

Explanation: HPE Primera's Quality of Service (QoS) settings allow IT teams to prioritize resources for critical applications and workloads, ensuring consistent performance even during unpredictable spikes in data traffic. By setting QoS policies, the retail company can manage and allocate resources dynamically to meet the demands of peak sales periods. Increasing storage capacity or implementing high-performance tiers can help, but they do not directly address the need for dynamic resource prioritization during peak times. Outsourcing and manual adjustments are less efficient and may not provide the immediate responsiveness required during these spikes.

Q250: Scenario-Based Question Your company, Tech Innovators Inc., has recently expanded its data center operations and adopted HPE SimpliVity for its hyper-converged infrastructure needs. During a recent review, the IT team discovered that the backup operations for critical databases are taking longer than expected, impacting the nightly maintenance window. The IT manager has asked you, as the GreenLake Administrator, to optimize the backup performance. After analyzing the current configuration, you found that all virtual machines (VMs) are running on a single node, which might be causing resource contention. What is the best approach to optimize backup performance in this situation?

A) Increase the memory allocation for the VMs involved in the backup process.

B) Migrate some VMs to another node to balance the load.

C) Enable deduplication and compression on the backup volumes.

D) Upgrade the network bandwidth between nodes.

E) Schedule backups during off-peak hours to minimize contention.

F) Use external backup software to manage the process.

Answer: B

Explanation: In a hyper-converged infrastructure like HPE SimpliVity, distributing the workload evenly across nodes is crucial for optimizing performance. When all VMs are concentrated on a single node, it can lead to resource contention, especially during intensive operations like backups. By migrating some VMs to another node, you can balance the load, thereby reducing contention and improving backup performance. Increasing memory allocation or upgrading network bandwidth might help in specific scenarios but won't address the root cause of resource contention. Enabling deduplication and compression is more about storage efficiency than performance. Scheduling backups during off-peak hours is a temporary fix that doesn't address the load imbalance. External backup software adds complexity without solving the underlying issue. Thus, redistributing VMs to balance the load across nodes is the most effective solution.

Q251: True/False Question HPE SimpliVity allows for the creation of backup policies that can automatically protect virtual machines based on their resource usage patterns.
A) True

B) False

Answer: B

Explanation: HPE SimpliVity provides robust data protection features, including the ability to create backup policies. However, these policies are not automatically generated based on resource usage patterns. Administrators must manually define backup policies based on organizational needs, recovery point objectives (RPOs), and recovery time objectives (RTOs). While SimpliVity offers automation for backup scheduling and retention, the creation of policies based on specific usage patterns requires administrative input and configuration.

Q252: Standard Multiple-Choice Question Which feature of HPE SimpliVity is specifically designed to optimize storage efficiency and reduce the data footprint?

A) Virtual Machine Snapshots

B) Inline Deduplication and Compression

C) Automated Data Tiering

D) Live Migration

E) Network Load Balancing

F) High Availability Clustering

Answer: B

Explanation: HPE SimpliVity's inline deduplication and compression are key features specifically designed to optimize storage efficiency. These processes occur in real-time, reducing the data footprint by eliminating duplicate data and compressing information before it is stored on disk. This results in significant space savings and enhances overall storage performance. Other options, such as virtual machine snapshots and live migration, serve different purposes, like facilitating backup and workload mobility. Automated data tiering is not a feature of HPE SimpliVity, and network load balancing and high availability clustering focus on network performance and system resilience, respectively.

Q253: Standard Multiple-Choice Question What is the primary benefit of using HPE SimpliVity's built-in backup capabilities over traditional backup methods?

A) Faster restore times

B) Lower cost of storage media

C) Simplified integration with third-party software

D) Enhanced user interface

E) Increased network redundancy

F) Greater compatibility with legacy systems

Answer: A

Explanation: The primary benefit of using HPE SimpliVity's built-in backup capabilities is faster restore times. SimpliVity's architecture allows for rapid backups and restores by leveraging its deduplication and compression technology, which minimizes the amount of data that needs to be moved and processed. This significantly reduces the time required to restore data compared to traditional backup methods, which often involve more complex processes and longer durations. While cost, integration, and interface improvements may be benefits, they are not the primary advantage in the context of backup and restore performance. Network redundancy and compatibility with legacy systems are unrelated to the core benefits of SimpliVity's backup capabilities.

Q254: Fill-in-the-Gap Multiple-Choice Question When managing an HPE SimpliVity environment, it is crucial to monitor the system's health regularly. Which HPE tool provides a centralized view of the health and status of SimpliVity clusters?

A) HPE InfoSight

B) HPE OneView

C) HPE Smart Storage Administrator

D) HPE Insight Control

E) HPE Systems Insight Manager

F) HPE SimpliVity OmniStack

Answer: A

Explanation: HPE InfoSight is the tool designed to provide a centralized view of the health and status of HPE SimpliVity clusters, among other HPE infrastructure components. It offers predictive analytics and proactive support, helping administrators to monitor system health, diagnose issues, and optimize performance. InfoSight's machine learning capabilities help identify potential problems before they impact operations. Other tools like HPE

OneView and HPE SimpliVity OmniStack are useful for different management tasks, but InfoSight specifically excels in providing comprehensive health monitoring and predictive analytics. HPE Smart Storage Administrator and HPE Systems Insight Manager focus on different aspects of infrastructure management and do not provide the same level of centralized health monitoring for SimpliVity clusters.

Q255: Scenario-Based Question You are the IT manager for a mid-sized company that recently adopted HPE GreenLake to manage its virtual infrastructure. The company aims to leverage GreenLake's cloud services to scale operations seamlessly with fluctuating demand. Recently, the company experienced a significant increase in website traffic, which led to performance bottlenecks in the virtual machines (VMs) hosting the web servers. As the administrator, your task is to optimize the performance of these VMs within the GreenLake environment. You are considering options such as resizing the VMs, adjusting resource allocation, and evaluating workloads. What is the most efficient first step you should take to address the performance issues?

A) Immediately resize all VMs to a larger configuration.

B) Implement auto-scaling policies to adjust resources dynamically.

C) Conduct a detailed performance analysis to identify bottlenecks.

D) Migrate workloads to a different region with better network latency.

E) Schedule downtime to reboot all VMs for clearing cache.

F) Upgrade the underlying hardware for all VMs to the latest version.

Answer: C

Explanation: Conducting a detailed performance analysis is the most efficient first step in addressing performance issues. This approach allows you to identify specific bottlenecks, such as CPU, memory, or I/O constraints. Without understanding the root cause, resizing or upgrading resources might not solve the problem and could lead to unnecessary costs. An analysis ensures that you apply targeted solutions, such as optimizing specific workloads or re-allocating resources, rather than taking broad actions that may not be necessary or effective.

Q256: True/False Question In HPE GreenLake, virtual machines can be managed through a unified dashboard that provides real-time analytics and performance monitoring. This enables administrators to make informed decisions quickly.

A) True

B) False

Answer: A

Explanation: True. HPE GreenLake offers a unified dashboard that provides real-time analytics and performance monitoring for virtual machines. This feature allows administrators to have a consolidated view of their virtual infrastructure, leading to quicker and more informed decision-making. The dashboard's insights can be used to optimize resource allocation, monitor usage trends, and ensure that performance meets business needs efficiently.

Q257: Standard Multiple-Choice Question Which of the following tools or features in HPE GreenLake is primarily used to automate the deployment and management of virtual machines to improve operational efficiency?

A) HPE OneView

B) HPE SimpliVity

C) HPE Synergy

D) HPE CloudPhysics

E) HPE InfoSight

F) HPE GreenLake Central

Answer: F

Explanation: HPE GreenLake Central is a key feature that provides a comprehensive platform for automating the deployment and management of virtual machines. It integrates various services and tools, allowing administrators to efficiently manage their infrastructure with minimal manual intervention. This automation capability is critical in improving operational efficiency and reducing the potential for human error, making it ideal for managing complex and dynamic virtual environments.

Q258: Fill-in-the-Gap Question In the context of HPE GreenLake, _____ is responsible for providing predictive analytics and AI to optimize the performance and capacity planning of virtual machines.

A) HPE OneSphere

B) HPE Aruba

C) HPE InfoSight

D) HPE Nimble Storage

E) HPE ProLiant

F) HPE SimpliVity

Answer: C

Explanation: HPE InfoSight is the tool responsible for providing predictive analytics and AI capabilities within the HPE GreenLake environment. It is designed to optimize performance and assist in capacity planning for virtual machines by analyzing data patterns and predicting potential issues before they occur. This proactive approach helps in maintaining high availability and performance of the VMs, ensuring that resources are utilized efficiently and potential disruptions are minimized.

Q259: Standard Multiple-Choice Question When managing VMs in HPE GreenLake, which best practice should be followed to ensure that resources are used efficiently and costs are minimized?

A) Always allocate maximum resources to each VM to prevent potential bottlenecks.

B) Regularly review and adjust VM resource allocations based on usage patterns.

C) Disable monitoring features to reduce overhead on the system.

D) Maintain a static allocation of resources irrespective of workload changes.

E) Use manual scaling instead of auto-scaling to maintain control over resources.

F) Deploy all VMs in a single availability zone to simplify management.

Answer: B

Explanation: Regularly reviewing and adjusting VM resource allocations based on usage patterns is a best practice to ensure efficient use of resources and minimize costs. This approach allows administrators to align resources with actual demand, avoiding over-provisioning and under-utilization. By continuously monitoring and adapting to changes in workload, businesses can optimize their infrastructure, leading to cost savings and better performance. Static allocations or maximum resource assignments can lead to unnecessary expenses and inefficiencies, emphasizing the importance of dynamic management.

Q260: A mid-sized retail company, RetailMart, has recently transitioned its IT infrastructure to HPE GreenLake to better manage its dynamic resource demands during peak shopping seasons. The company's IT team is tasked with monitoring resource usage across their environments to ensure optimal performance and cost efficiency. The team notices that during the Black Friday sales, the system's resources are being excessively utilized, leading to performance bottlenecks. To address this issue, the team needs to implement more effective monitoring strategies to predict and mitigate such bottlenecks in the future. Which of the following strategies should RetailMart's IT team prioritize to effectively monitor and manage resource usage during peak periods?

A) Implement real-time monitoring dashboards to visualize current resource usage and trends.

B) Schedule automated reports on resource usage only after the peak period has ended.

C) Rely solely on historical data reports to forecast future resource needs.

D) Use GreenLake's default alerts without customization for specific workload demands.

E) Manually check resource usage during peak hours without automated tools.

F) Reduce monitoring activities to avoid additional system load during peak times.

Answer: A

Explanation: Implementing real-time monitoring dashboards is crucial for RetailMart as it provides immediate insights into resource usage, enabling the IT team to quickly identify trends and potential bottlenecks. Real-time dashboards offer visual representations of data that are easier to interpret at a glance, which is especially beneficial during high-demand periods like Black Friday. This proactive approach allows the team to make timely decisions, such as allocating additional resources or adjusting workloads, to maintain performance and prevent system slowdowns. In contrast, relying solely on post-peak reports, historical data, or default alerts limits the team's ability to respond swiftly to dynamic changes in resource demands.

Q261: True or False: Customizing alert thresholds in HPE GreenLake is unnecessary as the default settings are sufficient for all business environments.
A) True

B) False

Answer: B

Explanation: Customizing alert thresholds in HPE GreenLake is essential because different business environments have unique operational demands and performance benchmarks. Default settings are designed to provide a general framework that might not align with specific organizational needs or workload characteristics. By customizing these thresholds, businesses can tailor alerts to better reflect their critical performance indicators and resource usage patterns. This customization helps ensure that alerts are meaningful and actionable, allowing IT teams to respond more effectively to potential issues before they escalate.

Q262: When using HPE GreenLake to monitor resource utilization, which of the following metrics is most critical for evaluating the efficiency of VM deployments in a cloud environment?

A) Network latency

B) Disk I/O operations

C) CPU utilization percentage

D) Number of active user sessions

E) Power consumption levels

F) Server uptime

Answer: C

Explanation: CPU utilization percentage is a key metric for evaluating the efficiency of VM deployments as it directly indicates how effectively the virtual machines are using the available CPU resources. High CPU utilization can signal that the VMs are operating near their capacity, which may necessitate scaling or optimization efforts to improve performance. Conversely, low CPU utilization might suggest over-provisioning or underutilization, indicating potential cost savings through resource reallocation. While other metrics like disk I/O and network latency are important, they do not provide the same direct insight into the overall efficiency of CPU resource usage in virtual environments.

Q263: An IT manager at a financial services firm is responsible for ensuring their HPE GreenLake infrastructure maintains optimal performance during end-of-quarter processing. The manager wants to set up automated alerts to monitor resource usage. Which resource metric should the manager prioritize for alert configuration to prevent potential slowdowns during this critical period?

A) Memory utilization

B) Backup completion times

C) Network bandwidth usage

D) Storage capacity threshold

E) Application response time

F) Database query execution time

Answer: A

Explanation: Memory utilization is a critical metric to prioritize when setting up automated alerts, especially during high-demand periods like end-of-quarter processing. Insufficient memory can lead to increased paging or swapping, significantly degrading system performance and affecting processing times. By monitoring memory utilization and setting alerts for potential issues, the IT manager can proactively manage resources to ensure there is adequate memory available to handle peak workloads. This approach helps prevent slowdowns and ensures the firm maintains operational efficiency during critical financial processing periods.

Q264: Fill-in-the-gap: In the context of HPE GreenLake, _____ is a method that helps in forecasting future resource needs by analyzing historical usage data and predicting trends.

A) Predictive analytics

B) Reactive monitoring

C) Post-event analysis

D) Manual data review

E) Intuitive guessing

F) System logs analysis

Answer: A

Explanation: Predictive analytics is a method used for forecasting future resource needs by leveraging historical usage data to identify patterns and predict trends. This approach allows organizations to anticipate changes in resource demands and plan accordingly, ensuring they have the necessary capacity to accommodate future workloads. By using predictive analytics, IT teams can optimize resource allocation, improve performance, and reduce costs by avoiding over-provisioning. This proactive strategy is essential in dynamic environments where demand can fluctuate significantly, such as in HPE GreenLake's cloud infrastructure.

Q265: Scenario-based Question A multinational corporation, XYZ Inc., operates in multiple regions and has recently adopted HPE GreenLake to manage its IT resources. The company needs to ensure that each regional office can independently manage its own IT workloads while maintaining overall governance and security standards from the corporate headquarters. The IT team at headquarters wants to implement a solution that allows resource isolation, efficient management, and cost allocation to respective regional offices. Considering the principles of multi-tenancy in HPE GreenLake, what would be the best approach to achieve this?

A) Create a single tenant environment for all regions and use role-based access control to manage permissions.

B) Set up separate GreenLake environments for each regional office to ensure complete isolation.

C) Implement a multi-tenant architecture with individual tenant spaces for each regional office.

D) Use a hybrid approach by combining on-premise solutions with GreenLake for each region.

E) Establish a centralized management system that delegates control using external third-party tools.

F) Leverage cloud-native solutions to automate resource allocation and management for the regional offices.

Answer: C

Explanation: To address the requirements of XYZ Inc., a multi-tenant architecture is the most suitable solution. This approach allows each regional office to have its own isolated tenant space within the GreenLake environment, enabling them to manage their workloads independently while maintaining global governance and security standards dictated by headquarters. Multi-tenancy ensures resource isolation, which is crucial for security and cost allocation, as it avoids resource and data overlap. Unlike a single tenant environment (option A), which could have security risks and management challenges, or setting up separate environments for each region (option B), which would be inefficient and costly, a multi-tenant architecture strikes the right balance. Additionally, it aligns with the centralized management desires of the headquarters without overcomplicating the system through external tools or hybrid models.

Q266: True/False Question Multi-tenancy in HPE GreenLake environments inherently provides tenants with complete autonomy over their infrastructure resources without any oversight from the service provider.

A) True

B) False

Answer: B

Explanation: In HPE GreenLake environments, while multi-tenancy offers individual tenants a significant degree of autonomy over their resources, the service provider retains oversight capabilities. This oversight is important to ensure compliance with security policies, efficient resource usage, and to provide troubleshooting and support services. It allows the service provider to maintain a stable and secure infrastructure, which is crucial for operational integrity across all tenants. Therefore, tenants do not have complete autonomy without oversight.

Q267: When configuring multi-tenancy in HPE GreenLake, which feature is crucial for ensuring that resource usage can be accurately tracked and billed to the correct tenant?

A) Role-based access control

B) Network segmentation

C) Usage metering and analytics

D) Data encryption

E) Integrated backup solutions

F) Shared virtual private networks

Answer: C

Explanation: Usage metering and analytics are crucial for tracking and billing resources accurately in a multi-tenant environment. This feature ensures that each tenant's resource consumption is monitored and reported, facilitating transparent and precise billing. While role-based access control (option A) and network segmentation (option B) are essential for security and access management, they do not directly contribute to billing accuracy. Data encryption (option D) ensures data security, and integrated backup solutions (option E) enhance data protection, but neither addresses billing needs directly. Shared virtual private networks (option F) offer connectivity solutions but do not aid in billing processes.

Q268: In the context of HPE GreenLake's multi-tenancy support, which of the following challenges is most effectively mitigated by implementing strict identity and access management (IAM) policies?

A) Physical hardware failure

B) Unauthorized data access

C) Network latency issues

D) Resource allocation inefficiency

E) Insufficient backup frequency

F) High operational costs

Answer: B

Explanation: Strict identity and access management (IAM) policies are critical in preventing unauthorized data access, especially in a multi-tenant environment where multiple tenants share the same physical infrastructure. By implementing stringent IAM policies, each tenant's data access is restricted according to their roles and permissions, minimizing the risk of unauthorized access. This is particularly important in a multi-tenant setting to maintain confidentiality and integrity of sensitive data. While IAM does not directly address hardware failures (option A), network latency (option C), resource allocation (option D), backup issues (option E), or operational costs (option F), it plays a pivotal role in securing access to resources.

Q269: Which of the following is a significant advantage of implementing a multi-tenant architecture in HPE GreenLake environments?

A) Simplified infrastructure management

B) Enhanced performance for a single tenant

C) Reduced need for security measures

D) Increased hardware redundancy

E) Lower cost through resource sharing

F) Unlimited scalability potential

Answer: E

Explanation: One of the significant advantages of a multi-tenant architecture in HPE GreenLake environments is the lower cost achieved through resource sharing. By allowing multiple tenants to share the same physical infrastructure, costs associated with hardware, maintenance, and administration are distributed among the tenants. This not only makes it more cost-effective but also optimizes resource utilization. Simplified infrastructure management (option A) and enhanced performance for a single tenant (option B) are not inherent benefits of multi-tenancy. Security measures (option C) are still essential, and multi-tenancy does not inherently increase hardware redundancy (option D) or provide unlimited scalability (option F).

Q270: Scenario-Based Question A global retail company, RetailPro, has recently adopted HPE GreenLake for its data management and processing needs. The company operates in various regions, each with different network setups and bandwidth capabilities. As a GreenLake administrator, you need to ensure optimal network performance and reliability for data transfers between the regional offices and the central data center. During peak shopping seasons, the data transfer load increases significantly, requiring efficient bandwidth allocation and network monitoring. How should you configure the network management capabilities within GreenLake to address these challenges?

A) Implement Quality of Service (QoS) policies to prioritize critical data transfers.

B) Deploy additional physical network interfaces in each regional office.

C) Use a VPN to secure all data transfers, regardless of performance impact.

D) Configure static IP addresses for all devices to ensure stable connections.

E) Set up automated alerts for any network downtime occurrences.

F) Increase the overall bandwidth capacity for each regional office.

Answer: A

Explanation: Implementing QoS policies is crucial in managing network traffic effectively, especially during peak periods. QoS allows administrators to prioritize critical data transfers, ensuring that essential business operations are not disrupted by increased load. This approach is more strategic and cost-effective than simply increasing bandwidth, which may not be feasible or necessary in all regions. Additionally, relying solely on static IP configurations or VPNs may not adequately address performance challenges and could complicate network management.

Q271: True/False Question True or False: HPE GreenLake's network management capabilities automatically adjust bandwidth allocation based on real-time data transfer needs without any administrator intervention.

A) True

B) False

Answer: B

Explanation: While HPE GreenLake provides robust network management tools, automatic bandwidth adjustment without administrator intervention is not a built-in feature. Administrators must configure network policies and settings to optimize performance based on specific needs and conditions. This requires a proactive approach to network management, including setting up QoS, monitoring traffic, and making necessary adjustments.

Q272: Standard Multiple-Choice Question Which of the following GreenLake network management features is most effective for monitoring real-time network performance and identifying potential bottlenecks?

A) Network Traffic Analyzer

B) Dynamic Bandwidth Scaling

C) Automated IP Assignment

D) Secure Sockets Layer (SSL) Encryption

E) Virtual Private Network (VPN) Tunnels

F) Network Address Translation (NAT)

Answer: A

Explanation: The Network Traffic Analyzer is a powerful tool within GreenLake that provides insights into real-time network performance. It helps administrators identify bottlenecks and potential issues by analyzing traffic patterns and usage. This feature is essential for maintaining optimal network performance and ensuring that resources are allocated efficiently. Other options, such as SSL encryption and VPN tunnels, focus on security rather than performance monitoring.

Q273: Fill-in-the-Gap Multiple-Choice Question In HPE GreenLake, _____
allows administrators to define specific policies that manage and prioritize
network traffic to improve performance during peak usage.

A) Dynamic DNS

B) Quality of Service (QoS)

C) Load Balancing

D) Data Encryption

E) DNS Caching

F) Network Isolation

Answer: B

Explanation: Quality of Service (QoS) is a critical feature in network management that
enables administrators to define policies for traffic prioritization. By setting QoS rules, you
can ensure that important applications and data transfers receive the bandwidth they
require, especially during peak times. This proactive management helps maintain
performance levels and prevents network congestion, unlike options such as DNS caching
or load balancing, which serve different purposes.

Q274: Advanced Configuration Question To enhance network security and
performance in HPE GreenLake, which approach should be taken to ensure
secure data transmission without significantly impacting bandwidth?

A) Implement SSL/TLS encryption for all data transmissions.

B) Utilize a dedicated firewall for each network segment.

C) Apply network segmentation to isolate sensitive data.

D) Use a hybrid approach combining VPN and QoS.

E) Increase physical security measures for network devices.

F) Opt for proprietary encryption protocols.

Answer: D

Explanation: A hybrid approach that combines VPN and QoS offers a balanced solution for securing data transmission while maintaining network performance. VPNs ensure data confidentiality and integrity, while QoS manages traffic prioritization, preventing the performance issues that can arise from encryption overhead. This dual strategy allows administrators to safeguard sensitive information without compromising on speed or efficiency, unlike relying solely on encryption or physical security measures.

Q275: Scenario-Based Question A multinational corporation, TechGlobal Inc., is planning to expand its IT operations by integrating new cloud services through HPE GreenLake. The corporation operates in multiple regions, and each region has distinct compliance and data sovereignty requirements. The IT team must ensure that the onboarding process aligns with these regional regulations and minimizes any potential downtime. Additionally, TechGlobal Inc. aims to optimize resource allocation across regions to prevent over-provisioning and reduce costs. As an HPE GreenLake administrator, what should be your primary focus during the onboarding of these new services to meet the corporation's needs?

A) Focus on centralizing all data in a single location for easier management.

B) Prioritize the onboarding process based on the region with the least compliance requirements.

C) Implement a standardized onboarding process without considering regional differences.

D) Customize the onboarding process for each region to comply with local regulations and optimize resources.

E) Delay the onboarding process until a global compliance solution is available.

F) Outsource the onboarding to a third-party vendor to handle regional compliance.

Answer: D

Explanation: When onboarding new services in HPE GreenLake, especially for a multinational corporation like TechGlobal Inc., it is crucial to customize the process according to regional regulations to ensure compliance. Compliance with local laws regarding data sovereignty and privacy is mandatory to avoid legal issues. Additionally, optimizing resource allocation is essential for cost management and efficiency. By tailoring the onboarding process to fit each region's specific needs, the corporation can ensure a smooth transition, minimize downtime, and maintain compliance, which is vital for maintaining operational integrity and avoiding penalties.

Q276: True/False Question True or False: The HPE GreenLake platform automatically adjusts service configurations to meet regional compliance requirements without any input from administrators.

A) True

B) False

Answer: B

Explanation: HPE GreenLake provides a flexible and scalable platform for managing IT resources, but it does not automatically adjust service configurations to meet regional compliance requirements without input from administrators. While the platform offers tools and features that can help manage compliance, administrators must actively configure and monitor these settings to ensure that all regional legal and compliance standards are met. This requires an understanding of the specific compliance needs of each region and the application of those requirements during the onboarding process.

Q277: Standard Multiple-Choice Question During the onboarding of new services in HPE GreenLake, you are tasked with ensuring that cost management is a top priority while maintaining performance. Which of the following strategies should you employ to achieve this goal?

A) Allocate maximum resources to all services to ensure peak performance.

B) Use predictive analytics to forecast resource needs and dynamically adjust allocations.

C) Implement a fixed resource allocation model to control costs.

D) Onboard services during peak usage periods to test performance.

E) Ignore cost considerations to focus solely on performance metrics.

F) Defer all cost management decisions to the finance department.

Answer: B

Explanation: Using predictive analytics to forecast resource needs and dynamically adjust allocations is an effective strategy for managing costs while maintaining performance in HPE GreenLake. Predictive analytics tools can help anticipate future demands, allowing you to adjust resources proactively rather than reactively. This approach helps optimize resource usage, preventing both over-provisioning (which leads to unnecessary costs) and under-provisioning (which can degrade performance). By leveraging predictive analytics, you can strike a balance between cost efficiency and performance, ensuring that resources are used judiciously and that the system adapts to changing demands.

Q278: Fill-in-the-Gap/Multiple-Choice Question During the onboarding process, it is important to establish a robust monitoring system to ensure ongoing service reliability. Which component is critical for achieving proactive monitoring in HPE GreenLake?

A) Manual log inspections by the IT team.

B) Implementation of automated alerts and notifications.

C) Monthly performance reviews.

D) Third-party auditing services.

E) User feedback surveys.

F) Weekly manual system checks.

Answer: B

Explanation: Implementing automated alerts and notifications is critical for achieving proactive monitoring in HPE GreenLake. Automated monitoring systems provide real-time insights into the health and performance of IT services, allowing administrators to detect and resolve issues before they impact users. These systems can be configured to send alerts based on predefined thresholds, ensuring that the IT team is promptly informed of any anomalies or potential failures. This proactive approach reduces downtime and helps maintain the reliability and availability of the services, which is crucial for maintaining user satisfaction and operational continuity.

Q279: Multiple-Choice Question In the context of onboarding new services in HPE GreenLake, which of the following best describes the role of a Service Level Agreement (SLA)?

A) An SLA is a marketing document used to attract new clients.

B) An SLA is a legal contract that dictates the cost of the services.

C) An SLA outlines the expected performance and availability metrics of the services.

D) An SLA is an internal document for the IT team only.

E) An SLA provides a detailed description of the technical specifications of the services.

F) An SLA is primarily used for financial auditing purposes.

Answer: C

Explanation: A Service Level Agreement (SLA) outlines the expected performance and availability metrics of the services provided. It is a formal document that defines the level of service expected by a customer from a service provider, laying out the metrics by which service is measured, and the remedies or penalties, if any, should the agreed-upon levels not be achieved. SLAs are critical during the onboarding of new services in HPE GreenLake as they set clear expectations between the provider and the client and serve as a reference point for service delivery and performance. They are essential for establishing trust and ensuring that both parties have a mutual understanding of the service commitments.

Q280: Scenario-Based Question Your company, a mid-sized enterprise, has recently adopted the HPE GreenLake platform to manage its IT infrastructure. You are responsible for overseeing the GreenLake environment and ensuring that any technical issues are promptly addressed. Recently, your team encountered a recurring performance issue with one of the services. After preliminary troubleshooting, you determine that you need to open a support case with HPE. However, the issue is intermittent, and you need to provide detailed information to facilitate quick resolution. How should you proceed to ensure that the support case is managed effectively?

A) Open a support case immediately, describing the issue briefly, and ask HPE to monitor the situation.

B) Gather detailed logs, document the issue thoroughly, including the circumstances under which it occurs, and then open a support case.

C) Wait until the issue becomes persistent and more easily reproducible before contacting HPE Support.

D) Perform a complete system reboot to see if the issue resolves itself, then open a support case if it persists.

E) Attempt to resolve the issue internally for several weeks before opening a support case with HPE.

F) Open multiple support cases to increase the chances of a quicker response from HPE.

Answer: B

Explanation: When encountering a technical issue with HPE GreenLake, it is crucial to gather as much information as possible before opening a support case. This includes collecting detailed logs, documenting the conditions under which the issue occurs, and any troubleshooting steps already undertaken. This information will enable HPE Support to understand the problem context better and expedite the resolution process. Opening a case without sufficient details (Option A) or delaying the case submission until the issue becomes more severe (Option C) can lead to delays in resolution. Attempting a system reboot (Option D) or waiting several weeks (Option E) may not address the root cause and could lead to prolonged service disruptions. Opening multiple support cases (Option F) can cause confusion and inefficiencies in support response.

True/False Question Submitting detailed logs and documentation when opening a support case with HPE GreenLake is not necessary if the issue is already well-known.

A) True

B) False

Answer: B

Explanation: Even if the issue seems well-known, providing detailed logs and documentation is essential when opening a support case with HPE GreenLake. This practice ensures that the support team has all the relevant context and information specific to your environment, which can be crucial for diagnosing and resolving the issue efficiently. Assumptions about the issue's nature without comprehensive data can lead to incorrect troubleshooting paths and prolonged downtime.

Q282: Standard Multiple-Choice Question Which of the following is a best practice for managing support cases in HPE GreenLake?

A) Escalate the case to the highest level as soon as it is opened to ensure prompt attention.

B) Regularly update the support case with any new findings or changes in the issue's behavior.

C) Close the case as soon as you receive a response from the support team, even if the issue is not resolved.

D) Avoid mentioning any previous similar issues to keep the case focused on the current problem.

E) Only communicate with HPE Support via email to maintain a written record.

F) Assign multiple team members to manage the same support case to increase oversight.

Answer: B

Explanation: Regularly updating the support case with new findings or changes in the issue's behavior is a best practice because it keeps the support team informed and engaged. This proactive approach can lead to quicker and more accurate resolutions. Premature escalation (Option A) can overwhelm the support process, and closing the case too soon (Option C) can leave issues unresolved. Previous similar issues (Option D) provide valuable context that can aid in diagnosis. While written records (Option E) are important, using multiple communication channels can be more effective. Assigning multiple team members (Option F) can lead to miscommunication and confusion.

Q283: Fill-in-the-Gap Question When encountering a critical issue that affects business operations, it is crucial to _____ the support case to ensure it receives the appropriate level of attention and resources from HPE Support.

A) immediately escalate

B) carefully describe

C) temporarily close

D) downgrade

E) ignore

F) duplicate

Answer: A

Explanation: In a situation where a critical issue impacts business operations, it is essential to immediately escalate the support case. Escalation ensures that the case is prioritized appropriately and receives the necessary attention and resources from HPE Support. This action can facilitate a faster resolution, minimizing business disruptions. Carefully describing the issue (Option B) is important but does not replace the need for escalation in critical situations. Temporarily closing (Option C), downgrading (Option D), ignoring (Option E), or duplicating (Option F) the case would not address the urgency required for critical issues.

Q284: Standard Multiple-Choice Question What is the most effective way to close a support case with HPE GreenLake once the issue has been resolved?

A) Close the case immediately after the first sign of resolution, regardless of confirmation.

B) Confirm with HPE Support that the issue is resolved and request case closure.

C) Wait for a week after resolution to ensure the issue does not reoccur, then close the case.

D) Close the case without confirming resolution if the support team's initial suggestion seemed correct.

E) Automatically close the case if no further communication from support is received within 48 hours.

F) Assign the case closure to the person who originally opened it, regardless of their current involvement.

Answer: B

Explanation: The most effective way to close a support case with HPE GreenLake is to confirm with HPE Support that the issue has been resolved and then request case closure. This ensures that both parties agree on the resolution and that no loose ends remain. Closing the case prematurely (Option A) or without confirmation (Option D) can lead to unresolved issues. Waiting unnecessarily (Option C) or relying on automatic closure (Option E) can leave cases open longer than necessary. Case closure should be managed by the person currently overseeing the resolution process, ensuring continuity and accountability, rather than the original opener (Option F).

Q285: Scenario-Based Question A medium-sized enterprise with a global presence relies heavily on its IT infrastructure for daily operations. The company has deployed HPE GreenLake to manage its hybrid cloud environment, which includes a mix of on-premises and cloud resources. The IT team is responsible for ensuring that the infrastructure is up-to-date with the latest patches and software updates to maintain security and performance. During a recent review, it was discovered that several critical updates were missed, leading to vulnerabilities in the system. The team must now implement a more effective patching process. What should be their first step in developing a robust patch management strategy to avoid future issues?

A) Conduct a comprehensive audit of all existing systems and inventory their current patch levels.

B) Immediately apply all available patches to all systems without further delay.

C) Defer patching until a new automated system is fully implemented.

D) Focus on patching only the most critical systems and ignore non-essential ones.

E) Outsource the patch management process to an external vendor.

F) Notify all users to manually update their systems and applications.

Answer: A

Explanation: Conducting a comprehensive audit of all existing systems is crucial for understanding the current state of the infrastructure. This step helps identify which systems are vulnerable and require immediate attention. It establishes a baseline for future updates and ensures that the team has a complete inventory of all systems and their patch levels. This information is vital for planning and prioritizing patches, scheduling updates during non-peak hours to minimize disruption, and ensuring that all systems comply with security policies. Implementing this step first aids in creating a structured and efficient patch management process.

A) Schedule updates during business peak hours for immediate feedback.

B) Apply updates as soon as they are released to avoid any delay.

C) Use rolling updates to minimize downtime by staggering updates across systems.

D) Disable automatic updates to prevent unexpected disruptions.

E) Only update systems annually to reduce frequency of disruptions.

F) Update all systems simultaneously to ensure uniformity.

Answer: C

Explanation: Rolling updates involve staggering updates across different systems or components to minimize downtime and ensure continuity of service. This approach allows the IT team to update portions of the infrastructure incrementally, reducing the risk of a complete system outage. It is particularly effective in environments where high availability is critical. By applying updates in a controlled manner, the team can monitor the impact of changes and address any issues that arise promptly, ensuring a smooth update process with minimal business disruption.

A) True

B) False

Answer: B

Explanation: While applying patches promptly is important for maintaining security, it is not always recommended to apply them immediately upon release. Patches should first be tested in a controlled environment to ensure they do not introduce new issues or conflicts within the existing infrastructure. This testing phase allows the IT team to assess the patch's impact on system performance and compatibility with other applications. Proper testing helps avoid potential disruptions or downtime in the production environment, making a staged rollout a safer approach.

Q288: Fill-in-the-Gap In the context of HPE GreenLake, what is the primary objective of implementing a patch management policy?

A) To reduce the frequency of updates needed.

B) To eliminate the need for system monitoring.

C) To ensure compliance with industry regulations and standards.

D) To increase the complexity of IT operations.

E) To prevent all security incidents.

F) To manage user access more effectively.

Answer: C

Explanation: The primary objective of implementing a patch management policy is to ensure compliance with industry regulations and standards. Such a policy helps maintain the security and integrity of the IT infrastructure by providing a systematic approach to identifying, testing, and deploying patches. Compliance with regulations like GDPR, HIPAA, or PCI DSS often requires organizations to keep their systems up-to-date to protect sensitive data and maintain customer trust. A well-defined patch management policy helps organizations stay compliant and mitigate the risk of security breaches.

Q289: Advanced Multiple Choice When considering automated patch management solutions in HPE GreenLake, which feature is most critical for ensuring that updates do not negatively impact system performance?

A) The ability to customize the patch schedule to fit business needs.

B) The inclusion of a detailed reporting system for tracking update status.

C) The integration with existing security information and event management (SIEM) systems.

D) The capability to automatically roll back updates if issues are detected.

E) Support for multiple operating systems and software applications.

F) The provision of user notifications prior to updates.

Answer: D

Explanation: The capability to automatically roll back updates if issues are detected is crucial for ensuring that system performance is not negatively impacted. This feature allows the IT team to quickly revert changes in the event of unexpected problems, minimizing downtime and maintaining system stability. It provides a safety net that enables more aggressive patching strategies, knowing that any adverse effects can be mitigated promptly. Rollback capabilities are particularly important in environments where uptime and performance are critical, as they help maintain business continuity while ensuring systems are secure and up-to-date.

Q290: A mid-sized retail company has recently transitioned to using HPE GreenLake for their infrastructure needs. The IT department is tasked with ensuring optimal performance and cost efficiency. The retail company experiences seasonal spikes in demand, particularly during the holiday season, which significantly impacts resource utilization. The IT manager wants to use the Performance Insights feature to predict and prepare for these changes. As the GreenLake administrator, you need to determine which performance insights metric will be most helpful in forecasting and responding to these fluctuations. What should you focus on to ensure the company is ready for demand spikes?

A) Average CPU utilization over the past year

B) Peak memory usage during non-peak seasons

C) Daily resource consumption trends over the last month

D) Weekly storage capacity growth rate

E) Monthly network throughput during peak seasons

F) Historical data analysis of resource usage during previous holiday seasons

Answer: F

Explanation: In this scenario, the retail company experiences predictable seasonal spikes, particularly during the holiday season. As a GreenLake administrator, focusing on historical data analysis of resource usage during previous holiday seasons (Option F) will provide a more accurate forecast of upcoming demand spikes. This approach allows the IT team to leverage past data to predict future trends, ensuring that the company can allocate resources efficiently to handle increased loads. While other options provide valuable insights, they do not specifically address the need to prepare for predictable seasonal variations, making historical data analysis the most effective choice.

Q291: Which of the following metrics is least likely to provide actionable insights for optimizing storage performance in HPE GreenLake?
A) IOPS (Input/Output Operations Per Second)

B) Data deduplication ratio

C) Network latency

D) Data transfer rate

E) Storage tiering efficiency

F) Disk failure rate

Answer: F

Explanation: While all the options listed can be relevant to storage performance, the disk failure rate (Option F) is least likely to provide actionable insights for optimizing performance in a proactive manner. It is more of a reactive metric that indicates hardware issues rather than an optimization parameter. The other options, such as IOPS, data deduplication ratio, and storage tiering efficiency, provide insights into how effectively the storage system is performing and can be directly used to make adjustments for optimization. Network latency and data transfer rate are also critical as they affect the speed and efficiency of data access and movement.

Q292: True or False: Monitoring the trend of peak network utilization is more critical for capacity planning in HPE GreenLake than monitoring average network utilization.
A) True

B) False

Answer: A

Explanation: Monitoring peak network utilization (Option A) is indeed more critical for capacity planning than average utilization because peak utilization represents the maximum demand on network resources. Being prepared for peak demand ensures that the infrastructure can handle the highest loads without performance degradation. Average utilization, while useful for understanding general usage patterns, may not reflect the needs during peak times, potentially leading to under-provisioning and performance issues.

Therefore, peak utilization is a more crucial metric for ensuring the network can support business operations during the highest demand periods.

Q293: Fill in the gap: To effectively use HPE GreenLake's Performance Insights for identifying underutilized resources, administrators should focus on analyzing _____ to make informed decisions about resource allocation.

A) Monthly billing reports

B) Real-time alert notifications

C) Historical usage patterns

D) Incident response times

E) User satisfaction surveys

F) Vendor service level agreements

Answer: C

Explanation: Analyzing historical usage patterns (Option C) is essential for identifying underutilized resources within HPE GreenLake. This analysis allows administrators to track how resources have been used over time, highlighting periods of low utilization that may indicate opportunities for reallocation or downsizing. Monthly billing reports and real-time alerts provide immediate financial and operational insights, but they do not offer the comprehensive view necessary for making strategic decisions about resource allocation. Historical data is critical for understanding trends and optimizing the infrastructure to meet actual needs efficiently.

Q294: In a scenario where an enterprise is using HPE GreenLake to support a hybrid IT environment, which performance metric should be prioritized to ensure seamless integration and data flow between on-premises and cloud resources?

A) On-premises server CPU load

B) Cloud storage availability

C) Network bandwidth between sites

D) On-premises memory usage

E) Cloud service uptime

F) Security compliance reports

Answer: C

Explanation: In a hybrid IT environment, ensuring seamless integration and data flow between on-premises and cloud resources relies heavily on the network bandwidth between sites (Option C). Adequate bandwidth ensures that data can move efficiently between different parts of the infrastructure, preventing bottlenecks that could disrupt operations. While other metrics such as server CPU load and storage availability are important for individual components, they do not directly address the connectivity and data transfer requirements of a hybrid setup. Prioritizing network bandwidth helps maintain high performance and reliability across the entire system, facilitating smooth integration and operational continuity.

Q295: Scenario: A mid-sized manufacturing company, XYZ Corp, uses HPE GreenLake to manage its hybrid cloud environment. They have recently experienced performance issues during peak production times, impacting their ability to meet customer orders. An analysis reveals that the workload intensities vary significantly based on production schedules, and there is a need to optimize resource allocation without incurring additional costs. As the GreenLake administrator, you are tasked with tuning the system to enhance performance during these peak periods. Given this context, which of the following best practices should you prioritize to achieve optimal performance without increasing the cost?

A) Implementing predictive analytics to forecast workload demands.

B) Increasing the total available compute resources permanently.

C) Utilizing auto-scaling features to adjust resources in real-time.

D) Scheduling intensive workloads during off-peak hours.

E) Reducing the number of virtual machines to lessen overhead.

F) Over-provisioning resources to handle peak loads.

Answer: C

Explanation: Auto-scaling allows for dynamic adjustment of compute resources based on real-time demand, which helps optimize performance during peak periods without the need for permanent resource increases, thus keeping costs in check. Predictive analytics, while useful, is more about planning and not immediate tuning. Increasing resources permanently or over-provisioning would lead to higher costs. Scheduling workloads might not always be feasible due to production constraints, and reducing virtual machines could lead to underperformance during high-demand times.

Q296: True/False: When tuning performance in HPE GreenLake, utilizing resource throttling can lead to more efficient workload management by preventing any single process from monopolizing system resources.
A) True

B) False

Answer: A

Explanation: Resource throttling is a technique used to limit the resources that a particular process can consume. This ensures that no single workload dominates the system, allowing for more balanced and efficient performance across all workloads. It is particularly beneficial in environments where multiple applications or services are competing for the same resources, as it prevents one from starving others of necessary compute or memory.

Q297: Which of the following metrics is most critical to monitor for identifying performance bottlenecks in an HPE GreenLake environment?

A) Network latency

B) CPU utilization

C) Disk I/O throughput

D) Memory usage

E) Application response time

F) Power consumption

Answer: B

Explanation: CPU utilization is a key performance indicator that can reveal if the compute resources are being maxed out, which is a common cause of performance bottlenecks. While network latency, disk I/O, and memory usage are also important, CPU utilization provides a direct insight into whether the processing power is sufficient for the workloads. High CPU usage often indicates that the system is struggling to keep up with demand, necessitating optimization or scaling.

Q298: Fill in the gap: To ensure that resource allocation is aligned with business priorities in HPE GreenLake, administrators should implement _____ to prioritize critical workloads.

A) Vertical scaling

B) Horizontal scaling

C) Quality of Service (QoS) policies

D) Load balancing

E) Resource pooling

F) Server consolidation

Answer: C

Explanation: Quality of Service (QoS) policies are used to assign priority levels to different workloads, ensuring that critical applications receive the necessary resources over less important ones. This alignment with business priorities is crucial for maintaining performance where it matters most. Vertical and horizontal scaling deal with resource allocation but don't prioritize workloads. Load balancing and server consolidation focus on distribution and efficiency, respectively, not prioritization.

Q299: In a scenario where an HPE GreenLake administrator needs to optimize storage performance for a database application, which strategy is recommended?

A) Increasing the size of the storage pool

B) Implementing a tiered storage system

C) Switching to a different storage vendor

D) Using RAID 0 for faster write speeds

E) Increasing the cache size on storage controllers

F) Reducing the number of concurrent database connections

Answer: B

Explanation: Implementing a tiered storage system is an effective strategy for optimizing storage performance, especially for database applications. By automatically moving frequently accessed data to faster storage tiers, it ensures that critical operations have quick access to the data they need, improving overall performance. Increasing storage pool size and cache may help but doesn't address the access speed directly. RAID 0 offers faster writes but at the risk of data loss; switching vendors is a complex, last-resort option, and reducing connections might not be feasible or effective.

Q300: Scenario-Based Question A technology services company, TechSolutions Inc., is transitioning to a hybrid cloud environment to better support its growing global client base. They have chosen HPE GreenLake to manage both on-premises and cloud resources efficiently. As a GreenLake administrator, you're tasked with ensuring seamless integration of legacy systems and new cloud services, while maintaining data compliance and security. There are concerns about resource allocation, cost management, and performance optimization. During a strategy meeting, the CIO asks for your recommendation on the best practices to follow to ensure operational efficiency and data security within the GreenLake environment.

A) Implement role-based access control and regular audits for data security.

B) Focus on cost management by optimizing resource allocation using HPE OneView.

C) Prioritize performance optimization by deploying workload-specific infrastructure.

D) Enable automated scaling and monitoring for demand fluctuations.

E) Integrate GreenLake with existing legacy systems to ensure compatibility.

F) Establish a dedicated GreenLake team for continuous operational management.

Answer: A

Explanation: In any hybrid cloud deployment, especially when integrating legacy systems with new cloud services, security and compliance are critical. Implementing role-based access control (RBAC) ensures that only authorized users have access to sensitive data and resources, minimizing the risk of data breaches. Regular audits help maintain compliance with regulatory standards and identify potential security vulnerabilities. While cost management and performance optimization are important, they should not compromise data security. Automated scaling and integration with legacy systems are operational considerations but must be underpinned by strong security practices.

Q301: True/False Question The HPE GreenLake platform allows organizations to manage resources across on-premises and cloud environments with a single interface, but it does not support third-party service integration.

A) True

B) False

Answer: B

Explanation: The statement is false. HPE GreenLake is designed to provide a unified management interface for resources across both on-premises and cloud environments. Furthermore, it supports integration with third-party services, allowing organizations to extend their capabilities and tailor their IT environment to meet specific business needs. This flexibility is one of the key advantages of using GreenLake, as it enables businesses to leverage a wide range of technologies and services without being locked into a single vendor.

Q302: Multiple-Choice Question Which of the following is an essential step to ensure business continuity when implementing HPE GreenLake in a multi-site deployment?

A) Establish a centralized data center with dedicated backup services.

B) Implement a comprehensive disaster recovery plan across all sites.

C) Focus on real-time data synchronization between locations.

D) Utilize HPE GreenLake's built-in analytics for predictive maintenance.

E) Prioritize network redundancy to prevent site-specific failures.

F) Ensure all sites have identical hardware configurations.

Answer: B

Explanation: Business continuity in a multi-site deployment hinges on the ability to recover from failures and maintain operations. Implementing a comprehensive disaster recovery (DR) plan is critical to ensuring that if one site experiences an issue, operations can continue at another location with minimal downtime. While network redundancy and real-time data synchronization are important, they are components of a broader DR strategy. A centralized data center or identical hardware configurations do not inherently ensure continuity without a robust recovery plan in place. HPE GreenLake's analytics can aid in maintenance but are not substitutes for a DR plan.

Q303: Multiple-Choice Question When configuring HPE GreenLake for optimal cost management, which feature should be prioritized to track and manage resource usage effectively?

A) HPE GreenLake Central's cost analytics dashboard.

B) Real-time usage alerts and notifications.

C) Integration with third-party financial software.

D) Detailed usage reports and trend analysis.

E) Automated billing reconciliation.

F) Customizable resource tagging for cost allocation.

Answer: A

Explanation: For optimal cost management in HPE GreenLake, leveraging the cost analytics dashboard available in HPE GreenLake Central is crucial. This feature provides visibility into resource usage patterns and associated costs, allowing administrators to make informed decisions on resource allocation and budgeting. While real-time alerts, integration with financial software, and detailed reports can enhance cost management processes, the cost analytics dashboard is specifically designed to centralize and streamline these efforts. Automated billing and resource tagging are supportive features but are secondary to the overarching visibility provided by the dashboard.

Q304: Multiple-Choice Question If a company wants to enhance its operational efficiency using HPE GreenLake, which approach should be taken to maximize the benefits of the platform?

A) Invest in extensive training for all IT staff on GreenLake functionalities.

B) Develop a custom integration solution with existing IT systems.

C) Utilize GreenLake's AI-driven recommendations for resource optimization.

D) Focus on migrating all workloads to GreenLake as quickly as possible.

E) Establish a cross-functional team to oversee GreenLake operations.

F) Standardize all IT processes around GreenLake's capabilities.

Answer: C

Explanation: To enhance operational efficiency with HPE GreenLake, utilizing the platform's AI-driven recommendations for resource optimization is key. These recommendations can help identify underutilized resources, suggest improvements, and automate routine tasks, thereby increasing efficiency. While training, integration, and cross-functional teams are important, they do not directly leverage the advanced capabilities of GreenLake's AI tools. Migrating workloads quickly or standardizing processes can be disruptive if not strategically planned, whereas AI-driven insights offer a balanced approach to optimizing operations without unnecessary upheaval.

Q305: Scenario-Based Question A mid-sized financial firm has adopted HPE GreenLake for its cloud services to manage its growing data analytics workloads efficiently. The company is experiencing frequent spikes in data processing requirements at the end of each fiscal quarter. To address this, the IT manager needs to ensure that resources are optimally provisioned to handle these peak loads without impacting performance or incurring unnecessary costs during the off-peak periods. The manager considers using GreenLake's capabilities to dynamically adjust resources. Which strategy should the IT manager implement to best manage these workload fluctuations?

A) Pre-allocate maximum resources at all times to ensure performance during peak periods.

B) Manually adjust resource allocations at the end of each quarter.

C) Use HPE GreenLake's auto-scaling feature to dynamically adjust resources based on workload demands.

D) Schedule regular downtime for maintenance during peak periods to free up resources.

E) Implement a hybrid model with additional on-premises resources for peak times.

F) Use predictive analytics to forecast demand and adjust resources manually.

Answer: C

Explanation: The best strategy for managing workload fluctuations in the HPE GreenLake environment is to use the auto-scaling feature. Auto-scaling allows resources to be dynamically adjusted based on real-time workload demands, ensuring optimal performance during peak times without incurring unnecessary costs during off-peak periods. Pre-allocating maximum resources at all times (option A) would lead to higher costs, while manual adjustments (option B) and predictive analytics (option F) require active monitoring and may not respond quickly enough to sudden changes. Scheduling downtime (option D) is not practical during peak periods, and a hybrid model (option E) could increase complexity and costs.

Q306: True/False Question True or False: HPE GreenLake allows for the integration of third-party cloud services to expand workload management capabilities.
A) True

B) False

Answer: A

Explanation: True. HPE GreenLake is designed to be a flexible and scalable cloud service that can integrate with third-party cloud services. This integration enhances workload management capabilities by allowing organizations to leverage additional tools and resources from other cloud providers, thereby expanding their operational scope and efficiency. This flexibility is one of the key advantages of using GreenLake, as it enables businesses to customize their cloud environment to better suit their specific needs.

Q307: Standard Multiple Choice Question Which of the following is NOT a recommended practice when provisioning workloads in HPE GreenLake?

A) Regularly reviewing and optimizing resource allocations to match workload requirements.

B) Using predefined templates to quickly deploy standard workloads.

C) Ignoring resource usage analytics and sticking to initial provisioning settings.

D) Implementing role-based access control to manage user permissions.

E) Monitoring performance metrics to ensure workloads are running efficiently.

F) Automating routine management tasks to reduce manual intervention.

Answer: C

Explanation: Ignoring resource usage analytics and sticking to initial provisioning settings is not a recommended practice. Effective workload provisioning in HPE GreenLake involves continuously reviewing and optimizing resource allocations based on analytics to ensure resources match current workload requirements, thereby avoiding waste and ensuring cost efficiency. Predefined templates (option B), role-based access control (option D), performance monitoring (option E), and automation (option F) are all practices that enhance the efficiency and security of workload management.

Q308: Fill-in-the-gap Question In HPE GreenLake, _____ allows administrators to automatically adjust storage capacity based on workload demands.

A) Capacity Planning

B) Workload Balancer

C) Auto-Scaling

D) Resource Orchestration

E) Dynamic Provisioning

F) Elastic Storage Management

Answer: F

Explanation: Elastic Storage Management in HPE GreenLake allows administrators to automatically adjust storage capacity based on workload demands. This feature is crucial for maintaining optimal performance and cost-effectiveness as it ensures that storage resources are available when needed and scaled down during times of low demand. Other options such as Capacity Planning (option A) and Resource Orchestration (option D) are important for overall resource management but do not directly address the automatic adjustment of storage capacity.

Q309: Standard Multiple Choice Question What is the primary benefit of using HPE GreenLake's centralized management console for workload management?
A) It allows for complex scripting and manual configuration of resources.

B) It provides a unified view of all cloud services and resources, simplifying management.

C) It restricts access to only predefined users, improving security.

D) It offers detailed financial reports for cost management.

E) It enables direct integration with hardware without the need for additional software.

F) It facilitates third-party API integration for expanded functionality.

Answer: B

Explanation: The primary benefit of using HPE GreenLake's centralized management console is that it provides a unified view of all cloud services and resources, simplifying management. This centralized perspective allows administrators to efficiently monitor, manage, and optimize resources across the entire cloud environment. While other options, such as security (option C) and financial reports (option D), are beneficial features, the core advantage of the centralized console is its ability to streamline and simplify workload management through comprehensive visibility and control.

Q310: Scenario-Based Question A mid-sized retail company, XYZ Retail, has been experiencing rapid growth, leading to increased demand for IT resources. The current infrastructure is struggling to cope with peak business hours, resulting in slow response times and occasional outages. To address these issues, the IT Manager has been tasked with implementing a scalable solution that can handle fluctuating demands efficiently. After evaluating various options, the IT Manager considers requesting new services through HPE GreenLake. What is the most critical first step the IT Manager should take when planning to request new services through HPE GreenLake?

A) Conduct a comprehensive workload assessment to determine precise resource requirements.

B) Opt for the largest available HPE GreenLake configuration to ensure future scalability.

C) Immediately request additional compute resources to address the current shortfall.

D) Schedule a consultation with an HPE GreenLake specialist to discuss potential solutions.

E) Implement a temporary workaround by reallocating existing resources.

F) Analyze historical data to predict future resource usage trends.

Answer: A

Explanation: The first critical step in planning to request new services through HPE GreenLake is to conduct a comprehensive workload assessment. This assessment will help determine the precise resource requirements based on current and projected usage. By understanding the specific needs, the IT Manager can ensure that the requested services are appropriately sized to handle both current demands and future growth. Simply opting for the largest configuration or requesting additional resources without a thorough assessment could lead to over-provisioning or under-provisioning, both of which have financial and operational implications. Engaging with an HPE specialist is a useful step but should follow the internal assessment to provide informed insights during the consultation.

Q311: True/False Question HPE GreenLake allows IT administrators to request new services and infrastructure through a self-service portal without any need for additional approvals from HPE.

A) True

B) False

Answer: B

Explanation: HPE GreenLake provides a self-service portal that facilitates the request process for new services and infrastructure. However, these requests typically require approval both from within the organization and from HPE to ensure alignment with service level agreements (SLAs) and to verify the feasibility of the requested resources. This ensures that the deployed infrastructure is optimal for the organization's needs and complies with HPE's provisioning capabilities.

Q312: Multiple-Choice Question When evaluating the need for new infrastructure through HPE GreenLake, which factor is least likely to influence the decision-making process?

A) Current energy consumption of existing infrastructure.

B) The geographical distribution of the workforce.

C) Historical ticket resolution times in IT support.

D) Vendor lock-in concerns with existing providers.

E) Compliance with industry-specific regulations.

F) The color palette of the HPE GreenLake management interface.

Answer: F

Explanation: The color palette of the HPE GreenLake management interface is the least likely factor to influence the decision-making process when evaluating the need for new infrastructure. Critical factors typically include technical, operational, and strategic considerations such as energy efficiency, workforce distribution, regulatory compliance, and support efficiency. These aspects directly impact the performance, cost, and compliance of the IT environment, while user interface aesthetics generally have minimal impact on strategic decision-making.

Q313: Multiple-Choice Question In the context of HPE GreenLake, which of the following steps should be performed to ensure that requested services align with budgetary constraints?

A) Submit a request based on estimated costs and adjust the budget accordingly.

B) Develop a cost-benefit analysis to justify the expenditure.

C) Request a detailed quote from HPE after deployment of services.

D) Trust in HPE GreenLake's scalability to provide cost-effective solutions.

E) Implement a pilot project to evaluate cost implications before full-scale deployment.

F) Seek approval from the finance department only after service deployment.

Answer: B

Explanation: Developing a cost-benefit analysis is a crucial step to ensure that requested services align with budgetary constraints. This analysis helps justify the investment by comparing the expected benefits, such as increased efficiency and scalability, against the costs. It allows decision-makers to understand the financial implications of the new services and provides a basis for seeking financial approval. Estimating costs without detailed analysis, requesting quotes post-deployment, or assuming scalability alone will ensure cost-effectiveness can lead to budget overruns and financial inefficiencies.

Q314: Multiple-Choice Question Which of the following is a primary advantage of using HPE GreenLake for requesting new IT services and infrastructure?

A) The ability to completely eliminate on-premises hardware requirements.

B) Instantaneous deployment of requested services without any lead time.

C) Enhanced data security through proprietary HPE encryption methods.

D) Flexible consumption models that align costs with actual usage.

E) Guaranteed reduction of IT operational staff due to automation.

F) Exclusive access to HPE's experimental technologies before market release.

Answer: D

Explanation: A primary advantage of using HPE GreenLake is its flexible consumption models, which align costs with actual usage. This "pay-as-you-go" approach enables organizations to scale their infrastructure according to demand, avoiding the need for large upfront capital expenditures and reducing the risk of over-provisioning. This flexibility is particularly beneficial for businesses with fluctuating resource requirements, as it allows them to adjust their infrastructure dynamically while only paying for the resources they consume. While other advantages like enhanced security and automation exist, the key value proposition of HPE GreenLake lies in its consumption-based pricing model.

Q315: Scenario-Based Question Your company, Tech Innovations Inc., has recently adopted HPE GreenLake to manage its IT infrastructure. The company operates in three distinct regions: North America, Europe, and Asia. Each region has its own set of applications and resources, which need to be managed separately to meet regional compliance and performance needs. Additionally, the company wants to set up a global dashboard view for the executive team to monitor the overall resource utilization and performance metrics. As the GreenLake administrator, you are tasked with configuring resource management and grouping to meet these requirements. Which approach should you take to effectively group and manage the resources across regions while providing a comprehensive global view?

A) Create a single global resource pool and use tags to differentiate resources by region.

B) Set up separate resource groups for each region and use aggregation tools for global insights.

C) Use a single resource group for all regions and filter resources through custom queries.

D) Establish a hierarchical resource group structure with regional sub-groups under a global group.

E) Deploy dedicated GreenLake instances for each region to ensure complete isolation.

F) Use a third-party tool to integrate and manage regional resources outside of GreenLake.

Answer: B

Explanation: To manage resources effectively across multiple regions while providing a global overview, setting up separate resource groups for each region is essential. This approach allows for regional compliance and performance optimization by isolating resources specific to each location. Additionally, using aggregation tools within HPE GreenLake enables the creation of a comprehensive global view for the executive team. This configuration ensures that resources are managed efficiently and monitored accurately, while also facilitating compliance with regional regulations and enhancing performance metrics reporting.

In the context of HPE GreenLake, what is the primary benefit of using resource tags for resource management and grouping?

A) Tags automatically enforce security policies across resources.

B) Tags provide a method to automate the scaling of resources.

C) Tags help in identifying and organizing resources for billing purposes.

D) Tags enable the application of software updates to grouped resources.

E) Tags allow for the isolation of resources to prevent unauthorized access.

F) Tags facilitate the integration of third-party applications with GreenLake resources.

Answer: C

Explanation: Resource tags in HPE GreenLake are primarily used for identifying and organizing resources, which is especially beneficial for billing purposes. By tagging resources, administrators can track usage and costs associated with specific projects, departments, or business units, enabling precise billing and cost allocation. This practice enhances financial transparency and accountability, ensuring that each sector of the business is charged appropriately for the resources it consumes.

Q317: True/False Question In HPE GreenLake, resource groups can be dynamically resized based on demand without manual intervention.

A) True

B) False

Answer: B

Explanation: Resource groups in HPE GreenLake do not automatically resize based on demand. While HPE GreenLake offers scalability options, such as adding or removing resources, these adjustments typically require manual intervention or predefined automation scripts. Dynamic resizing would require automated monitoring and scaling solutions, which are not inherently part of the resource grouping functionality within GreenLake.

Q318: Fill-in-the-Gap Multiple-Choice Question When configuring alerts for resource management in HPE GreenLake, administrators should use _____ to ensure they receive timely notifications about resource thresholds being exceeded.

A) API calls

B) Webhooks

C) Email notifications

D) SNMP traps

E) SMS alerts

F) Dashboard widgets

Answer: C

Explanation: Email notifications are a reliable method for administrators to receive timely alerts about resource thresholds being exceeded in HPE GreenLake. By configuring email alerts, administrators can ensure that they are promptly informed about critical issues, allowing for swift remedial action. This method is especially useful in environments where constant monitoring is required to maintain optimal performance and prevent resource overuse or outages.

Q319: Advanced Multiple-Choice Question Which feature of HPE GreenLake allows administrators to automate the deployment of resources based on predefined templates, ensuring consistency across environments?

A) Resource tagging

B) Blueprinting

C) Capacity planning

D) Policy management

E) Resource cloning

F) Workload balancing

Answer: B

Explanation: Blueprinting in HPE GreenLake allows administrators to automate the deployment of resources based on predefined templates. This feature ensures consistency and standardization across different environments by allowing administrators to define the configuration of resources and then deploy them uniformly. Blueprinting is particularly useful in large-scale deployments where maintaining consistency is crucial for operational efficiency and compliance. By using blueprints, organizations can streamline the provisioning process, reduce errors, and ensure that all deployments adhere to established standards and policies.

Q320: Scenario-Based Question XYZ Corporation has recently migrated its IT infrastructure to HPE GreenLake to enhance scalability and flexibility. The IT department has been tasked with optimizing resource allocation and minimizing costs. They need to review the service consumption history to identify any trends or anomalies that could indicate underutilization or overutilization of resources. During a quarterly review meeting, the IT manager notices a sharp increase in storage utilization over the past month, which was unexpected given the stable nature of their operations. To address this, the IT manager needs to determine the root cause and decide on the appropriate actions to optimize resource usage. What should the IT manager prioritize to effectively analyze the consumption history and make informed decisions? ---

A) Implement a real-time monitoring tool to continuously track resource usage patterns.

B) Review detailed usage reports focusing on storage metrics from the past three months.

C) Conduct a survey among the teams to understand recent changes in data generation.

D) Increase the storage capacity to prevent any potential service disruptions.

E) Schedule a meeting with HPE GreenLake consultants to discuss optimization strategies.

F) Compare the storage utilization with the industry benchmarks for similar-sized businesses.

Answer: B

Explanation: To effectively analyze the sharp increase in storage utilization, the IT manager should prioritize reviewing the detailed usage reports focusing on storage metrics from the past three months. This approach allows the manager to identify specific trends, patterns, or events that may have contributed to the spike in usage. Understanding historical data is crucial for recognizing anomalies or periods of increased demand, which could be due to increased data generation, changes in business operations, or other factors. Implementing real-time monitoring tools and consulting with experts can be beneficial in the long term; however, they are not immediate solutions for understanding past consumption trends. Increasing storage capacity without understanding the cause may lead to unnecessary costs. Comparing benchmarks or conducting surveys, while useful, do not directly address the immediate need for historical data analysis.

Q321: True/False Question The service consumption history in HPE GreenLake can be used to track and forecast future resource needs accurately. ---
A) True

B) False

Answer: A

Explanation: The service consumption history in HPE GreenLake is a valuable tool for tracking past and current resource usage, which can provide insights into trends and patterns. By analyzing this historical data, organizations can forecast future resource needs more accurately. This capability is essential for planning and scaling resources efficiently, ensuring that businesses can meet demand without over-provisioning or under-provisioning. Accurate forecasting helps in optimizing costs and maintaining the necessary service levels to support business operations effectively.

Q322: When reviewing the service consumption history, which metric is most crucial for understanding the efficiency of resource utilization in HPE GreenLake? ---

A) Total cost of ownership (TCO)

B) Utilization rate of allocated resources

C) Number of active users

D) Total data throughput

E) Peak usage times

F) Number of service requests

Answer: B

Explanation: The utilization rate of allocated resources is the most crucial metric for understanding the efficiency of resource utilization in HPE GreenLake. This metric provides insight into how effectively the allocated resources are being used, indicating whether they are being underutilized, optimally used, or overutilized. By focusing on the utilization rate, administrators can make informed decisions about scaling resources up or down, thereby optimizing costs and ensuring that the infrastructure aligns with actual business needs. Other metrics, like TCO or peak usage times, offer valuable information but do not directly measure the efficiency of resource utilization.

Q323: Which of the following steps is least effective when attempting to identify anomalies in service consumption history within HPE GreenLake? ---

A) Setting up automated alerts for unusual usage patterns

B) Conducting regular audits of resource usage reports

C) Comparing current usage to historical averages

D) Reviewing detailed billing statements

E) Analyzing metadata of stored information

F) Implementing predictive analytics tools

Answer: E

Explanation: While analyzing metadata of stored information can provide additional context about the data being stored, it is the least effective step when attempting to identify anomalies in service consumption history. Anomalies are typically identified through patterns and trends in usage data, which are best captured by setting up automated alerts, conducting audits, and comparing current usage against historical averages. Detailed billing statements can highlight financial anomalies, and predictive analytics can forecast potential future issues. Metadata analysis is more relevant for understanding data characteristics rather than consumption anomalies.

Q324: Which approach should be avoided when trying to optimize resource allocation based on service consumption history in HPE GreenLake?

A) Analyzing past usage trends to forecast future needs

B) Automatically scaling resources without manual intervention

C) Collaborating with cross-functional teams to understand usage patterns

D) Reviewing detailed usage and billing reports regularly

E) Aligning resource allocation with business growth projections

F) Continuously monitoring real-time usage data

Answer: B

Explanation: Automatically scaling resources without manual intervention should be avoided when trying to optimize resource allocation based on service consumption history. While automation can improve efficiency, it may lead to resource misallocation if not guided by informed human oversight. Automated scaling might react to short-term spikes or dips in usage without understanding the underlying context, potentially leading to overprovisioning or underprovisioning. Analyzing past trends, collaborating with teams, reviewing reports, aligning with business growth, and monitoring usage data are essential practices that provide a comprehensive approach to resource optimization by ensuring decisions are based on accurate and relevant data.

Q325: Scenario-Based Question Acme Corp, a global technology firm, is in the process of migrating its infrastructure to HPE GreenLake. The IT department is tasked with ensuring that the right roles and permissions are configured for various teams. The finance team needs access to billing and usage dashboards without the ability to make configuration changes, while the operations team requires full administrative access to manage resources. Meanwhile, the security team should have read-only access to audit logs. What is the best way to configure these roles in HPE GreenLake to meet the specific access requirements of each team?

A) Assign the Finance team to the 'Billing Admin' role, the Operations team to the 'Super Admin' role, and the Security team to the 'Audit Viewer' role.

B) Assign the Finance team to the 'Read-Only User' role, the Operations team to the 'Resource Admin' role, and the Security team to the 'Security Analyst' role.

C) Assign the Finance team to the 'Usage Analyst' role, the Operations team to the 'Infrastructure Admin' role, and the Security team to the 'Compliance Officer' role.

D) Assign the Finance team to the 'Financial Operator' role, the Operations team to the 'Global Admin' role, and the Security team to the 'Audit Reader' role.

E) Assign the Finance team to the 'Billing Viewer' role, the Operations team to the 'Admin User' role, and the Security team to the 'Read-Only User' role.

F) Assign the Finance team to the 'Finance Viewer' role, the Operations team to the 'Admin Operator' role, and the Security team to the 'Security Viewer' role.

Answer: A

Explanation: In HPE GreenLake, roles are designed to align with specific operational needs and access levels. The 'Billing Admin' role provides access to billing and usage dashboards, which suits the finance team's requirement for viewing billing without making changes. The

'Super Admin' role offers comprehensive access for resource management, ideal for the operations team. The 'Audit Viewer' role allows read-only access to audit logs, providing the security team with necessary oversight without the ability to alter records. This configuration ensures that each team has access aligned with their responsibilities, maintaining both operational efficiency and security compliance.

Q326: True/False Question In HPE GreenLake, the 'Resource Admin' role provides the capability to manage user access and configure network settings.

A) True

B) False

Answer: B

Explanation: The 'Resource Admin' role in HPE GreenLake is primarily focused on managing resources such as compute, storage, and network resources. However, it does not inherently include permissions to manage user access or configure network settings at the administrative level. These tasks are typically reserved for a higher-level role such as 'Super Admin' or 'Global Admin', which have broader permissions including the ability to manage user roles and access settings.

Q327: Which role in HPE GreenLake should be assigned to a user who needs to generate detailed usage reports and analyze service consumption patterns without altering any configurations?

A) Usage Analyst

B) Read-Only User

C) Service Auditor

D) Financial Operator

E) Report Generator

F) Data Observer

Answer: A

Explanation: The 'Usage Analyst' role is specifically designed for users who need to generate and analyze reports related to service consumption and usage patterns. It allows access to detailed analytics and reporting tools without granting permissions to change configurations or settings. This role is perfect for users whose primary responsibility is to monitor and analyze resource utilization to inform strategic decision-making without the risk of unintended configuration changes.

Q328: When configuring roles in HPE GreenLake, which role would be most appropriate for a user responsible for monitoring system health and performance, but not authorized to make system-wide changes?

A) System Monitor

B) Performance Analyst

C) Health Supervisor

D) Infrastructure Viewer

E) Operations Observer

F) System Auditor

Answer: D

Explanation: The 'Infrastructure Viewer' role is tailored for users who need to monitor the system's health and performance metrics without the authority to make any changes. This role provides access to dashboards and monitoring tools, enabling users to track system performance and health indicators, ensuring they can identify issues without the risk of modifying system configurations. This separation of duties helps maintain system integrity and security while providing necessary oversight.

Q329: In HPE GreenLake, which role is best suited for a user whose primary task is to ensure compliance and security policy enforcement across all organizational units, with permissions to view but not modify configurations?

A) Compliance Officer

B) Security Policy Viewer

C) Audit Supervisor

D) Security Enforcer

E) Governance Officer

F) Risk Manager

Answer: A

Explanation: The 'Compliance Officer' role in HPE GreenLake is designed for users who need to ensure that security policies and compliance regulations are being followed across the organization. This role provides access to compliance and security reports and dashboards, allowing the user to view and assess compliance statuses without the ability to alter configurations. This ensures that compliance officers can effectively oversee policy adherence while maintaining system security and integrity.

Q330: In a mid-sized enterprise, the IT department has recently adopted HPE GreenLake to manage its hybrid cloud environment. The organization has different teams responsible for various functions such as development, testing, and production. Each team requires specific access to resources relevant to their roles, and the security policy mandates that no team should have access beyond what they need to perform their duties. The IT administrator must configure role-based access control to meet these needs. Which of the following strategies should the IT administrator implement to ensure that each team has the appropriate level of access while maintaining security compliance?

A) Assign all users to the same role with full access to all resources.

B) Create a single role with minimal access for all teams.

C) Define separate roles for each team and assign permissions based on their specific needs.

D) Use a default role for all users and manually adjust permissions for individual users.

E) Allow teams to request additional permissions as needed without predefined roles.

F) Implement a role hierarchy with inherited permissions for simplicity.

Answer: C

Explanation: Role-based access control (RBAC) is essential for managing user permissions effectively in an IT environment. By defining separate roles for each team, the IT administrator can allocate permissions that align with the specific tasks and responsibilities of each team, thereby adhering to the principle of least privilege. This approach not only enhances security by preventing unauthorized access but also simplifies management by grouping users with similar access needs. Options A and B are too broad and can lead to security risks, while D and E involve more manual intervention and can result in inconsistent access control. Option F might complicate permission management without addressing the specific needs of each team.

Q331: True or False: In HPE GreenLake, role-based access control (RBAC) can be used to restrict user access to specific services and resources within a hybrid cloud environment.
A) True

B) False

Answer: A

Explanation: True. HPE GreenLake's role-based access control (RBAC) is designed to provide granular access management by allowing administrators to define roles with specific permissions. This capability ensures that users can only access the services and resources necessary for their roles, thereby enhancing security and operational efficiency. By restricting access based on roles, organizations can prevent unauthorized access and reduce the risk of accidental or malicious changes to the system.

Q332: Which of the following is a best practice when configuring role-based access control (RBAC) for a new HPE GreenLake deployment?

A) Assign roles based on user seniority within the organization.

B) Grant all users the highest level of access initially and revoke as needed.

C) Regularly review and update roles and permissions to reflect changes in user responsibilities.

D) Limit the number of roles to simplify management, even if it means broader access.

E) Use role-based access control only for external users.

F) Disable RBAC if not needed immediately to simplify initial deployment.

Answer: C

Explanation: Regularly reviewing and updating roles and permissions is a best practice in any RBAC implementation, including HPE GreenLake. As user responsibilities and organizational needs change, it's crucial to adjust access controls to ensure they remain aligned with current requirements. This proactive approach minimizes security risks and ensures compliance with internal policies and regulatory requirements. Options A and B can lead to inappropriate access levels, while D could compromise security. Option E is incorrect because internal users also require controlled access, and F undermines the purpose of RBAC by eliminating its protective benefits.

Q333: In an HPE GreenLake environment, a user reports that they cannot access certain resources required for their role. As an administrator, what is the first step you should take to resolve this issue?

A) Immediately grant the user full access to all resources.

B) Check the user's role assignment and validate that it includes the necessary permissions.

C) Reassign the user to a different role with broader access.

D) Contact HPE support to troubleshoot the issue.

E) Reset the user's password to ensure it's not an authentication problem.

F) Ask the user to log out and log back in to refresh their session.

Answer: B

Explanation: The first step in troubleshooting RBAC issues is to verify the user's role assignment and ensure that it includes the necessary permissions for accessing the required resources. This involves checking the configuration of the roles and comparing them with the expected access rights for the user's responsibilities. By addressing the root cause of the access issue, administrators can resolve the problem efficiently without compromising security or functionality. Options A and C could lead to unnecessary exposure of resources, while D, E, and F may not address the underlying RBAC configuration issue.

Q334: In a large corporation using HPE GreenLake, the compliance team requires a report detailing user access changes over time to ensure audit readiness. Which feature would best facilitate this requirement within the RBAC framework?

A) Role templates

B) Access logs

C) Permission inheritance

D) Real-time access control updates

E) Multi-factor authentication

F) Automated role assignment

Answer: B

Explanation: Access logs are a critical feature in the RBAC framework for tracking and documenting user access changes over time. They provide a detailed record of who accessed what resources and when, which is crucial for compliance audits and ensuring accountability. By using access logs, organizations can demonstrate adherence to security policies and regulations and quickly identify any unauthorized access attempts. Options A and C relate to role configuration rather than monitoring, while D, E, and F do not directly address the need for historical access reporting.

Q335: Your company, a mid-sized logistics firm, is facing challenges with managing IT resources across multiple locations. The IT department is tasked with optimizing resource allocation and ensuring seamless operations. Recently, the company decided to adopt a hybrid cloud strategy to enhance scalability and flexibility. As the lead IT administrator, you are evaluating the HPE GreenLake Edge-to-Cloud Console for its capabilities in managing this hybrid environment. Which feature of the HPE GreenLake Edge-to-Cloud Console is most beneficial for efficiently managing resources across your distributed locations?

A) Automated billing and invoicing.

B) Centralized management of on-premises and cloud resources.

C) Enhanced data analytics for market trends.

D) Built-in customer relationship management (CRM) tools.

E) Integrated social media monitoring.

F) Advanced email filtering and security.

Answer: B

Explanation: The HPE GreenLake Edge-to-Cloud Console is designed to offer centralized management capabilities, which is crucial for a company that operates across multiple locations. By providing a single pane of glass for managing both on-premises and cloud resources, the console allows for efficient resource allocation and streamlined operations in a hybrid cloud environment. Options like automated billing, enhanced analytics, and CRM tools, while beneficial, do not directly address the challenge of managing distributed IT resources. Centralized management is essential for ensuring that IT resources are utilized effectively, reducing the complexity of managing a hybrid infrastructure, and supporting the company's scalability and flexibility objectives.

Q336: True or False: The HPE GreenLake Edge-to-Cloud Console can only manage HPE-specific hardware and does not support third-party infrastructure.

A) True

B) False

Answer: B

Explanation: The statement is false because the HPE GreenLake Edge-to-Cloud Console is designed to be versatile and support a wide range of infrastructure, not limited to HPE-specific hardware. It is built to integrate with various third-party systems, enabling organizations to manage a diverse IT environment under a unified management framework. This capability is crucial for businesses that use heterogeneous infrastructures, allowing them to leverage the full benefits of the GreenLake solution without being constrained to a single vendor's products.

Q337: A retail company is planning to deploy new applications across its chain of stores and needs to ensure consistent performance and monitoring. How does the HPE GreenLake Edge-to-Cloud Console assist in achieving this objective?

A) By offering virtual private network (VPN) services.

B) By providing centralized application performance monitoring.

C) By implementing blockchain technology for transaction security.

D) By offering a marketplace for third-party applications.

E) By scheduling regular system maintenance tasks.

F) By sending automated customer satisfaction surveys.

Answer: B

Explanation: The HPE GreenLake Edge-to-Cloud Console provides centralized application performance monitoring, which is essential for ensuring consistent application performance across multiple locations. This feature allows IT administrators to monitor application performance metrics, identify bottlenecks, and ensure that applications meet performance expectations. While options like VPN services and blockchain technology are beneficial in their respective domains, they do not directly contribute to centralized performance monitoring. This capability is particularly valuable in a retail environment where consistent application performance is crucial for maintaining efficient operations and customer satisfaction.

Q338: In what way does the HPE GreenLake Edge-to-Cloud Console support compliance and security for a financial services company dealing with sensitive data?

A) By providing built-in AI-driven fraud detection.

B) By offering customizable compliance reporting tools.

C) By integrating directly with stock market data feeds.

D) By offering low-latency trading platforms.

E) By hosting virtual shareholder meetings.

F) By tracking and analyzing consumer spending habits.

Answer: B

Explanation: The HPE GreenLake Edge-to-Cloud Console supports compliance and security by offering customizable compliance reporting tools, which are essential for financial services companies that deal with sensitive data. These tools enable organizations to tailor compliance reports to meet specific regulatory requirements, ensuring that they can demonstrate adherence to industry standards and regulations. While AI-driven fraud detection and other options may be relevant to security, customizable compliance reporting directly addresses the need for regulatory compliance, making it an invaluable feature for financial services institutions seeking to maintain data integrity and regulatory adherence.

Q339: Fill in the gap: The HPE GreenLake Edge-to-Cloud Console enhances operational efficiency by providing _____, allowing IT teams to quickly adapt to changing business needs.

A) Pre-configured social media dashboards

B) Real-time resource allocation and scaling

C) Built-in video conferencing capabilities

D) Augmented reality development tools

E) Customizable employee training modules

F) Automated customer feedback collection

Answer: B

Explanation: The HPE GreenLake Edge-to-Cloud Console enhances operational efficiency by providing real-time resource allocation and scaling. This capability allows IT teams to quickly adapt to changing business needs by dynamically adjusting resources to meet demand. Real-time resource allocation ensures that companies can efficiently manage workloads, optimize resource usage, and respond promptly to fluctuations in demand, which is particularly critical in today's fast-paced business environment. Other options, while useful in specific contexts, do not directly contribute to the core functionality of enhancing operational efficiency through dynamic resource management.

Q340: Scenario-Based Question A multinational corporation, TechGlobal Inc., recently adopted the HPE GreenLake platform to streamline their IT infrastructure across different regions. The company's IT department is particularly concerned about ensuring that their data complies with international security standards and regulations such as GDPR and HIPAA. The platform needs to integrate with existing security protocols and provide robust data protection and encryption features. Additionally, TechGlobal Inc. wants the ability to monitor security events in real-time and have comprehensive reporting capabilities. Given these requirements, which security feature of the HPE GreenLake platform should TechGlobal Inc. prioritize to satisfy their compliance and security monitoring needs?   ---

A) Role-based access control (RBAC)

B) End-to-end data encryption

C) Unified security management console

D) Integration with third-party security tools

E) Distributed denial-of-service (DDoS) protection

F) Advanced persistent threat (APT) detection

Answer: C

Explanation: The unified security management console is a crucial feature for TechGlobal Inc. as it provides centralized visibility and control over all security aspects of the HPE GreenLake platform. This feature allows the company to monitor security events in real-time, ensuring compliance with international regulations like GDPR and HIPAA by providing detailed security and compliance reports. While other options like end-to-end data encryption and role-based access control are important, the unified console directly addresses the need for comprehensive monitoring and reporting capabilities, making it the most suitable choice for TechGlobal Inc.

Q341: Which security feature of the HPE GreenLake platform is responsible for ensuring that only authorized users can access specific resources, thereby minimizing the risk of unauthorized data access?   ---

A) Multi-factor authentication (MFA)

B) Role-based access control (RBAC)

C) Data loss prevention (DLP)

D) Network segmentation

E) Intrusion detection systems (IDS)

F) Secure socket layer (SSL) encryption

Answer: B

Explanation: Role-based access control (RBAC) is a security feature that ensures only authorized users have access to specific resources based on their roles within the organization. By defining roles and assigning permissions accordingly, RBAC minimizes the risk of unauthorized data access and helps maintain a secure environment. This feature is particularly important in multi-user environments, such as those managed through the HPE GreenLake platform, where different users have varying levels of access and responsibility.

Q342: True or False: HPE GreenLake's security features include end-to-end encryption to protect data both at rest and in transit within the platform.   ---

A) True

B) False

Answer: A

Explanation: True. HPE GreenLake incorporates end-to-end encryption to protect data both at rest and in transit. This ensures that sensitive information is encrypted as it moves through the network and when it is stored, safeguarding it against potential intercepts or breaches. End-to-end encryption is a critical component of data security, particularly for organizations that handle sensitive or regulated information, as it helps maintain confidentiality and integrity.

Q343: In the context of HPE GreenLake, what is the primary benefit of integrating the platform with third-party security tools? ---

A) Simplifies user management

B) Provides cost-effective storage solutions

C) Enhances compliance reporting capabilities

D) Improves performance and scalability

E) Increases flexibility and customization of security measures

F) Reduces the need for on-site IT staff

Answer: E

Explanation: Integrating HPE GreenLake with third-party security tools primarily increases flexibility and customization of security measures. This integration allows organizations to leverage existing security investments and tailor security protocols to their specific needs. By combining the robust features of GreenLake with specialized third-party tools, organizations can create a more comprehensive and adaptable security framework that can address unique challenges and compliance requirements.

Q344: Fill in the gap: The HPE GreenLake platform includes a feature that allows for the detection and prevention of unauthorized access by analyzing patterns and behaviors. This feature is known as _____.

A) User behavior analytics (UBA)

B) Data integrity verification

C) Security information and event management (SIEM)

D) Single sign-on (SSO)

E) Distributed denial-of-service (DDoS) protection

F) Identity and access management (IAM)

Answer: A

Explanation: User behavior analytics (UBA) is a security feature that detects and prevents unauthorized access by analyzing user patterns and behaviors. UBA can identify anomalies or deviations from normal user activities, which may indicate potential security threats or breaches. By leveraging machine learning and advanced analytics, UBA enhances the security posture of the HPE GreenLake platform by providing proactive threat detection and response capabilities.

Q345: Scenario-Based Question Your company, a midsize enterprise specializing in e-commerce solutions, has recently decided to migrate its on-premises infrastructure to HPE GreenLake to improve scalability and manage costs. During the initial setup meeting, the IT team decides to activate several services, including compute, storage, and networking. However, due to the complexity of your existing environment and the need for high availability, your team is unsure of the best practices for configuring the GreenLake platform to ensure seamless integration and activation of these services. As the lead administrator, you are tasked with guiding this process to avoid common pitfalls and ensure optimal performance.

A) Prioritize the activation of compute services to ensure application performance, followed by networking and storage.

B) Activate networking services first to establish foundational connectivity, then proceed with compute and storage activation.

C) Simultaneously activate all services to reduce setup time and streamline the integration process.

D) Begin with storage services activation to ensure data availability, followed by compute and networking.

E) Conduct a thorough dependency analysis before activating any services, followed by a staggered activation based on the analysis.

F) Activate services based on vendor recommendations without considering the existing environment.

Answer: E

Explanation: When integrating new services within HPE GreenLake, especially in complex environments requiring high availability, conducting a dependency analysis is crucial. This approach ensures that all interdependencies are identified and accounted for, reducing the risk of activation errors or performance issues. A staggered activation based on the analysis allows for troubleshooting at each step, ensuring a smooth transition. Prioritizing service activation without considering dependencies (options A, B, D) or simultaneous activation (option C) can lead to misconfigurations and service disruptions. Relying solely on vendor recommendations (option F) without context may not address specific business needs.

Q346: Multiple Choice Question During the service activation process in HPE GreenLake, which component is essential for ensuring that all activated services can communicate effectively within the hybrid cloud environment?

A) Virtual Machine configurations

B) Load Balancer settings

C) Network Fabric

D) Storage Tiering

E) API Gateway

F) Identity and Access Management roles

Answer: C

Explanation: The network fabric is crucial for ensuring effective communication between services within a hybrid cloud environment like HPE GreenLake. It provides the necessary connectivity and bandwidth to support data flow and application interactions across different services and locations. Virtual Machine configurations and Load Balancer settings (options A and B) are important but pertain to specific applications and traffic management.

Storage Tiering (option D) relates to data management, while an API Gateway (option E) facilitates API interactions, and Identity and Access Management (option F) focuses on security and permissions, not communication infrastructure.

Q347: True/False Question True or False: In the HPE GreenLake service activation process, it is mandatory to perform a comprehensive security audit after activating each service to ensure compliance with organizational policies.

A) True

B) False

Answer: A

Explanation: A comprehensive security audit after each service activation is a mandatory step to ensure that the deployment complies with organizational security policies and industry standards. It helps identify potential vulnerabilities introduced during activation and ensures that all security controls are implemented properly. This process is critical for maintaining the integrity, confidentiality, and availability of services and data within HPE GreenLake.

Q348: Fill-in-the-Gap Question In the initial setup process of HPE GreenLake, it is important to configure _____ to manage and monitor service utilization effectively, ensuring that resources are allocated according to business priorities.

A) Cost Management Dashboard

B) Resource Pools

C) Service Level Agreements

D) Capacity Planning Tools

E) Automation Scripts

F) User Access Policies

Answer: B

Explanation: Resource Pools are essential in managing and monitoring service utilization within HPE GreenLake. They allow administrators to allocate and control resources based on business priorities, ensuring that each department or application receives the necessary compute, storage, and networking resources. This configuration helps optimize performance and cost-efficiency. While Cost Management Dashboard (option A) and Capacity Planning Tools (option D) are important for financial and capacity insights, Resource Pools actively manage the allocation. Service Level Agreements (option C) define performance expectations, Automation Scripts (option E) aid in task automation, and User Access Policies (option F) control access to services.

Q349: Multiple Choice Question Which of the following best describes the role of the HPE GreenLake Central interface during the service activation process?

A) It provides a centralized location for deploying additional hardware resources.

B) It serves as a dashboard for monitoring environmental conditions in data centers.

C) It acts as a user-friendly interface for managing, monitoring, and optimizing cloud services.

D) It functions as a repository for storing backup configurations.

E) It is used to automate the deployment of software patches.

F) It serves as a communication tool for internal IT teams during activation.

Answer: C

Explanation: HPE GreenLake Central is a unified interface designed for managing, monitoring, and optimizing cloud services. It provides administrators with a comprehensive view of their cloud resources and performance metrics, allowing them to manage services effectively and ensure they align with business objectives. While options A, B, D, E, and F describe useful IT tools and functions, they do not accurately capture the central role and capabilities of the HPE GreenLake Central interface in the service activation and management process.

Q350: Scenario-Based Question Your company, Tech Innovators Inc., recently migrated its infrastructure to HPE GreenLake. The IT department has been tasked with optimizing service request processes to improve efficiency. During a high-priority project, a team member submits a service request for additional storage resources. However, the request seems to be delayed, affecting project timelines. Upon investigation, you discover that the request was incorrectly categorized as a low-priority issue. To prevent such occurrences in the future, you decide to implement a more rigorous request categorization process. What step should be prioritized to ensure accurate categorization of service requests?

A) Implement a machine learning algorithm to automatically categorize requests based on historical data.

B) Require mandatory training for all team members on service request submission protocols.

C) Assign a dedicated team to manually review and categorize each service request.

D) Integrate a priority checklist in the service request form to guide users.

E) Develop a more detailed service-level agreement (SLA) with specific categorization guidelines.

F) Conduct monthly audits of all service requests to identify categorization errors.

Answer: D

Explanation: Integrating a priority checklist in the service request form helps users accurately categorize their requests by providing clear guidelines at the point of submission. This step is practical and ensures that the categorization process is user-friendly and consistent. While other options like machine learning and manual review teams could enhance accuracy, they require more resources and time to implement. Training and SLAs can be beneficial but do not directly address the immediate issue of incorrect categorization during submission. Monthly audits are useful for long-term improvements but do not prevent initial errors.

Q351: True/False Question In HPE GreenLake, all service requests are automatically assigned the highest priority when submitted to ensure quick processing.

A) True

B) False

Answer: B

Explanation: Not all service requests are assigned the highest priority. HPE GreenLake, like many service platforms, uses a priority system to manage requests based on urgency and impact. Requests are categorized into different priority levels, and only those that meet specific criteria are given high priority. This system ensures that resources are allocated efficiently and critical issues are addressed promptly without overwhelming the support team.

Q352: Standard Multiple-Choice Question Which of the following is NOT a typical component of the HPE GreenLake support process?

A) Incident logging and tracking

B) Automated resource scaling

C) Root cause analysis

D) Service level management

E) Change management

F) Knowledge base access

Answer: B

Explanation: Automated resource scaling is not a component of the support process itself but rather a feature of the HPE GreenLake service model. The support process typically includes activities like incident logging, root cause analysis, service level management, change management, and providing access to a knowledge base. These elements are designed to help manage and resolve service issues efficiently. Automated scaling pertains to the operational capabilities of the infrastructure rather than support processes.

Q353: Fill-in-the-Gap Multiple-Choice Question In the context of HPE GreenLake, the _____ is responsible for ensuring that service requests align with the organization's overall IT strategy and objectives.

A) Service Request Manager

B) IT Operations Analyst

C) Chief Information Officer (CIO)

D) Project Manager

E) Support Engineer

F) Business Relationship Manager

Answer: F

Explanation: The Business Relationship Manager (BRM) plays a crucial role in aligning service requests with the organization's IT strategy and objectives. The BRM acts as a liaison between the business units and IT, ensuring that the services provided support the broader business goals. While other roles like the CIO and IT Operations Analyst have strategic responsibilities, the BRM specifically focuses on translating business needs into IT solutions, making them vital in the service request process.

Q354: Standard Multiple-Choice Question Which tool or method is most effective for tracking and managing the lifecycle of service requests in HPE GreenLake?

A) Excel spreadsheets for manual tracking

B) Email threads for request communication

C) A centralized IT service management (ITSM) platform

D) Daily stand-up meetings for status updates

E) A shared document repository

F) A custom-built internal tracking application

Answer: C

Explanation: A centralized IT service management (ITSM) platform is the most effective tool for tracking and managing the lifecycle of service requests in HPE GreenLake. ITSM platforms provide a structured approach to handling service requests, incidents, and changes, ensuring that all relevant information is logged and can be easily accessed. They offer features such as automated workflows, reporting capabilities, and integration with other systems, which enhance efficiency and reduce manual errors. While other options like Excel and email may be used in smaller setups, they lack the scalability and functionality of an ITSM platform.

Q355: Scenario-based Question Your company, TechSolutions Inc., has recently decided to adopt the HPE GreenLake platform to streamline its backup services. You have been tasked with setting up these services for the company's three major departments: Finance, HR, and IT. Each department has specific data retention policies and compliance requirements. The Finance department requires daily backups with a retention period of seven years, while HR needs weekly backups with a retention period of three years. The IT department requires more frequent backups due to constant system updates, with a retention cycle of 30 days. What is the best way to configure the HPE GreenLake backup services to accommodate these varied departmental needs efficiently?

A) Create a single backup policy for all departments with the most extended retention period required.

B) Establish separate backup policies for each department according to their specific requirements.

C) Use HPE GreenLake's default backup settings for quick deployment and adjust later as needed.

D) Configure a centralized backup policy with exceptions for departments with unique needs.

E) Implement a tiered backup strategy, starting with a baseline policy and customizing for each department.

F) Set up automated alerts to review and adjust backup policies quarterly.

Answer: B

Explanation: The most efficient way to accommodate the varied backup requirements of different departments is to establish separate backup policies for each. By doing so, each department's specific needs and compliance requirements are precisely met. This approach avoids unnecessary resource usage and ensures that each department's data is protected according to its unique retention schedule. Creating a single policy with the longest retention period (Option A) would result in inefficient use of storage resources. Options C and D would require frequent manual adjustments, leading to potential oversight and non-compliance risks. Option E could lead to unnecessary complexity and resource waste, while Option F is more about policy review than setup.

Q356: True/False Question In HPE GreenLake, backup policies can be applied universally across all departments without customization for specific department needs.
A) True

B) False

Answer: B

Explanation: HPE GreenLake's backup services are designed to be flexible to meet the specific needs of different departments or business units. Applying a universal backup policy without considering individual departmental requirements could lead to compliance issues and inefficient resource use. Customization is crucial to ensure each department's data is backed up in accordance with its unique retention policies and regulatory requirements. Therefore, it's false to state that backup policies can be applied universally without customization.

Q357: Which of the following components of HPE GreenLake should be configured first to ensure that backup services meet compliance and regulatory standards?

A) Storage resource pools

B) Data encryption settings

C) Network bandwidth allocation

D) User access controls

E) Backup policy templates

F) Audit logging and reporting

Answer: E

Explanation: Configuring backup policy templates first ensures that the backup services are aligned with compliance and regulatory standards. These templates dictate how data is backed up, retained, and protected, which are critical factors in meeting compliance requirements. Storage resource pools (A) and data encryption settings (B) are important but secondary to establishing the foundational policies. Network bandwidth allocation (C) and user access controls (D) are operational considerations, while audit logging and reporting (F) are essential for compliance verification but should be configured after the backup policies.

Q358: During the setup of HPE GreenLake backup services, which feature is essential for ensuring that backups are not only performed but also verified for integrity?

A) Automated backup scheduling

B) Data deduplication

C) Backup verification checks

D) Redundant storage configuration

E) Snapshot management

F) Compliance reporting

Answer: C

Explanation: Backup verification checks are crucial for ensuring the integrity of backups. This feature confirms that the data has been backed up correctly and is recoverable in case of data loss. Automated backup scheduling (A) ensures regular backups, while data deduplication (B) optimizes storage usage. Redundant storage configuration (D) provides additional data protection but doesn't verify backup data. Snapshot management (E) is useful for point-in-time data recovery, and compliance reporting (F) helps with regulatory adherence but doesn't verify backup integrity.

Q359: Which HPE GreenLake feature allows administrators to efficiently manage and monitor backup operations across multiple geographic locations?
A) Centralized management console

B) Multi-region backup replication

C) Localized data centers

D) Distributed backup nodes

E) Unified analytics dashboard

F) Cross-region data mirroring

Answer: A

Explanation: The centralized management console in HPE GreenLake enables administrators to efficiently manage and monitor backup operations across multiple geographic locations. This feature provides a single point of control for viewing and managing backup tasks, ensuring consistency and compliance across different regions. Multi-region backup replication (B) and cross-region data mirroring (F) are related to data availability but not management. Localized data centers (C) and distributed backup nodes (D) focus on infrastructure distribution, while a unified analytics dashboard (E) provides insights rather than direct management capabilities.

Q360: A multinational corporation, TechGlobal Inc., has integrated HPE GreenLake to manage their IT infrastructure across various regions. The company's IT department is responsible for ensuring that all Service Level Agreements (SLAs) are met, especially those related to uptime and performance. During a quarterly review, the IT director notices discrepancies in the SLA reports generated by the HPE GreenLake platform. The reports show varying uptime percentages across different regions, despite similar infrastructure setups and workloads. As an HPE GreenLake administrator, you're tasked with identifying the root cause of these discrepancies and ensuring consistent SLA reporting moving forward. What should be your first step in addressing this issue?

A) Verify the accuracy of the time zone settings for each regional data center.

B) Conduct a manual audit of the reported uptime data for each region.

C) Analyze network latency and bandwidth differences across regions.

D) Reconfigure the SLA parameters to ensure alignment with corporate standards.

E) Implement additional monitoring tools to cross-verify HPE GreenLake reports.

F) Schedule regular meetings with regional IT teams to discuss and align on SLA expectations.

Answer: A

Explanation: The first step in addressing the discrepancies in SLA reports across different regions is to verify the accuracy of the time zone settings for each regional data center.

Incorrect time zone configurations can lead to inaccurate calculations of uptime, as the reporting tool might not correctly align downtime events with the appropriate time frames. Ensuring that all data centers are configured with the correct local time settings will help standardize the reporting process and eliminate discrepancies caused by time zone misalignments. This step is critical before considering other potential issues like network latency or manual data audits.

Q361: In the context of HPE GreenLake SLA reporting, which of the following metrics is most critical for evaluating the performance aspect of the SLA?

A) Uptime percentage

B) Response time for technical support

C) Data throughput rate

D) Incident resolution time

E) Cost per usage unit

F) Number of service requests

Answer: C

Explanation: The data throughput rate is the most critical metric for evaluating the performance aspect of an SLA within HPE GreenLake. This metric measures the volume of data processed over a given period and directly impacts the perceived performance and efficiency of the services provided. High throughput rates indicate that the system can handle large volumes of data efficiently, which is essential for maintaining service quality and meeting performance SLAs. While uptime percentage and incident resolution time are also important, they pertain more to availability and support aspects of SLAs, respectively.

Q362: True or False: HPE GreenLake's SLA tracking tools automatically adjust SLA parameters based on historical performance data.

A) True

B) False

Answer: B

Explanation: False. HPE GreenLake's SLA tracking tools do not automatically adjust SLA parameters based on historical performance data. Instead, they provide detailed insights and reports on SLA compliance, allowing administrators to manually analyze performance trends and make necessary adjustments to the SLA configurations. Users must review these reports and take proactive measures to ensure that SLAs are aligned with business objectives and performance expectations.

Q363: When configuring SLA notifications in HPE GreenLake, which of the following actions should an administrator take to ensure timely alerts for potential SLA breaches?

A) Set notification thresholds to the maximum allowable deviation from SLA targets.

B) Enable notifications only for critical SLA parameters.

C) Configure real-time alerts for any deviation from SLA targets.

D) Schedule weekly summary reports to monitor SLA compliance.

E) Integrate SLA notifications with a third-party incident management system.

F) Assign dedicated personnel to manually monitor SLA dashboards.

Answer: C

Explanation: Configuring real-time alerts for any deviation from SLA targets is the most effective way to ensure timely alerts for potential SLA breaches. This proactive approach allows administrators to respond quickly to issues as they arise, preventing minor deviations from escalating into significant SLA violations. While integrating with third-party systems and scheduling reports can complement this strategy, real-time alerts are essential for maintaining SLA compliance and ensuring that corrective actions are taken promptly.

Q364: An HPE GreenLake administrator is preparing a quarterly SLA compliance report for senior management. The report must highlight key performance indicators (KPIs) and any SLA breaches that occurred. Which of the following data points is least relevant to include in this report?

A) Number of SLA breaches and their impact on business operations

B) Historical trends in uptime and performance metrics

C) Feedback from end-users regarding service quality

D) Details of maintenance activities and scheduled downtimes

E) Cost savings achieved through HPE GreenLake optimization

F) Comparison of SLA compliance against industry benchmarks

Answer: E

Explanation: While cost savings achieved through HPE GreenLake optimization can be valuable information, it is the least relevant data point in the context of a quarterly SLA compliance report focusing on key performance indicators and SLA breaches. The primary purpose of the report is to assess SLA adherence and identify areas for improvement in service delivery. Therefore, data points directly related to SLA performance, such as breaches, uptime, and user feedback, are more pertinent to the report's objectives. Cost savings are more relevant to financial and strategic assessments rather than SLA compliance evaluations.

Q365: Scenario-Based Question XYZ Corporation is planning to migrate its existing on-premises data storage to an HPE GreenLake cloud environment. The company has a mix of structured and unstructured data, and it experiences variable data growth rates throughout the fiscal year. The IT team estimates a 30% increase in data storage requirements during the holiday season due to increased customer transactions. The team is concerned about over-provisioning during off-peak times while ensuring sufficient capacity during peak periods. What strategy should the IT team adopt to efficiently manage storage provisioning and capacity allocation in HPE GreenLake?   ###

A) Implement a fixed capacity allocation strategy to ensure consistent performance year-round.

B) Use HPE GreenLake's elastic resource pool to dynamically adjust capacity based on real-time usage.

C) Pre-allocate extra capacity for the holiday season and deallocate after the peak period.

D) Set up multiple small storage pools to cater to different types of data and adjust them individually.

E) Use predictive analytics to forecast demand and manually adjust provisioning accordingly.

F) Allocate the maximum anticipated capacity year-round to avoid any risk of under-provisioning.

Answer: B

Explanation: HPE GreenLake's elastic resource pool allows for dynamic adjustment of storage capacity based on current usage, making it ideal for organizations with variable data growth rates. This approach prevents over-provisioning during off-peak periods and ensures that additional capacity is available during peak times, such as the holiday season. By using elastic pools, XYZ Corporation can optimize costs and performance without manual intervention, leveraging HPE GreenLake's ability to scale resources up or down as needed. This strategy provides a balance between cost efficiency and capacity assurance, aligning with the organization's needs for flexibility and scalability.

Q366: Multiple-Choice Question What feature of HPE GreenLake helps organizations track and manage their storage usage to avoid over-provisioning? ###

A) Predictive analytics dashboard

B) Capacity management alerts

C) Automated scaling protocols

D) Resource utilization reports

E) Fixed provisioning templates

F) User-initiated scaling tools

Answer: D

Explanation: Resource utilization reports in HPE GreenLake provide detailed insights into how storage resources are being used over time. These reports enable organizations to identify patterns and trends in resource consumption, which can help in planning for future capacity needs. By analyzing these reports, the IT team can make informed decisions to avoid over-provisioning, ensuring that the organization pays only for what it needs. This feature supports cost optimization while maintaining the necessary performance levels.

Q367: Fill-in-the-Gap Question HPE GreenLake allows administrators to set _____ to ensure that specific applications always have access to the necessary storage resources, even during peak usage times. ###

A) Elastic limits

B) Static allocations

C) Priority tiers

D) Service level agreements (SLAs)

E) Dynamic thresholds

F) Manual overrides

Answer: D

Explanation: Service level agreements (SLAs) in HPE GreenLake are used to define the performance and availability standards for specific applications. By setting SLAs, administrators can ensure that critical applications always receive the necessary storage resources, even when demand spikes. This approach helps maintain application performance and reliability, aligning with business requirements for uptime and efficiency. The use of SLAs is a strategic tool for capacity allocation, ensuring that key services remain unaffected during peak usage times.

Q368: True/False Question True or False: HPE GreenLake automatically adjusts storage capacity in real-time without any input from the administrator.   ###
A) True

B) False

Answer: A

Explanation: HPE GreenLake is designed to provide a cloud-like experience with on-premises infrastructure, offering real-time adjustments to storage capacity based on current usage patterns. This automatic scaling is a key feature of GreenLake's service model, reducing the need for manual intervention by administrators. By leveraging this capability, organizations can ensure they always have the right amount of resources without the risk of under- or over-provisioning, optimizing both performance and cost.

Q369: Multiple-Choice Question Which of the following is NOT a benefit of using HPE GreenLake for storage provisioning and capacity allocation?
A) On-demand resource scaling

B) Predictable monthly billing

C) Increased capital expenditure

D) Enhanced performance monitoring

E) Simplified IT management

F) Reduced environmental impact

Answer: C

Explanation: HPE GreenLake is designed to convert capital expenditure (CapEx) into operational expenditure (OpEx) by offering a consumption-based pricing model, which typically reduces the need for large upfront investments. This pricing model results in predictable monthly billing based on actual usage, simplifying budgeting and financial planning. Additionally, HPE GreenLake enhances performance monitoring and IT management, while potentially reducing environmental impact by optimizing data center and resource usage. Increased capital expenditure is not a benefit of HPE GreenLake, as it aims to minimize CapEx and streamline costs.

Q370: Scenario-based A large retail company, RetailTech Inc., has been experiencing challenges with scaling its IT infrastructure to meet fluctuating demand, especially during peak shopping seasons. The company is considering transitioning to a subscription-based IT consumption model through HPE GreenLake to achieve better resource utilization and cost management. The IT manager, Sarah, is tasked with presenting the benefits and potential challenges of this model to the executive board. Which of the following points would be most relevant for Sarah to emphasize regarding the advantages of adopting a subscription-based IT consumption model?

A) It eliminates all IT infrastructure management responsibilities.

B) It ensures a fixed monthly IT cost regardless of usage.

C) It provides on-demand scalability to match business needs.

D) It requires a significant upfront capital investment.

E) It guarantees zero downtime during the transition phase.

F) It allows for better alignment of IT spending with business outcomes.

Answer: C

Explanation: The primary advantage of a subscription-based IT consumption model like HPE GreenLake is its ability to offer on-demand scalability. This means RetailTech Inc. can adjust its IT resources to meet varying demands, such as during peak shopping seasons, without over-provisioning or under-utilizing infrastructure. This flexibility leads to optimized resource use and cost efficiency, as the company only pays for what it uses. While option F is also a benefit, the ability to scale resources on-demand is a more immediate and tangible advantage in the context of RetailTech Inc.'s needs. Options A, B, and D are incorrect as they misrepresent the nature of subscription-based models, which typically involve some management responsibility and variable costs based on usage, rather than a significant upfront investment. Option E is incorrect as downtime depends on various factors, including the execution of the transition strategy.

Q371: True/False True or False: In a subscription-based IT consumption model, the customer owns the IT infrastructure.
A) True

B) False

Answer: B

Explanation: In a subscription-based IT consumption model, like HPE GreenLake, the customer does not own the IT infrastructure. Instead, the infrastructure is provided and managed by the service provider, while the customer pays for the usage as a service. This model shifts the capital expenditure (CapEx) of owning hardware to an operational expenditure (OpEx), where customers pay based on consumption, allowing for more flexible financial management and removing the burden of owning and maintaining physical assets.

Q372: Which of the following is a key challenge that organizations might face when adopting a subscription-based IT consumption model?
A) Increased upfront capital requirements

B) Difficulty in predicting IT costs due to variable usage

C) Lack of access to the latest technology

D) Inability to scale resources quickly

E) Limited customization options

F) Reduced security compared to on-premises solutions

Answer: B

Explanation: A potential challenge with subscription-based IT consumption models is the difficulty in predicting IT costs, as they tend to vary based on actual resource usage. This can make budgeting more complex compared to traditional models with fixed costs. However, this variability is also a strength, as it aligns costs more closely with actual business needs. Option A is incorrect because one of the benefits of this model is reduced upfront capital requirements. Option C is incorrect, as these models often provide access to the latest technologies. Option D is incorrect because scalability is a key advantage of subscription models. Option E is incorrect as these models typically offer significant customization to meet specific business needs. Option F is incorrect as security is generally enhanced through the use of advanced, provider-managed infrastructure.

Q373: In the context of HPE GreenLake, which of the following best describes the financial benefit to businesses of using a subscription-based IT consumption model?

A) Increased long-term fixed costs

B) Enhanced cash flow management through reduced capital expenditure

C) Requirement for long-term financial commitments

D) Decreased flexibility in resource allocation

E) Mandatory minimum usage commitments

F) Increased complexity in resource tracking and billing

Answer: B

Explanation: One of the significant financial benefits of using a subscription-based IT consumption model like HPE GreenLake is enhanced cash flow management. This is achieved by reducing the need for large capital expenditures, as businesses pay for IT resources based on consumption rather than purchasing equipment outright. This model allows companies to allocate financial resources more effectively and invest in other strategic areas. Option A is incorrect as it refers to fixed costs, which are not typical in consumption-based models. Option C is incorrect because these models offer flexibility in terms of financial commitments. Option D is incorrect as they enhance flexibility in resource allocation. Option E and F are incorrect as they do not accurately represent the typical benefits of such a model.

Q374: Fill in the gap: One of the key distinguishing features of a subscription-based IT consumption model is the ability to _____ based on current business needs, which helps in optimizing resource utilization and cost-efficiency.

A) lock hardware resources

B) scale resources dynamically

C) limit software upgrades

D) increase fixed IT costs

E) delay technology refreshes

F) enforce strict usage limits

Answer: B

Explanation: The ability to scale resources dynamically is a core feature of subscription-based IT consumption models. This flexibility allows businesses to adjust their IT resources according to current demands, ensuring that they are not overpaying for unused capacity during low-demand periods or under-resourced during peak times. This dynamic scaling leads to optimized resource utilization and cost efficiency, aligning IT spending more closely with business outcomes. Option A is incorrect as it suggests inflexibility. Option C and E are incorrect as they do not pertain to the core features of these models. Option D and F are incorrect as they misrepresent the financial and operational flexibility that such models offer.

Q375: Scenario-Based A mid-sized financial services company has recently migrated its data center to HPE GreenLake to leverage on-demand capacity and optimize costs. The IT team is responsible for ensuring that the company maintains adequate capacity to handle peak workloads while minimizing excess. Recently, the company experienced a surge in demand for its online services, leading to concerns about capacity planning and subscription costs. The CIO has asked the IT team to provide a report detailing the most efficient way to manage subscription unit metrics to avoid over-provisioning while ensuring availability during peak times. Which strategy should the IT team recommend to best align with the business needs?

A) Allocate maximum capacity to handle unexpected surges at all times.

B) Use historical usage data to predict peak demand and adjust capacity accordingly.

C) Maintain the current capacity and purchase additional units only when necessary.

D) Implement a hybrid model combining on-premises and cloud-based resources.

E) Schedule regular assessments to adjust capacity based on weekly usage trends.

F) Develop a custom predictive analytics model to forecast demand and capacity needs.

Answer: B

Explanation: To effectively manage capacity in HPE GreenLake, aligning capacity with historical usage patterns is crucial. By analyzing historical usage data, the IT team can predict peak demand periods and adjust capacity proactively, avoiding the costs associated with over-provisioning. This approach ensures resources are available when needed, without continuously maintaining excess capacity. Options like maintaining maximum capacity or relying solely on reactive measures (such as purchasing additional units only when necessary) can lead to unnecessary costs or potential service disruptions. Therefore, using historical data for predictive capacity planning is the most efficient strategy.

Q376: True/False In HPE GreenLake, subscription unit metrics are primarily used to track only the physical hardware resources consumed by a customer.

A) True

B) False

Answer: B

Explanation: HPE GreenLake's subscription unit metrics encompass more than just physical hardware resources. They include various consumption metrics such as compute, storage, and networking resources utilized, allowing for a comprehensive view of the resources consumed. This holistic approach ensures that customers only pay for what they use, enabling more precise billing and capacity planning. Therefore, it is incorrect to state that these metrics are limited to physical hardware tracking.

Q377: Multiple-choice Which of the following factors is least likely to affect subscription unit metrics in an HPE GreenLake environment?

A) Seasonal business cycles

B) Software licensing agreements

C) Unexpected system downtimes

D) Regulatory compliance changes

E) Virtual machine sprawl

F) Changes in network bandwidth usage

Answer: D

Explanation: While subscription unit metrics in HPE GreenLake are influenced by various operational and usage factors, regulatory compliance changes are least likely to have a direct impact. These metrics are more directly related to resource consumption patterns, such as seasonal business cycles, software licensing, virtual machine sprawl, and network usage, which drive capacity needs. Regulatory compliance changes may indirectly affect operations but do not directly influence the metrics themselves.

Q378: Multiple-choice When planning for future capacity needs in an HPE GreenLake environment, which analytic tool would most effectively help to predict future subscription unit requirements?

A) A/B testing

B) Regression analysis

C) SWOT analysis

D) Root cause analysis

E) Fishbone diagram

F) Pareto analysis

Answer: B

Explanation: Regression analysis is a statistical tool used to identify relationships between variables and forecast future trends, making it highly effective for predicting future subscription unit requirements. By analyzing past consumption data, regression analysis can help identify patterns and predict future capacity needs. Other tools like A/B testing and SWOT analysis are more suited for testing hypotheses and strategic planning, respectively, rather than predicting future resource requirements in a data-driven manner.

Q379: Multiple-choice A company utilizing HPE GreenLake has noticed fluctuations in its capacity usage metrics. Which approach should be taken to ensure accurate capacity planning without incurring additional costs?

A) Increase the minimum commitment to cover peak usage

B) Use predictive analytics to anticipate future demands

C) Regularly switch service providers for better rates

D) Allocate resources based solely on current demand

E) Implement strict user quotas to limit resource usage

F) Schedule quarterly reviews to adjust capacity agreements

Answer: B

Explanation: Utilizing predictive analytics enables organizations to forecast future capacity needs based on historical data and trends, allowing them to adjust resources efficiently and cost-effectively. This approach minimizes the risk of incurring unnecessary costs from over-provisioning or underestimating demand. Simply increasing commitments or switching providers may not address the core issue of accurate demand forecasting. Predictive analytics offers a proactive solution to effectively manage and plan for future capacity needs in an HPE GreenLake environment.

Q380: A mid-sized financial services company is planning to migrate its customer relationship management (CRM) application to HPE GreenLake. The CRM application is mission-critical and requires high availability and data security due to compliance with financial regulations. The current on-premises setup utilizes a combination of dedicated servers and a private cloud. As the IT manager, you are tasked with ensuring that the transition to GreenLake not only meets the performance and compliance requirements but also optimizes cost efficiency. What initial step should you prioritize to ensure a successful migration?

A) Conduct a detailed cost-benefit analysis of the migration.

B) Perform a comprehensive workload assessment to understand application dependencies.

C) Develop a disaster recovery plan specific to GreenLake.

D) Engage with HPE support to discuss potential technical challenges.

E) Train your IT staff on GreenLake capabilities and management tools.

F) Run a pilot migration with a non-critical application to test the process.

Answer: B

Explanation: When migrating a mission-critical application like CRM, it is crucial to perform a comprehensive workload assessment to identify application dependencies, performance metrics, and compliance requirements. Understanding these factors will help in designing the architecture on GreenLake that meets high availability and data security needs. This assessment is foundational to ensuring that the transition is smooth, the system operates as expected post-migration, and that it adheres to financial regulations. While cost analysis, training, and a disaster recovery plan are important, they are subsequent steps that rely on the initial workload assessment to be accurate and thorough.

Q381: True or False: When migrating an application to HPE GreenLake, it is essential to refactor all applications to be cloud-native for better performance and integration.

A) True

B) False

Answer: B

Explanation: Not all applications need to be refactored to be cloud-native when migrating to HPE GreenLake. The decision to refactor should be based on the specific needs of the application and the business goals. In many cases, a lift-and-shift approach can be sufficient, especially if the application is already optimized for cloud performance. Refactoring can offer improved performance and integration but requires more resources and time. Thus, it's not a mandatory step for all applications migrating to GreenLake.

Q382: During the application migration process to HPE GreenLake, it is crucial to ensure data consistency and integrity. Which of the following strategies is most effective in achieving this goal?

A) Implementing end-to-end encryption during data transfer.

B) Scheduling migrations during peak business hours for immediate troubleshooting.

C) Utilizing GreenLake's built-in data replication tools to mirror data in real-time.

D) Conducting a full data audit post-migration to check for discrepancies.

E) Leveraging third-party migration tools for additional verification.

F) Performing a pre-migration data integrity assessment using checksum algorithms.

Answer: C

Explanation: Using GreenLake's built-in data replication tools to mirror data in real-time is the most effective strategy to ensure data consistency and integrity during migration. These tools are designed to handle data transfer efficiently and reliably, maintaining the integrity of the data as it moves to the new environment. While encryption, audits, and assessments are important, real-time replication directly addresses the consistency challenge by continuously syncing data and reducing the risk of discrepancies.

Q383: A retail company is transitioning its e-commerce application to HPE GreenLake. The application experiences seasonal spikes in traffic, particularly during holiday sales. Which GreenLake feature should the company leverage to handle these fluctuations efficiently without over-provisioning resources?

A) Fixed capacity allocation

B) Continuous performance monitoring

C) Automated scaling capabilities

D) Dedicated instance provisioning

E) Cloud-native application refactoring

F) Long-term resource forecasting

Answer: C

Explanation: Automated scaling capabilities in GreenLake allow the company to dynamically adjust resources based on demand, efficiently handling seasonal spikes without over-provisioning. This feature ensures that the application has the necessary resources during peak times and scales down during off-peak periods, optimizing cost and performance. Fixed capacity and dedicated instances would not provide the same flexibility, whereas continuous monitoring, refactoring, and forecasting, while useful, do not directly address the need for on-demand resource scaling.

Q384: When planning for application migration to HPE GreenLake, what is a critical factor to consider to minimize downtime and ensure business continuity?

A) Selecting the right GreenLake service tier

B) Implementing a robust change management process

C) Conducting user training post-migration

D) Opting for a phased migration approach

E) Utilizing only HPE native tools for migration

F) Prioritizing cost savings over performance

Answer: D

Explanation: Opting for a phased migration approach is critical to minimizing downtime and ensuring business continuity. By migrating applications in stages, the business can test each phase for stability and performance, reducing the risk of unforeseen issues. This method allows for immediate troubleshooting and adjustments, ensuring that critical applications remain operational throughout the process. While service tier selection, change management, and training are important, phased migration specifically addresses the challenge of minimizing downtime.

Q385: Scenario-Based Question A multinational corporation, Globex Corp, has adopted HPE GreenLake to manage its hybrid IT environment. The company operates in multiple regions and has several departments, each with its own IT budget. To ensure cost transparency and accountability, Globex Corp wants to implement a tagging strategy that will allow them to accurately track and charge back IT resource usage to the appropriate departments and regions. The finance team is particularly concerned about accurately attributing costs for shared resources, such as storage and network infrastructure, which are used by multiple departments. How should Globex Corp implement its tagging strategy to meet these requirements?

A) Use a single tag for each department and region to simplify cost tracking.

B) Tag resources based on usage patterns rather than departmental ownership.

C) Implement a dual tagging strategy, assigning both department and region tags to each resource.

D) Use a central tag management system to automate tag assignment based on predefined rules.

E) Tag only the most expensive resources to minimize administrative overhead.

F) Allow each department to define its own tagging taxonomy to ensure flexibility.

Answer: C

Explanation: The correct approach for Globex Corp is to implement a dual tagging strategy, assigning both department and region tags to each resource. This allows for accurate tracking and chargeback of resource usage across different departments and regions. By tagging resources with both department and region identifiers, the company can create detailed reports that allocate costs according to the actual usage by each department and region. This approach ensures transparency and accountability, which are critical for financial management and budget planning. Additionally, using a dual tagging strategy helps in managing shared resources by allowing costs to be split accurately based on consumption, addressing the finance team's concerns.

Q386: True/False Question True or False: In HPE GreenLake, it is recommended to use a standardized tagging convention across all departments to ensure consistency and ease of reporting.

A) True

B) False

Answer: A

Explanation: Using a standardized tagging convention is crucial in HPE GreenLake environments as it ensures consistency, which simplifies management and reporting. A standardized approach enables all departments to understand and use the same terms, reducing the likelihood of errors and miscommunications. It also facilitates smoother integration of data from various departments when generating reports, thereby enhancing the accuracy of chargeback and cost allocation models. Consistent tagging practices help maintain coherence across the organization, which is particularly important in large, complex setups like those often found in multinational corporations.

Q387: Standard Multiple-Choice Question Which of the following is a key benefit of implementing a chargeback model in an HPE GreenLake environment?

A) Eliminates the need for cost management tools.

B) Increases the overall IT budget for the organization.

C) Provides detailed visibility into departmental resource consumption.

D) Allows for the automatic shutdown of unused resources.

E) Reduces the complexity of managing hybrid IT environments.

F) Ensures compliance with all data privacy regulations.

Answer: C

Explanation: A chargeback model provides detailed visibility into departmental resource consumption, which is a significant benefit in an HPE GreenLake environment. By allocating costs based on actual usage, departments can better understand their consumption patterns and manage their budgets more effectively. This transparency encourages departments to optimize their resource usage, potentially leading to cost savings. It also fosters accountability as departments are responsible for their resource consumption, aligning IT spending with business objectives. While chargeback models may not directly eliminate the need for cost management tools or increase the IT budget, they do provide valuable insights that aid in strategic decision-making.

Q388: Fill-in-the-Gap Multiple-Choice Question In a well-implemented tagging strategy, tags should be _____ to ensure they serve their intended purpose.

A) Generic and flexible

B) Detailed and specific

C) Assigned randomly

D) Used sparingly

E) Created on-the-fly

F) Automatically generated without oversight

Answer: B

Explanation: Tags should be detailed and specific to ensure they serve their intended purpose effectively. Detailed and specific tags allow for precise tracking of resource usage and cost allocation, which is essential for accurate chargeback models and reporting. This level of detail helps organizations gain deeper insights into their IT environments, enabling better resource management and strategic planning. Generic or randomly assigned tags, on the other hand, can lead to confusion and inaccuracies in reporting, undermining the benefits of a tagging strategy. Therefore, it is important to define clear and specific tags that align with organizational goals and reporting requirements.

Q389: Standard Multiple-Choice Question When designing a chargeback model in HPE GreenLake, which of the following factors is least important?

A) Departmental budget limits

B) Predictable and recurring expenses

C) Historical usage data

D) Current market rates for cloud services

E) Real-time monitoring capabilities

F) Organizational hierarchy

Answer: D

Explanation: When designing a chargeback model in HPE GreenLake, current market rates for cloud services are generally less important than other factors such as departmental budget limits, historical usage data, and real-time monitoring capabilities. While understanding market rates can be useful for benchmarking purposes, the primary focus of a chargeback model is to allocate internal costs based on actual resource usage and organizational needs. Factors like budget limits, usage data, and monitoring capabilities directly influence how costs are tracked, reported, and managed within the organization. The organizational hierarchy is also important as it dictates how costs are distributed and reported across different departments and business units.

Q390: Scenario-Based Question A global retail company, RetailCo, has recently migrated its infrastructure to the HPE GreenLake platform. Their IT department is responsible for tracking costs across various departments such as Sales, Marketing, and Operations. RetailCo wants to implement a tagging strategy that not only helps in tracking the costs by department but also accounts for different geographic regions like North America, Europe, and Asia. Additionally, the company wants to ensure that resources used for short-term projects are easily identifiable. What would be the most effective tagging strategy for RetailCo to achieve these objectives while maintaining clarity and simplicity in their resource management? ---

A) Use tags for department names only.

B) Use tags for geographic regions only.

C) Use a combination of department and geographic region tags, but not project tags.

D) Use tags for department names, geographic regions, and project durations.

E) Use custom tags for each resource without a standardized format.

F) Use tags for project durations only.

Answer: D

Explanation: RetailCo's objective is to track costs by department, geographic region, and identify short-term projects. A comprehensive tagging strategy that includes department names, geographic regions, and project durations ensures that all these aspects are covered. It allows for granular tracking and reporting, which aids in cost management and resource allocation. Using standardized tags helps maintain consistency across the organization, making it easier to analyze and report on resource usage and costs. Option D is the most effective as it aligns with all of RetailCo's objectives.

Q391: True/False Style Question Tagging resources in HPE GreenLake is optional and does not significantly impact cost tracking and allocation. ---
A) True

B) False

Answer: B

Explanation: Tagging in HPE GreenLake is crucial for effective cost tracking and resource allocation. Tags allow organizations to categorize and organize their resources, making it easier to associate costs with specific departments, projects, or regions. Without tags, it becomes challenging to track resource utilization accurately, leading to potential inefficiencies and increased costs. Therefore, tagging is not just optional but a best practice for effective cost management.

Q392: Multiple-Choice Question In the context of HPE GreenLake, which of the following is NOT considered a best practice when establishing a tagging strategy for resources? ---

A) Using a consistent naming convention for all tags.

B) Creating tags that reflect organizational structure.

C) Using a minimal number of tags to simplify management.

D) Regularly reviewing and updating tags for relevance.

E) Allowing individual teams to create their own tags independently.

F) Ensuring tags are applied at the time of resource creation.

Answer: E

Explanation: Allowing individual teams to create their own tags independently can lead to inconsistencies and confusion, making it difficult to manage and analyze resources effectively. A best practice is to establish a standardized tagging strategy across the organization to ensure consistency and clarity. This approach facilitates better reporting, cost tracking, and resource management. Options A, B, D, and F support these goals, while C simplifies management but E can lead to fragmentation.

Q393: Multiple-Choice Question When designing a tagging strategy for short-term promotional campaigns within HPE GreenLake, which of the following tag attributes would be most beneficial for tracking and reporting purposes? ---

A) Campaign name

B) Start date of the campaign

C) End date of the campaign

D) Project manager's name

E) Budget allocated for the campaign

F) All of the above

Answer: F

Explanation: To effectively track and report on short-term promotional campaigns, including all relevant attributes such as the campaign name, start and end dates, project manager's name, and budget is beneficial. This comprehensive approach allows for detailed analysis of each campaign's performance and cost-effectiveness. It also aids in forecasting future campaigns and understanding resource utilization. Option F provides a holistic view, making it the most beneficial choice.

Q394: Multiple-Choice Question Which of the following scenarios would likely result in the most significant challenges when implementing a tagging strategy in HPE GreenLake?

A) A small startup with a limited number of resources and projects.

B) A large corporation with decentralized IT departments and diverse projects.

C) An organization with a single, focused product line.

D) A non-profit organization with a limited IT budget.

E) A tech company with a standardized IT infrastructure.

F) A financial institution with strict regulatory compliance requirements.

Answer: B

Explanation: A large corporation with decentralized IT departments and diverse projects poses significant challenges for implementing a tagging strategy. The diversity in projects and decentralization can lead to inconsistencies and difficulties in maintaining a unified tagging standard. Coordination among departments is necessary to ensure consistent application of tags, which can be complex in such environments. This scenario requires careful planning and ongoing management to ensure effective cost tracking and resource management.

Q395: Scenario-Based Question In a mid-sized enterprise, the IT department has recently migrated its infrastructure to HPE GreenLake to take advantage of consumption-based billing. After the first month, the finance team notices that the billed amount is significantly higher than the initial estimate. Upon further investigation, they find that the metered usage data does not align with the actual resource consumption reported by the IT team. The discrepancies mainly involve compute and storage resources. The IT team is confident that their internal monitoring tools are accurate. As the HPE GreenLake administrator, you are tasked with identifying and resolving these billing discrepancies to ensure alignment between reported usage and billing. What is the most likely cause of this discrepancy?

A) The HPE GreenLake metering service is configured to a different time zone than the internal monitoring tools.

B) The internal monitoring tools are not accounting for peak usage periods captured by HPE GreenLake.

C) The initial configuration of HPE GreenLake did not include all resource types, leading to inaccurate billing.

D) There is a delay in the HPE GreenLake billing cycle that causes outdated usage data to be billed.

E) The finance team made an error in converting the usage data into billable units.

F) The network latency between the on-premises environment and HPE GreenLake affects data synchronization.

Answer: B

Explanation: The most likely cause of the discrepancy is that the internal monitoring tools are not accounting for peak usage periods captured by HPE GreenLake. HPE GreenLake bills customers based on actual resource consumption, which includes peak usage times. Internal tools might average out the usage over time, potentially missing these peaks. It's essential to compare the metering intervals of both internal tools and HPE GreenLake to ensure they capture the same data points. Aligning the monitoring tools with HPE's billing cycles can help mitigate such discrepancies. Reviewing configuration settings and ensuring all resource types are accounted for also helps maintain accurate billing.

Q396: True/False Question HPE GreenLake automatically synchronizes its internal billing data with customer on-premises monitoring systems to ensure consistency.

A) True

B) False

Answer: B

Explanation: False. HPE GreenLake does not automatically synchronize billing data with customer on-premises monitoring systems. While GreenLake provides detailed usage data, it is the customer's responsibility to ensure that their internal systems are aligned with this data. Customers must manually verify and reconcile any differences between GreenLake's billing and their internal monitoring. This process involves understanding the billing metrics and ensuring internal tools are configured to capture the same data points for accurate comparison.

Q397: Standard Multiple-Choice Question Which of the following actions should an HPE GreenLake administrator take first when addressing a billing discrepancy related to storage resource consumption?

A) Update the internal monitoring tool to match HPE GreenLake's billing cycle.

B) Review the HPE GreenLake usage reports for any anomalies or errors.

C) Adjust the storage resource allocation to match the billed amount.

D) Contact HPE support to request a billing adjustment.

E) Reconfigure the network settings to improve data transfer rates.

F) Verify the accuracy of the finance team's calculations.

Answer: B

Explanation: The first step an administrator should take is to review HPE GreenLake usage reports for any anomalies or errors. These reports provide a detailed breakdown of resource consumption and can reveal discrepancies or unusual patterns that may have caused billing issues. By identifying specific anomalies, administrators can pinpoint the root cause of the issue, whether it be a configuration error, an overestimation of resource needs, or a misalignment with internal monitoring tools. This step is crucial before making any changes or contacting support.

Q398: Fill-in-the-Gap Multiple-Choice Question When analyzing discrepancies in HPE GreenLake billing, administrators should focus on the _____ to ensure accurate resource consumption reporting.

A) network bandwidth usage

B) peak usage periods

C) virtualization overhead

D) user access logs

E) security compliance reports

F) environmental impact reports

Answer: B

Explanation: Administrators should focus on peak usage periods to ensure accurate resource consumption reporting. HPE GreenLake billing is often based on the highest level of resource utilization, known as peak usage. If internal monitoring tools do not capture these peaks, it can lead to discrepancies in reported usage. By understanding and aligning with these peak periods, administrators can better reconcile differences between actual usage and billed amounts, ensuring consistent and accurate billing.

Q399: Advanced Multiple-Choice Question An enterprise notices a consistent discrepancy in billed compute hours every month. Which strategy should be employed to identify the root cause of the discrepancy effectively?

A) Implement an external audit of all HPE GreenLake configurations.

B) Cross-reference billed hours with detailed time-stamped logs from HPE GreenLake.

C) Increase the frequency of data synchronization between on-premises systems and HPE GreenLake.

D) Optimize resource allocation to reduce overall compute usage.

E) Use machine learning to predict future billing discrepancies.

F) Switch to a different cloud provider for a more accurate billing system.

Answer: B

Explanation: The most effective strategy to identify the root cause of the billed compute hour discrepancy is to cross-reference billed hours with detailed time-stamped logs from HPE GreenLake. These logs provide a chronological record of resource usage, allowing administrators to pinpoint when and where discrepancies occur. By comparing these logs with internal monitoring data, administrators can identify patterns or irregularities in the billing process. This methodical approach ensures that any discrepancies are thoroughly investigated and resolved, preventing future issues and maintaining accurate billing.

Q400: Scenario-Based Question Your company, GlobalTech Solutions, has recently transitioned to using HPE GreenLake for managing its IT infrastructure. While provisioning new resources for a critical project, the engineering team encounters errors stating that the resources cannot be allocated due to insufficient capacity, despite the dashboard showing available capacity. The project deadline is tight, and the team needs the resources urgently. The team's initial checks confirm that the usage metrics appear normal, and no alerts have been triggered. They are unsure if it's a software glitch or a misconfiguration in the provisioning process. As the HPE GreenLake administrator, what should you check first to resolve this issue?   Explanation: When encountering issues with resource allocation, especially with an error indicating insufficient capacity, it's crucial first to verify the configuration of the resource pool. Often, resource pools might be inadvertently limited due to misconfigurations or policy settings that restrict allocations. Checking the resource pool settings ensures that the available capacity is correctly defined and accessible for provisioning. While software glitches or updates could potentially cause issues, confirming the configuration is a more direct approach to identifying and resolving provisioning problems efficiently. This step helps to eliminate any configuration-related barriers before exploring other possibilities such as software issues or contacting support. ---

A) Verify if the resource pool is correctly configured and not inadvertently limited.

B) Check if there is a pending maintenance job that might be affecting resource availability.

C) Confirm if the capacity dashboard is updated with the latest data.

D) Investigate if there is a recent system update that might have introduced the issue.

E) Reset the provisioning process and attempt the operation again.

F) Contact HPE support for immediate assistance to check for backend issues.

Answer: A

Explanation: nan

Q401: True/False Style Question True or False: If a provisioning request in HPE GreenLake fails, the first step should always be to escalate the issue to HPE support.   Explanation: In the event of a provisioning failure, it is not always necessary to immediately escalate the issue to HPE support. The first step should be to perform initial troubleshooting by checking error logs, reviewing the configuration settings, and verifying the resource availability. Often, issues can be resolved internally without external assistance by following these basic troubleshooting steps. Escalation to HPE support should be considered if internal troubleshooting does not resolve the issue or if the problem is suspected to be a deeper system-level error that requires expert intervention. ---

A) True

B) False

Answer: B

Explanation: nan

Q402: In HPE GreenLake, which of the following could be a reason for a provisioning task to remain stuck in a 'pending' state? Explanation: A provisioning task remaining in a 'pending' state can often be attributed to a concurrent task taking precedence, which may delay the execution of subsequent provisioning requests. HPE GreenLake handles multiple provisioning tasks by prioritizing them based on resource availability and system constraints. While network configurations and permissions could affect task execution, a pending status typically indicates a queue or dependency issue within the provisioning process. Checking the task queue and understanding the system's task handling can provide insights into why a task is pending. ---

A) Incorrect network configuration blocking resource access.

B) An expired SSL certificate on the GreenLake platform.

C) A concurrent provisioning task taking precedence.

D) A misconfigured firewall rule on the client side.

E) Lack of administrative permissions for the user initiating the task.

F) An incorrect resource tagging configuration.

Answer: C

Explanation: nan

Q403: When troubleshooting a failed provisioning attempt in HPE GreenLake, which log would provide the most detailed information about the failure?
Explanation: The Provisioning Task Log is the most specific and detailed source of information regarding provisioning attempts in HPE GreenLake. It records all provisioning actions, including errors, execution details, and status updates. By reviewing this log, administrators can gain insights into what specifically went wrong during the provisioning process, allowing them to identify and rectify the issues more effectively. Other logs, while helpful for broader system insights, do not provide the detailed level of information necessary for diagnosing provisioning-specific failures. ---

A) System Event Log

B) User Activity Log

C) Resource Allocation Log

D) Security Audit Log

E) Provisioning Task Log

F) Network Traffic Log

Answer: E

Explanation: nan

Q404: Which of the following might cause provisioning issues due to resource misallocation in HPE GreenLake?   Explanation: Over-provisioning of resources beyond the agreed capacity can lead to misallocation issues in HPE GreenLake. This occurs when resource requests exceed what has been contractually agreed upon, often leading to allocation failures or resource contention.

Administrators must ensure that provisioning requests align with the capacity and limits set within the service agreement to avoid such issues. While other factors like network latency or configuration mismatches could affect system performance, they do not directly cause resource misallocation in the context of provisioning.

A) Incorrectly applied service level agreements (SLAs).

B) Network latency affecting data transmission.

C) The presence of unpatched security vulnerabilities.

D) Over-provisioning of resources beyond the agreed capacity.

E) A mismatch in resource configuration templates.

F) Hardware failure in the data center.

Answer: D

Explanation: nan

Q405: Scenario-Based Question A mid-sized retail company, TechMart, is expanding its online presence and expects a surge in data processing and storage needs. They are considering deploying HPE GreenLake to manage their IT infrastructure for scalability and cost-effectiveness. However, they have a legacy system that manages their inventory and sales, which is critical for day-to-day operations. The CIO is concerned about integration challenges and potential downtime that might affect their sales operations during the transition. What should TechMart prioritize when planning their HPE GreenLake deployment to ensure a smooth transition with minimal disruption?   ---

A) Prioritize a complete system overhaul to modernize the entire IT infrastructure.

B) Integrate HPE GreenLake with the legacy system to ensure data consistency across platforms.

C) Focus on training staff on HPE GreenLake's functionalities before deployment.

D) Start with a pilot deployment in a non-critical area to test integration.

E) Outsource the deployment process to a third-party vendor specializing in legacy systems.

F) Implement a parallel system to run both the legacy and HPE GreenLake systems concurrently for a period.

Answer: B

Explanation: When integrating a new system such as HPE GreenLake with an existing legacy system, it is crucial to ensure data consistency and smooth operation across both platforms. Prioritizing the integration of HPE GreenLake with the legacy system allows TechMart to maintain uninterrupted sales operations and avoid data silos. This approach minimizes business disruption and leverages the strengths of both systems, ensuring that the legacy system's critical functions continue while benefiting from the scalability and flexibility of GreenLake. A complete system overhaul (A) or outsourcing to a third-party (E) could introduce more complexity and risk of downtime. Training staff (C) and pilot deployments (D) are important but secondary to ensuring core business continuity, while running parallel systems (F) can be resource-intensive and may lead to data synchronization issues.

Q406: True/False Question True or False: HPE GreenLake can be deployed on-premises, in colocation facilities, and in cloud environments, providing flexibility in deployment locations.   ---

A) True

B) False

Answer: A

Explanation: HPE GreenLake is designed to provide a cloud-like experience on-premises and offers the flexibility to be deployed in various environments, including on-premises data centers, colocation facilities, and cloud environments. This flexibility allows organizations to choose the deployment model that best suits their specific needs, whether they require the control and security of on-premises infrastructure, the scalability of cloud resources, or a hybrid approach. This adaptability is a key advantage of HPE GreenLake, enabling businesses to optimize their IT infrastructure based on their operational and financial priorities.

Q407: When considering the deployment of HPE GreenLake, which factor is most critical for ensuring customer data security and compliance with industry regulations?   ---

A) Implementing a zero-trust security model across all IT environments.

B) Choosing a deployment location with the lowest latency to end-users.

C) Ensuring compatibility with existing networking equipment.

D) Regularly updating all software and firmware to the latest versions.

E) Establishing a comprehensive backup and disaster recovery strategy.

F) Conducting a detailed cost-benefit analysis of the deployment.

Answer: A

Explanation: Implementing a zero-trust security model is critical for ensuring customer data security and compliance with industry regulations when deploying HPE GreenLake. A zero-trust approach assumes that threats could exist both outside and inside the network, and therefore, it requires strict verification for every user and device attempting access to resources. This model helps in protecting sensitive data and maintaining compliance with regulations like GDPR, HIPAA, or PCI-DSS, which mandate rigorous data protection standards. While other options like updating software (D) and backup strategies (E) are important, they do not address the overarching framework needed for comprehensive security and compliance as effectively as a zero-trust model.

Q408: For a company planning to deploy HPE GreenLake, which of the following is the best approach to manage unpredictable workload demands and optimize resource utilization?   ---

A) Over-provisioning resources to ensure maximum availability during peak times.

B) Implementing a pay-as-you-go pricing model to scale resources as needed.

C) Utilizing predictive analytics to anticipate and prepare for workload spikes.

D) Establishing fixed resource allocations to simplify budgeting and planning.

E) Conducting quarterly resource audits to adjust capacity based on past usage.

F) Deploying resources in multiple geographic locations to balance load.

Answer: B

Explanation: Implementing a pay-as-you-go pricing model is the best approach for managing unpredictable workload demands and optimizing resource utilization in an HPE GreenLake deployment. This model allows organizations to scale resources dynamically based on actual usage rather than anticipated peaks, leading to cost savings and efficient resource management. Unlike over-provisioning (A) or fixed allocations (D), which can lead to wasted resources, a flexible pricing model provides the agility needed to handle variable workloads. Predictive analytics (C) and regular audits (E) complement this approach by offering insights into resource trends but do not inherently provide the same level of flexibility as pay-as-you-go.

A) Proximity to the company's headquarters for ease of access.

B) Availability of renewable energy sources to support sustainability goals.

C) Reputation of the facility in the industry for reliability and uptime.

D) Presence of advanced cooling technology to support high-density workloads.

E) Cost of leasing space and associated operational expenses.

F) Security certifications and compliance with international standards.

Answer: F

Explanation: When selecting a colocation facility to host part of the infrastructure for an HPE GreenLake deployment, the paramount consideration should be the facility's security certifications and compliance with international standards. This ensures that the facility meets rigorous security protocols and is compliant with relevant data protection regulations, which is crucial for safeguarding sensitive data and maintaining customer trust. While factors like proximity (A), renewable energy (B), and cost (E) are important, they do not directly address the critical need for security and compliance as effectively as ensuring that the facility is certified and adheres to international standards. This is especially vital for organizations operating in highly regulated industries.

Q410: A leading retail company, RetailPro Inc., has been experiencing fluctuating demand for its online services, especially during peak shopping seasons. The IT team is considering implementing a hybrid cloud infrastructure to manage these fluctuations efficiently. They are evaluating HPE GreenLake Cloud Services for this purpose. Their primary goal is to ensure cost-effectiveness while maintaining high-performance levels. Considering these requirements, which feature of HPE GreenLake Cloud Services would be most beneficial for RetailPro Inc.?

A) On-demand capacity management

B) Fixed capacity pricing model

C) Integrated security compliance

D) Multi-cloud workload orchestration

E) Long-term capacity commitment

F) Dedicated on-premises resources

Answer: A

Explanation: RetailPro Inc. is dealing with fluctuating demand, which suggests that they need a flexible and scalable solution to handle varying workloads. On-demand capacity management is a key feature of HPE GreenLake Cloud Services that allows businesses to scale resources up or down based on current demand. This feature ensures cost-effectiveness by providing the necessary resources only when needed, thus avoiding the costs associated with unused capacity. The fixed capacity pricing model and long-term capacity commitment are less suitable for a dynamic environment like RetailPro Inc.'s, where demand is not constant. Multi-cloud workload orchestration and integrated security compliance, while important, do not directly address the issue of fluctuating demand. Dedicated on-premises resources could lead to underutilization during off-peak periods, making on-demand capacity the most beneficial option.

Q411: True or False: HPE GreenLake allows businesses to operate with a pay-per-use model, which can lead to cost savings compared to a traditional capital expenditure model.

A) True

B) False

Answer: A

Explanation: HPE GreenLake's pay-per-use model is designed to align IT spending with actual usage, allowing companies to pay only for the resources they consume. This model contrasts with traditional capital expenditure models, where businesses must invest heavily in infrastructure upfront regardless of actual usage. By adopting the pay-per-use approach, organizations can achieve significant cost savings, particularly if their workloads fluctuate or if they want to avoid the risk of over-provisioning. This flexibility is one of the main advantages of HPE GreenLake, making the statement true.

Q412: When configuring HPE GreenLake for a global enterprise, which factor should be prioritized to ensure compliance with varying international data protection regulations?

A) Centralized data storage

B) Localized data sovereignty

C) Single-point data access

D) Unified global security policy

E) Cross-border data sharing

F) Decentralized user management

Answer: B

Explanation: Localized data sovereignty is crucial for global enterprises using HPE GreenLake, as different countries have distinct data protection regulations. Ensuring data is stored and processed within specific geographic boundaries helps organizations comply with local laws, such as the GDPR in Europe or the CCPA in California. Centralized data storage and cross-border data sharing might conflict with these regulations. While a unified global security policy and decentralized user management are important for security and accessibility, they do not specifically address compliance with international data protection laws as effectively as localized data sovereignty.

Q413: A medium-sized manufacturing company, TechFab, is transitioning to HPE GreenLake to improve its data analytics capabilities. The company wants to integrate third-party analytics tools with minimal disruption. Which HPE GreenLake feature should TechFab leverage to achieve this integration smoothly?

A) Built-in analytics solutions

B) HPE GreenLake Central

C) Third-party API support

D) Proprietary integration tools

E) Exclusive vendor partnership programs

F) Custom development services

Answer: C

Explanation: Third-party API support is essential for TechFab to integrate its existing analytics tools with HPE GreenLake seamlessly. This feature facilitates communication and data exchange between different software applications, allowing TechFab to maintain its current analytics capabilities while leveraging the benefits of HPE GreenLake. Built-in analytics solutions might not accommodate TechFab's specific needs, and proprietary integration tools could lead to vendor lock-in. Exclusive vendor partnerships and custom development services could result in higher costs and longer implementation times, making third-party API support the most efficient choice for smooth integration.

Q414: During the deployment of HPE GreenLake, an IT manager notices that resource utilization is consistently low, resulting in higher costs than anticipated. What immediate action should the IT manager take to optimize costs?

A) Increase resource allocation

B) Conduct a workload assessment

C) Implement a capacity ceiling

D) Switch to a fixed pricing model

E) Migrate workloads to public cloud

F) Enable auto-scaling features

Answer: B

Explanation: Conducting a workload assessment is the first step the IT manager should take to understand why resource utilization is low. This assessment will provide insights into whether resources are over-provisioned or if workloads are not optimally distributed. Based on this analysis, the IT manager can identify opportunities to adjust resource allocation, such as right-sizing or consolidating workloads, to reduce costs. Increasing resource allocation, implementing a capacity ceiling, and switching to a fixed pricing model may not address the underlying issue of low utilization. Migrating workloads to a public cloud or enabling auto-scaling features could be considered after understanding the workload characteristics and needs.

Q415: Scenario-based Your company, a mid-sized enterprise, has recently signed up for HPE GreenLake to manage its hybrid cloud resources more effectively. The IT department is tasked with optimizing resource allocation and ensuring compliance with industry regulations. You have been appointed as the lead administrator for HPE GreenLake Central. During a quarterly review meeting, the CFO raises concerns about resource usage spikes and cost predictability. You need to generate reports that provide insights into resource consumption trends, cost allocation by department, and compliance with internal and external policies. Which feature of the HPE GreenLake Central interface would best assist you in addressing the CFO's concerns? ---

A) Capacity Planner

B) Consumption Analytics

C) Resource Pooling

D) Deployment Tracker

E) Compliance Dashboard

F) Cost Management Tool

Answer: B

Explanation: The Consumption Analytics feature in HPE GreenLake Central is designed to offer detailed insights into resource usage and costs. It enables administrators to analyze consumption trends over time, allocate costs by department or project, and ensure predictable budgeting. By leveraging this tool, you can create comprehensive reports that address the CFO's concerns about resource usage spikes and facilitate better cost predictability. Although other features like Compliance Dashboard and Cost Management Tool may offer some relevant insights, Consumption Analytics provides the most direct and detailed analysis needed for this scenario.

True/False The HPE GreenLake Central interface allows administrators to integrate third-party cloud services into its dashboard for unified management.

A) True

B) False

Answer: A

Explanation: True. HPE GreenLake Central is designed to support a hybrid cloud environment by integrating with various third-party cloud services. This integration allows administrators to manage and monitor resources across different platforms from a single interface, facilitating better operational efficiency and strategic decision-making. By having a unified dashboard, organizations can streamline their cloud management processes and improve overall visibility.

Q417: Which component of the HPE GreenLake Central interface is primarily used for tracking the deployment status of IT projects within the organization?

A) Deployment Tracker

B) Resource Monitor

C) Project Manager

D) Status Dashboard

E) Implementation Tracker

F) Task Scheduler

Answer: A

Explanation: The Deployment Tracker component is specifically designed to monitor and report the status of IT deployments within the HPE GreenLake Central interface. It provides detailed insights into the progress of various IT projects, ensuring that administrators are kept informed of any delays or issues. This feature helps in maintaining project timelines and improving the coordination of resources. While other options like Project Manager and Status Dashboard may sound relevant, Deployment Tracker is explicitly focused on deployment status tracking.

Q418: In HPE GreenLake Central, which feature would you use to ensure that your clients' data handling processes comply with GDPR regulations?   ---

A) Data Privacy Module

B) Compliance Dashboard

C) Security Manager

D) Regulatory Monitor

E) Privacy Tracker

F) Risk Assessment Tool

Answer: B

Explanation: The Compliance Dashboard in HPE GreenLake Central is designed to help organizations monitor and manage compliance with various regulations, including GDPR. It provides a comprehensive view of compliance status and highlights areas that require attention. By using this feature, administrators can ensure that data handling processes align with legal requirements, thus reducing the risk of non-compliance. While other features like Security Manager and Risk Assessment Tool are important for overall security and risk management, the Compliance Dashboard is directly focused on regulatory compliance.

Q419: When using the HPE GreenLake Central interface, what is the primary benefit of utilizing the Resource Pooling feature?

A) Improved compliance tracking

B) Enhanced security measures

C) Increased resource utilization efficiency

D) Streamlined project management

E) Simplified user access control

F) Accelerated data processing speeds

Answer: C

Explanation: The Resource Pooling feature in HPE GreenLake Central is designed to optimize the utilization of available resources by grouping them together for more efficient allocation and management. This leads to increased resource utilization efficiency, as it allows for dynamic adjustment of resources based on demand, minimizing waste and reducing costs. While other aspects like compliance, security, and user access are critical, Resource Pooling specifically focuses on maximizing the effective use of IT infrastructure.

Q420: Scenario-Based Question A multinational retail corporation has recently adopted HPE GreenLake to optimize its IT operations and support its growing e-commerce platform. The company's DevOps team is tasked with deploying new applications rapidly to meet fluctuating customer demands during peak shopping seasons. However, they face challenges in managing multiple environments and ensuring that resource allocation aligns with the business's dynamic needs. The team is considering using HPE GreenLake's DevOps support features to streamline these processes and improve efficiency. Which HPE GreenLake feature should the DevOps team prioritize to effectively manage their deployment pipelines and ensure optimal resource utilization?
A) HPE GreenLake Central unified dashboard

B) HPE GreenLake Cloud Services for Containers

C) HPE GreenLake's cost optimization analytics

D) HPE GreenLake's security compliance tools

E) HPE GreenLake's hybrid cloud management capabilities

F) HPE GreenLake's disaster recovery services

Answer: B

Explanation: HPE GreenLake Cloud Services for Containers is designed to support DevOps teams in managing containerized applications across hybrid environments. This feature provides capabilities that align with the needs of the retail corporation's DevOps team by enabling efficient application deployment and scaling, which is crucial during peak shopping seasons. The use of container services allows for consistent and repeatable deployment processes, reducing the complexity of managing multiple environments. Additionally, it ensures that resources are allocated efficiently, addressing the corporation's need for dynamic resource management. Other options like dashboards and cost analytics are supportive but don't directly address deployment pipeline management or container orchestration.

Q421: Standard Multiple-Choice Question Which of the following is a key benefit of using HPE GreenLake's DevOps support for continuous integration and continuous deployment (CI/CD) processes?

A) Enhanced physical security of data centers

B) Improved scalability and flexibility of workloads

C) Guaranteed 100% uptime of all services

D) Reduction of energy consumption in data centers

E) Simplified legacy system integration

F) Increased manual intervention requirements

Answer: B

Explanation: HPE GreenLake's DevOps support provides improved scalability and flexibility, which are crucial for CI/CD processes. This is because it offers the ability to quickly allocate and deallocate resources as needed, ensuring that workloads can scale efficiently in response to changing demands. This flexibility is essential for maintaining the agility and speed that CI/CD pipelines require. Enhanced scalability supports the rapid deployment of code changes, leading to faster release cycles without compromising on performance or resource efficiency. Other options, while beneficial, do not specifically address the nature of CI/CD processes.

Q422: True/False Question HPE GreenLake provides built-in DevOps tools that allow for the seamless integration of third-party applications into the customer's existing CI/CD pipelines.

A) True

B) False

Answer: A

Explanation: True. HPE GreenLake offers built-in DevOps tools that facilitate the integration of third-party applications into existing CI/CD pipelines. This integration capability is a critical feature that allows organizations to leverage their existing DevOps tools and processes while taking advantage of the scalability and flexibility offered by HPE GreenLake. By supporting popular DevOps tools and frameworks, HPE GreenLake ensures that customers can continue using their familiar toolsets without disruption, promoting continuity and minimizing the learning curve for IT teams.

Q423: Fill-in-the-Gap Question HPE GreenLake's DevOps support is particularly beneficial for organizations looking to _____. This feature allows for the rapid deployment of applications and services, ensuring that development and operations teams can collaborate efficiently.

A) Implement machine learning models

B) Transition from on-premises to public cloud

C) Streamline software development and deployment

D) Enhance cybersecurity measures

E) Perform large-scale data analytics

F) Re-engineer network architectures

Answer: C

Explanation: The correct phrase to fill in the gap is "streamline software development and deployment." HPE GreenLake's DevOps support offers tools and services that enhance the efficiency of software development and deployment processes. This includes features like automated resource provisioning, container orchestration, and integration with CI/CD tools, all of which allow development and operations teams to work more collaboratively and effectively. This streamlining is essential for organizations that prioritize rapid innovation and require shortened development cycles to remain competitive in fast-paced markets.

Q424: Standard Multiple-Choice Question What primary challenge does HPE GreenLake's DevOps support address for enterprises with complex IT environments?

A) High electricity costs in data centers

B) Difficulty in managing multi-cloud environments

C) Lack of advanced data visualization tools

D) Inadequate customer support services

E) Limited on-premises storage capacity

F) Slow network connectivity

Answer: B

Explanation: HPE GreenLake's DevOps support is particularly effective in addressing the challenge of managing multi-cloud environments, which are often complex and difficult to oversee. Enterprises with diverse IT environments can benefit from HPE GreenLake's ability to unify management across different cloud platforms, providing a seamless experience that simplifies operations. The platform's integrated tools support consistent application deployment and management across clouds, reducing complexity and enhancing operational efficiency. While other options like electricity costs and storage capacity are relevant to IT operations, they are not the primary focus of DevOps support in the context of multi-cloud management.

Q425: Scenario-Based Question A major e-commerce company, XYZ Retail, is experiencing rapid growth in its customer base and is looking to optimize its infrastructure to ensure scalability and cost-effectiveness. The company is considering adopting HPE GreenLake for Containers to manage its Kubernetes workloads more efficiently. During a meeting, the CTO highlights the need for a solution that offers seamless integration with existing cloud services, enhanced security, and simplified management. Additionally, the IT team must be able to monitor container performance in real-time to quickly address any issues. Which feature of HPE GreenLake for Containers would best address the company's requirements for integration and management?

A) HPE Ezmeral Runtime Enterprise

B) HPE OneView

C) HPE GreenLake Central

D) HPE InfoSight

E) HPE Storage Optimizer

F) HPE Synergy

Answer: C

Explanation: HPE GreenLake Central provides a unified platform for managing cloud and on-premises environments, making it ideal for organizations like XYZ Retail that require seamless integration and simplified management. It offers real-time monitoring of workloads, which helps in quickly addressing performance issues. Furthermore, it supports enhanced security features and can integrate with existing cloud services, aligning with the company's needs for a scalable and cost-effective solution.

Q426: True/False Question HPE GreenLake for Containers offers built-in support for managing both Kubernetes and Docker container environments.
A) True

B) False

Answer: A

Explanation: True. HPE GreenLake for Containers is designed to provide comprehensive support for containerized workloads, including both Kubernetes and Docker environments. This capability ensures that organizations can manage a variety of container deployments under a single platform, offering flexibility and efficiency in operations.

Q427: Standard Multiple-Choice Question Which component of HPE GreenLake for Containers is primarily responsible for providing application lifecycle management and deployment of containerized applications?
A) HPE CloudPhysics

B) HPE Ezmeral Data Fabric

C) HPE Ezmeral Container Platform

D) HPE Apollo Systems

E) HPE SimpliVity

F) HPE 3PAR StoreServ

Answer: C

Explanation: HPE Ezmeral Container Platform is the component of HPE GreenLake for Containers specifically focused on application lifecycle management and deployment of containerized applications. It provides a robust environment for deploying, managing, and scaling containerized applications, leveraging Kubernetes orchestration.

To ensure optimal performance and resource allocation in HPE GreenLake for Containers, administrators should regularly use _____ to analyze and predict workload trends.

A) HPE OneView

B) HPE InfoSight

C) HPE Synergy Composer

D) HPE GreenLake Central

E) HPE CloudPhysics

F) HPE Ezmeral Runtime Enterprise

Answer: B

Explanation: HPE InfoSight is a predictive analytics tool that helps administrators analyze and predict workload trends, ensuring optimal performance and resource allocation. By using machine learning and AI, HPE InfoSight provides insights that allow proactive management of resources, minimizing downtime and improving efficiency.

Q429: Standard Multiple-Choice Question Which of the following best describes the role of HPE Ezmeral Runtime Enterprise within the HPE GreenLake for Containers ecosystem?

A) It provides network virtualization and security features for containerized applications.

B) It offers machine learning capabilities to optimize container performance.

C) It delivers a unified platform for managing hybrid cloud environments.

D) It enhances data storage and retrieval for containerized applications.

E) It provides an enterprise-grade platform for managing containerized applications.

F) It serves as a monitoring tool for real-time container traffic analysis.

Answer: E

Explanation: HPE Ezmeral Runtime Enterprise is designed to provide an enterprise-grade platform for managing containerized applications. It offers a robust environment for deploying, running, and managing containerized applications with a focus on security, scalability, and performance. This makes it integral to the HPE GreenLake for Containers ecosystem, supporting various enterprise use cases and operational needs.

Q430: Your company, a rapidly growing e-commerce business, is experiencing frequent downtime due to the inability of its current IT infrastructure to handle peak traffic loads. The IT team is considering transitioning to a composable infrastructure to improve resource allocation and flexibility. They are particularly interested in HPE Synergy for its promise of delivering infrastructure as code. The team needs to ensure that the solution can dynamically allocate resources based on real-time demand and integrate seamlessly with their existing DevOps tools. What aspect of HPE Synergy should the IT team focus on to meet these requirements?

A) HPE Synergy Image Streamer

B) HPE Synergy Composer

C) HPE Synergy Frame Link Modules

D) HPE Synergy Data Fabric

E) HPE Synergy Integrated Lights-Out (iLO)

F) HPE Synergy Power Management Module

Answer: B

Explanation: HPE Synergy Composer is the key component of the HPE Synergy architecture that enables dynamic resource allocation and integration with DevOps tools. It acts as the management interface, allowing IT administrators to compose and recompose resources on-demand using software-defined intelligence. This capability aligns perfectly with the company's need to dynamically allocate resources based on real-time demand. Additionally,

Synergy Composer integrates seamlessly with existing DevOps tools to automate and streamline the deployment process, making it an ideal solution for businesses looking to improve flexibility and reduce downtime.

Q431: In the context of HPE Synergy, what is the primary function of the Image Streamer?

A) To provide real-time monitoring and analytics of resource usage

B) To enable seamless integration with third-party cloud services

C) To manage power and cooling for the composable infrastructure

D) To deploy and manage operating system images for compute modules

E) To optimize network latency and bandwidth across the infrastructure

F) To offer centralized storage management for virtual machines

Answer: D

Explanation: The HPE Synergy Image Streamer is primarily used for deploying and managing operating system images for compute modules. It allows administrators to quickly provision and re-provision OS images, applications, and settings, making it an essential tool for environments that require rapid scaling and agility. This capability supports the infrastructure as code approach by enabling consistent and repeatable deployments, which is critical for maintaining efficiency and minimizing errors in dynamic IT environments.

Q432: True or False: HPE Synergy requires a separate management interface for each compute module.

A) True

B) False

Answer: B

Explanation: False. HPE Synergy is designed to provide a unified management interface that does not require separate management interfaces for each compute module. The Synergy Composer consolidates management tasks into a single tool, simplifying the administration of the entire composable infrastructure. This unified management approach reduces complexity, improves efficiency, and lowers the potential for misconfigurations, making it easier for IT teams to manage large-scale deployments.

Q433: Which of the following best describes the concept of composability in HPE Synergy?

A) The ability to integrate with any public cloud provider

B) The capability to assign resources based on fixed, pre-defined templates

C) The feature that allows dynamic resource allocation based on workload demands

D) The process of manually configuring hardware components for specific applications

E) The ability to use only HPE proprietary software and hardware

F) The necessity to upgrade all components simultaneously to ensure compatibility

Answer: C

Explanation: Composability in HPE Synergy refers to the capability to dynamically allocate resources based on workload demands. This is achieved through a software-defined approach that allows administrators to compose and recompose resources as needed, providing flexibility and efficiency. Composability eliminates the limitations of fixed, pre-defined templates, enabling IT teams to respond quickly to changing business needs and optimize resource utilization. This approach is central to the value proposition of composable infrastructure, offering a scalable and agile solution for modern IT environments.

An organization is evaluating HPE Synergy for its next-generation data center. The IT manager is particularly concerned about the ease of managing storage resources as part of this new infrastructure. Which HPE Synergy component should they focus on to address this concern?

A) HPE Synergy Power Management Module

B) HPE Synergy Frame Link Modules

C) HPE Synergy Composer

D) HPE Synergy Storage Modules

E) HPE Synergy Integrated Lights-Out (iLO)

F) HPE Synergy Image Streamer

Answer: D

Explanation: The HPE Synergy Storage Modules are specifically designed to manage storage resources within the Synergy environment. They provide a flexible and scalable approach to storage management, allowing administrators to provision and manage storage resources efficiently. By focusing on the Storage Modules, the IT manager can ensure that the organization benefits from seamless storage integration, high performance, and simplified management, which are critical for maintaining an agile and responsive data center. This component is vital for organizations looking to optimize storage usage and improve overall infrastructure performance.

Q435: In the context of HPE GreenLake's service level objectives, which of the following statements is true?

A) SLOs are primarily concerned with the financial management of IT resources.

B) SLOs are critical in defining the expected performance and availability levels of services.

Answer: B

Explanation: Service Level Objectives (SLOs) are a key component in managing cloud services, such as those provided by HPE GreenLake. They define specific performance and availability targets that must be met to ensure that services are delivered effectively to meet business needs. While financial management is an important aspect of cloud services, SLOs focus on technical performance metrics such as uptime, response times, and throughput. These metrics ensure that services meet the required standards to support business operations.

Q436: Which of the following best describes the relationship between Service Level Agreements (SLAs) and Service Level Objectives (SLOs) within HPE GreenLake?

A) SLAs and SLOs are interchangeable terms used to measure service performance.

B) SLAs are specific commitments made to customers, while SLOs are internal goals.

C) SLAs are broader business commitments, and SLOs are detailed technical targets.

D) SLOs define penalties for service failures, which are outlined in SLAs.

E) SLAs are focused on financial penalties, whereas SLOs focus on performance metrics.

F) SLAs are used for external reporting, while SLOs are used for internal assessment.

Answer: C

Explanation: Service Level Agreements (SLAs) and Service Level Objectives (SLOs) serve different purposes within service management. SLAs are formal agreements that outline the expected service levels and may include penalties or compensations if these levels are not met. They are broader business commitments made to customers. On the other hand, SLOs are specific, detailed targets set internally to achieve the broader goals defined in SLAs. SLOs help in monitoring and managing the performance of services to ensure that the commitments made in SLAs are met.

Q437: When setting Service Level Objectives (SLOs) for an HPE GreenLake deployment, which factor is least likely to influence the determination of these objectives?

A) Historical performance data of similar services.

B) Industry benchmarks and best practices.

C) The financial budget allocated for IT services.

D) The geographic location of end-users.

E) Regulatory compliance requirements.

F) The personal preferences of the IT manager.

Answer: F

Explanation: Setting SLOs is a strategic process that involves understanding various factors that impact service delivery. These include historical performance data, industry benchmarks, financial constraints, regulatory requirements, and the end-users' geographic location, which can affect latency and performance. However, the personal preferences of the IT manager are the least relevant in this context, as SLOs should be based on objective data and organizational needs rather than individual opinions.

Q438: Fill in the gap: The primary purpose of setting service level objectives (SLOs) in HPE GreenLake is to _____.

A) Ensure compliance with IT governance frameworks.

B) Establish clear performance targets and measure service success.

C) Reduce the overall costs associated with IT infrastructure.

D) Enhance the security posture of the IT environment.

E) Simplify the process of resource procurement.

F) Facilitate the transition to a multi-cloud strategy.

Answer: B

Explanation: The primary purpose of setting service level objectives (SLOs) is to establish clear, measurable performance targets that define what success looks like for IT services. By setting these targets, organizations can monitor service performance, ensure that it aligns with business needs, and take corrective actions when necessary. SLOs provide a framework for evaluating service success and ensuring that IT resources are effectively supporting business operations. While factors like cost reduction and security are important, SLOs specifically focus on performance and availability metrics.

Q439: Scenario-Based Question Imagine you are the IT administrator for a mid-sized financial services company that utilizes HPE GreenLake for its storage solutions. The company has recently expanded its operations globally and is concerned about data integrity and availability across its international branches. You have been tasked with implementing a robust snapshot and replication strategy to ensure minimal data loss and quick recovery in case of a disaster. The primary data center is located in New York, and there are secondary data centers in London and Tokyo. The company requires that snapshots be taken every hour and retained for a week, while replicated data should be available in near real-time at all locations. Which configuration should be implemented to meet the company's requirements?

A) Implement synchronous replication with hourly snapshots retained for one week.

B) Use asynchronous replication with daily snapshots retained for one week.

C) Set up point-in-time replication with hourly snapshots retained for one month.

D) Configure synchronous replication with real-time snapshots retained for one day.

E) Implement asynchronous replication with hourly snapshots retained for one week.

F) Use real-time replication with daily snapshots retained for one month.

Answer: E

Explanation: To meet the company's requirements of having near real-time data availability across international locations, asynchronous replication is most suitable. Synchronous replication would ensure immediate consistency but might not perform well over long distances due to latency. Asynchronous replication allows for data to be replicated with minimal performance impact, which is crucial for global operations. Taking hourly snapshots ensures that the data can be restored to almost any point in time within the past week, aligning with the requirement for minimal data loss. Retaining snapshots for one week strikes a balance between data recovery options and storage efficiency.

Q440: True/False Question True or False: In an HPE GreenLake environment, storage snapshots consume the same amount of physical space as the original data.

A) True

B) False

Answer: B

Explanation: In HPE GreenLake, storage snapshots are typically implemented using a Copy-on-Write (CoW) or Redirect-on-Write (RoW) mechanism, which means that snapshots only store changes made to the data since the last snapshot. This makes them highly space-efficient, as they do not consume the same amount of physical space as the original data. Instead, they only occupy additional storage for the differences between the current state and the snapshot state. This efficiency is one of the key advantages of using snapshots for data protection and recovery.

Q441: Standard Multiple-Choice Question When configuring snapshot schedules in HPE GreenLake, which factor is NOT typically considered?

A) Frequency of data changes

B) Network bandwidth

C) Data retention policy

D) User access patterns

E) Time zone differences

F) Hardware compatibility

Answer: F

Explanation: When setting up snapshot schedules, administrators must consider factors such as the frequency of data changes (to determine how often snapshots should be taken), network bandwidth (to ensure snapshots do not impact network performance), data retention policies (to comply with organizational and legal requirements), user access patterns (to schedule snapshots during low-activity periods), and time zone differences (to coordinate snapshots across different regions). Hardware compatibility is generally not a concern at the snapshot scheduling level, as snapshots are software-managed features that do not typically depend on specific hardware configurations.

Q442: Fill-in-the-Gap Question In an HPE GreenLake environment, the primary purpose of data replication is to provide _____.

A) Enhanced data analytics

B) Improved storage capacity

C) Disaster recovery and data availability

D) Faster data processing

E) Simplified data migration

F) Cost reduction

Answer: C

Explanation: The primary purpose of data replication in an HPE GreenLake environment is to ensure disaster recovery and data availability. Replication involves creating copies of data and storing them in different locations to protect against data loss due to hardware failure, natural disasters, or other unforeseen events. By having multiple copies of data, organizations can quickly recover and maintain operational continuity. This is particularly important for businesses that require high availability and reliability of their critical data.

Which of the following best describes the difference between a snapshot and a replica in an HPE GreenLake storage environment?

A) Snapshots are full copies of data, while replicas are incremental changes.

B) Snapshots are stored locally, while replicas are stored remotely.

C) Snapshots are read-only, while replicas allow read-write access.

D) Snapshots preserve data state at a point in time, while replicas maintain continuous data consistency.

E) Snapshots require more storage space than replicas.

F) Snapshots are used for testing, while replicas are used for production environments.

Answer: D

Explanation: In an HPE GreenLake storage environment, a snapshot is a read-only point-in-time copy of data. It captures the state of the data at a specific moment, allowing for data recovery to that exact state if needed. A replica, on the other hand, is a continuously updated copy of the data that ensures data consistency across different locations or systems. Replicas are used to maintain up-to-date copies of data for redundancy and failover purposes. Snapshots are typically used for backup and recovery, while replicas are essential for disaster recovery and high availability.

Q444: Scenario-Based Question ABC Corporation is a rapidly growing company with fluctuating demands for its IT resources due to seasonal business spikes. The company decided to implement HPE GreenLake to gain flexibility and scalability. During their procurement process, they faced challenges with accurately forecasting their resource needs over a 12-month period. They are concerned about the cost implications of underutilization or over-provisioning of resources. The IT manager is tasked with ensuring that the ordering process aligns perfectly with the dynamic needs and financial constraints of ABC Corporation. What should the IT manager prioritize to efficiently manage the HPE GreenLake ordering process?

A) Establish a fixed resource allocation plan based on last year's data.

B) Engage in a detailed consultation with HPE to tailor a scalable solution.

C) Opt for the maximum available configuration to avoid resource shortages.

D) Use a third-party tool to estimate future resource needs.

E) Implement a pay-as-you-go model without any consultation.

F) Rely solely on vendor recommendations without internal assessments.

Answer: B

Explanation: When implementing HPE GreenLake, it's crucial for the IT manager to work closely with HPE to develop a solution that is tailored to their specific needs. This ensures that the system is scalable and can adapt to the company's fluctuating demand. By engaging in a detailed consultation, the IT manager can leverage HPE's expertise to forecast needs more accurately and avoid the pitfalls of over-provisioning or underutilization. This collaborative approach helps align the ordering process with the company's financial constraints and dynamic requirements, leading to a more efficient and cost-effective deployment.

Q445: True/False Question The HPE GreenLake ordering process requires a one-size-fits-all approach, regardless of the customer's unique business requirements.

A) True

B) False

Answer: B

Explanation: The HPE GreenLake ordering process is designed to be flexible and customizable to meet the specific needs of each customer. Unlike a one-size-fits-all approach, GreenLake allows businesses to tailor their infrastructure to their unique requirements, ensuring that they only pay for what they use and can scale resources as needed. This adaptability is one of the key benefits of the GreenLake model, allowing businesses to align IT consumption with their operational and financial goals.

Q446: Standard Question During the HPE GreenLake ordering process, what is a critical factor to consider to ensure a successful deployment?

A) Selecting the most popular configuration used by other companies.

B) Ignoring future growth projections to save on initial costs.

C) Regularly reviewing and adjusting resource allocations post-deployment.

D) Avoiding any customizations to streamline the ordering process.

E) Outsourcing the entire process to a third-party vendor without oversight.

F) Choosing the smallest configuration to minimize immediate expenses.

Answer: C

Explanation: Regularly reviewing and adjusting resource allocations post-deployment is essential to ensure a successful HPE GreenLake implementation. This practice allows businesses to adapt to changing demands and optimize resource utilization continuously. By monitoring usage patterns and making necessary adjustments, companies can prevent underutilization or resource shortages, leading to better cost management and improved operational efficiency. This proactive approach ensures that the solution remains aligned with the business's evolving needs.

Q447: Fill-in-the-Gap Question In the context of the HPE GreenLake ordering process, the primary advantage of engaging in a detailed needs assessment is to

_____.

A) Reduce the overall project timeline.

B) Ensure alignment with long-term strategic goals.

C) Minimize initial capital expenditure.

D) Eliminate the need for ongoing support.

E) Avoid any form of customization.

F) Simplify the contract negotiation process.

Answer: B

Explanation: Engaging in a detailed needs assessment during the HPE GreenLake ordering process ensures alignment with the company's long-term strategic goals. This assessment helps identify the specific requirements and potential growth areas of the business, allowing the solution to be tailored accordingly. By aligning the IT infrastructure with strategic objectives, businesses can ensure that the deployed solution supports future growth and innovation, ultimately contributing to their competitive advantage and success.

Q448: Multiple-Choice Question What is a common pitfall to avoid during the HPE GreenLake ordering process?
A) Conducting thorough market research before making decisions.

B) Engaging multiple stakeholders in the decision-making process.

C) Relying solely on past usage data to predict future needs.

D) Customizing the solution to fit unique business requirements.

E) Implementing a robust monitoring and management solution post-deployment.

F) Regularly updating the deployment plan to reflect changing needs.

Answer: C

Explanation: Relying solely on past usage data to predict future needs is a common pitfall in the HPE GreenLake ordering process. While historical data can provide insights into usage patterns, it does not account for potential changes in demand or business strategy. Businesses must consider factors such as anticipated growth, market trends, and emerging technologies to accurately forecast future resource needs. By incorporating these considerations into the planning process, companies can avoid over-provisioning or underutilizing resources, ensuring that the deployment is both efficient and cost-effective.

Q449: Scenario-based Question A global retail company, XYZ Corp, has recently migrated its IT infrastructure to HPE GreenLake to leverage its Consumption-Based IT model. With operations in multiple continents, XYZ Corp needs to ensure accurate usage metering to avoid unexpected costs and ensure fair departmental chargebacks. The company has departments with varying IT resource demands, such as marketing, which experiences spikes during campaigns, and R&D, which requires steady resources for simulations. As the HPE GreenLake administrator, you must decide on the best usage metering mechanism to align with the company's dynamic and varied usage patterns while ensuring transparency and predictability in billing. What is the most suitable approach to achieve this? ---

A) Implement a flat-rate metering mechanism across all departments.

B) Use real-time usage metering with dynamic thresholds for each department.

C) Adopt a tiered usage metering strategy based on historical consumption patterns.

D) Employ peak usage metering to account for the maximum resource demands.

E) Use predictive analytics to forecast usage and adjust metering accordingly.

F) Establish a manual tracking system for resource usage in each department.

Answer: C

Explanation: A tiered usage metering strategy based on historical consumption patterns is suitable for XYZ Corp's diverse and fluctuating departmental demands. It allows for a more predictable billing structure by categorizing usage into different levels or tiers, reflecting the actual consumption patterns observed historically. This approach provides transparency and helps in budget forecasting, ensuring departments are charged based on their typical usage while accommodating occasional spikes. Real-time metering or peak usage metering could lead to unpredictable costs due to the natural variability in demand, particularly for departments like marketing. Predictive analytics and manual tracking, while potentially useful, do not directly address the need for a fair, transparent, and straightforward billing mechanism, which is critical for departmental chargebacks and ensuring no unexpected financial burdens. A flat-rate model would not reflect actual usage, leading to potential inefficiencies and inequities in cost distribution.

Q450: True/False Question HPE GreenLake's usage metering system can automatically adjust billing rates based on seasonal usage patterns without manual intervention.   ---

A) True

B) False

Answer: B

Explanation: HPE GreenLake's usage metering system is designed to measure and report resource consumption accurately. However, it does not automatically adjust billing rates based on seasonal usage patterns without manual intervention. Billing rates are typically pre-defined and based on contractual agreements or specific metering mechanisms chosen by the organization, such as tiered or real-time metering. While the system can report on usage patterns, any adjustment in billing rates or metering strategy to accommodate seasonal variations typically requires administrative action or a pre-configured dynamic pricing model. The system's primary role is to provide transparent and precise usage data, which can then inform any necessary manual adjustments or strategy changes.

Q451: When configuring usage metering in HPE GreenLake for a company with highly variable workloads, which metering mechanism can help in minimizing unexpected cost spikes and ensuring cost predictability? ---

A) Flat-rate metering

B) Peak usage metering

C) Real-time usage metering

D) Tiered usage metering

E) Predictive analytics-based metering

F) Seasonal adjustment metering

Answer: D

Explanation: Tiered usage metering is effective for companies with highly variable workloads as it divides consumption into different usage levels or tiers, allowing for cost predictability. This method charges based on predefined consumption categories, which can be aligned with typical usage patterns, offering a buffer against unexpected cost spikes due to temporary workload increases. Flat-rate metering might not accurately reflect actual usage, and peak or real-time metering could lead to fluctuations in costs. Predictive analytics-based and seasonal adjustment metering, while valuable for forecasting, do not directly prevent unexpected billing changes based on immediate usage spikes.

Q452: In HPE GreenLake's usage metering, which feature would most effectively allow a company to allocate costs internally based on actual departmental consumption? ---

A) Real-time usage alerts

B) Cost forecasting tools

C) Departmental usage reports

D) Automated billing adjustments

E) Historical usage data analysis

F) Consumption-based chargeback system

Answer: F

Explanation: A consumption-based chargeback system is specifically designed to allocate costs internally based on actual departmental consumption, making it the most effective feature for this purpose. This system uses detailed usage data to directly associate costs with the departments using the resources, promoting accountability and transparency. Real-time alerts, cost forecasting, and historical data analysis are supportive features that aid in planning and monitoring, but they do not directly facilitate cost allocation. Automated billing adjustments relate to external billing processes, while departmental usage reports provide visibility but not the cost distribution mechanism.

Q453: Which strategy can enhance the accuracy of usage metering in HPE GreenLake, especially for a company experiencing rapid growth and frequent infrastructure changes?

A) Static resource allocation

B) Periodic manual audits

C) Dynamic resource scaling

D) Automated resource tagging

E) Predictive usage modeling

F) Fixed usage thresholds

Answer: D

Explanation: Automated resource tagging significantly enhances the accuracy of usage metering, especially for companies experiencing rapid growth and frequent infrastructure changes. By tagging resources dynamically and automatically, the system can accurately track and associate usage with specific projects, departments, or initiatives, even as resources are added or reallocated. This ensures that metering reflects the current state of resource allocation and consumption. Static resource allocation, periodic manual audits, and fixed usage thresholds might not keep pace with rapid changes, while dynamic scaling and predictive modeling are more about resource management and forecasting rather than improving metering accuracy.

Q454: You are an HPE GreenLake administrator for a multinational corporation that has recently transitioned to a hybrid cloud model. The CFO has requested a quarterly report that highlights the cost savings achieved through infrastructure optimization. The report must pull data from multiple sources, including on-premises and cloud resources, and present it in an easily digestible format for executive review. To achieve this, you decide to create a custom dashboard using HPE GreenLake's reporting tools. What is the first step you should take in creating a custom dashboard to meet the CFO's requirements?

A) Define the key performance indicators (KPIs) that align with the CFO's objectives.

B) Gather the historical data from the on-premises infrastructure.

C) Set up data synchronization for real-time cloud resource monitoring.

D) Choose a template from the HPE GreenLake dashboard library.

E) Schedule a workshop with the finance team to understand their reporting needs.

F) Install the latest HPE GreenLake software updates.

Answer: A

Explanation: The first step in creating a custom dashboard is to define the KPIs that align with the specific objectives of the report—in this case, cost savings from infrastructure optimization. This ensures that the dashboard is tailored to highlight the relevant data and insights needed by the CFO. Once the KPIs are established, you can then gather the necessary data and configure the dashboard to display this information. By starting with the KPIs, you ensure that the dashboard serves its intended purpose and provides value to its intended audience.

Q455: True or False: HPE GreenLake custom dashboards automatically update all widgets to reflect changes in data sources without the need for manual intervention.

A) True

B) False

Answer: B

Explanation: False. While HPE GreenLake dashboards can be configured to automatically update using real-time data feeds, not all widgets will automatically update without manual intervention. Some widgets may require manual configuration to refresh or update based on changes to data sources. It is essential to configure each widget appropriately to ensure that the dashboard remains accurate and up-to-date.

Q456: When configuring data sources for a custom dashboard in HPE GreenLake, which of the following is a best practice to ensure data consistency and accuracy?

A) Use only real-time data sources for all dashboard widgets.

B) Frequently switch between different data source types to maintain diversity.

C) Validate data sources by cross-referencing with external data.

D) Limit the number of data sources to avoid overloading the dashboard.

E) Rely solely on cloud-based data sources for flexibility.

F) Prioritize data sources that provide the most visually appealing results.

Answer: C

Explanation: Validating data sources by cross-referencing with external data ensures data consistency and accuracy. This practice helps verify that the data being presented is reliable and reflects the true state of the resources being monitored. It is vital to ensure that the data sources used in the dashboard are trustworthy, especially when making strategic business decisions based on the insights provided by the dashboard.

Q457: A retail company has deployed HPE GreenLake to manage its IT infrastructure across several regions. The IT team wants to create a custom dashboard to monitor server utilization and network performance metrics across all regions. Which feature of HPE GreenLake custom dashboards should they utilize to ensure scalability and ease of access for the entire team?

A) Role-based access control for secure access.

B) The ability to export dashboard data to CSV.

C) Multi-region data aggregation.

D) Pre-built dashboard templates for quick setup.

E) Interactive data visualization widgets.

F) Scheduled email reports for regular updates.

Answer: C

Explanation: Multi-region data aggregation is essential for monitoring server utilization and network performance metrics across various regions. This feature allows the team to compile and view data from multiple locations within a single dashboard, providing a comprehensive overview of infrastructure performance. Scalability is achieved by leveraging this feature, ensuring that the dashboard can grow with the organization's needs and provide insights across all regions efficiently.

Q458: During a routine review, you notice that a custom dashboard in HPE GreenLake is showing outdated data for storage usage metrics. To resolve this issue, what should you do first?

A) Reboot the HPE GreenLake platform to reset data feeds.

B) Manually update the dashboard widgets with new data.

C) Check the data source connections for any errors or disruptions.

D) Recreate the dashboard from scratch using a new template.

E) Increase the data refresh frequency in the dashboard settings.

F) Contact HPE support for technical assistance.

Answer: C

Explanation: The first action to take when a dashboard shows outdated data is to check the data source connections for any errors or disruptions. Ensuring that data sources are correctly connected and functioning allows the dashboard to pull updated information. This step helps identify if the issue is with data connectivity rather than the dashboard configuration itself. Once any issues with the data sources are resolved, the dashboard should automatically update with the latest data.

Q459: Scenario-Based Question XYZ Corporation, a global retail company, is in the process of migrating its legacy data protection systems to HPE GreenLake. The company has several regional data centers and a growing amount of sensitive customer data. They've experienced data loss in the past due to inadequate backup solutions and are keen on leveraging GreenLake's capabilities to enhance their data protection strategy. The company's IT team is particularly concerned about ensuring data consistency and reliability across different regions and wants to optimize costs by using a pay-per-use model. Given these requirements, which feature of HPE GreenLake should XYZ Corporation prioritize to address their data protection needs?

A) HPE GreenLake's integrated machine learning algorithms for predictive analytics.

B) HPE GreenLake's multi-cloud management capabilities.

C) HPE GreenLake's global data deduplication feature.

D) HPE GreenLake's capacity reservation options.

E) HPE GreenLake's compliance and security automation tools.

F) HPE GreenLake's disaster recovery as a service (DRaaS) offering.

Answer: F

Explanation: XYZ Corporation needs a robust data protection strategy that ensures data consistency and reliability, particularly in the event of a disaster. HPE GreenLake's DRaaS offering is specifically designed to provide businesses with a flexible and cost-effective disaster recovery solution that leverages a pay-per-use model. This feature allows companies to scale their disaster recovery resources up or down as needed, ensuring that they only pay for what they use. The DRaaS solution also ensures data integrity and availability across different regions, which is critical for a global company like XYZ Corporation. Additionally, the DRaaS offering integrates seamlessly with existing infrastructure, providing an efficient and comprehensive approach to data protection.

Q460: True/False Question HPE GreenLake's data protection services include built-in support for encryption at rest and in transit, ensuring that all customer data is secured throughout the entire lifecycle.
A) True

B) False

Answer: A

Explanation: HPE GreenLake is designed with security as a priority, incorporating advanced data protection features such as encryption at rest and in transit. This ensures that customer data remains secure and protected from unauthorized access throughout its entire lifecycle, from storage to transmission. This capability is crucial for meeting compliance requirements and protecting sensitive data from potential breaches. By providing built-in support for encryption, HPE GreenLake enables businesses to maintain high levels of security without the need for additional third-party solutions.

Q461: Which of the following HPE GreenLake features can help an organization minimize data loss and ensure rapid recovery in the event of a system failure?

A) Advanced data analytics dashboard

B) Automated data tiering

C) Continuous data protection (CDP)

D) Dynamic capacity management

E) Network load balancing

F) Cloud cost optimization

Answer: C

Explanation: Continuous Data Protection (CDP) is a key feature of HPE GreenLake that helps organizations minimize data loss by capturing every change made to data in real-time. This ensures that data can be recovered to any point in time, significantly reducing data loss and enabling rapid recovery in the event of a system failure. Unlike traditional backup methods that rely on periodic snapshots, CDP provides a more granular level of data protection, which is essential for businesses with mission-critical applications. By implementing CDP, organizations can ensure business continuity and protect against data loss due to unexpected failures or corruption.

Q462: Which HPE GreenLake capability allows for automatic scaling of storage resources in response to fluctuating data protection requirements?

A) Elastic Compute Services

B) Predictive resource management

C) Storage resource pooling

D) Automated storage scaling

E) Hybrid cloud orchestration

F) Virtualized environment management

Answer: D

Explanation: Automated storage scaling is a capability of HPE GreenLake that enables the automatic adjustment of storage resources based on changing data protection requirements. This feature leverages advanced monitoring and analytics to predict shifts in demand and dynamically allocate or deallocate storage capacity as needed. This ensures that organizations can efficiently manage their storage resources, avoid over-provisioning, and reduce costs by only using the resources they need at any given time. Automated storage scaling is particularly beneficial for businesses experiencing variable workloads, as it provides the flexibility to adapt to changes without manual intervention.

Q463: In the context of HPE GreenLake's data protection solutions, what is the primary advantage of using centralized data management for geographically dispersed data centers?

A) Simplifies the integration of third-party applications

B) Enhances data visibility and control across locations

C) Improves the speed of data processing and analytics

D) Reduces network latency between data centers

E) Increases the redundancy of data storage

F) Lowers the total cost of ownership for IT infrastructure

Answer: B

Explanation: Centralized data management in HPE GreenLake offers the primary advantage of enhanced data visibility and control across geographically dispersed data centers. This capability allows organizations to manage their data protection strategies from a single pane of glass, ensuring consistent policies, compliance, and security measures are implemented across all locations. Centralized management simplifies the monitoring and administration of data, enabling IT teams to efficiently identify and resolve issues, optimize resource allocation, and ensure data integrity. This holistic approach is crucial for businesses with multiple data centers, as it ensures that data protection efforts are cohesive and aligned with organizational goals.

Q464: Imagine a multinational corporation, Globex Inc., is utilizing the HPE Consumption Analytics Portal to manage its IT resources across various continents. The IT team has noticed that the resource consumption in their Asia-Pacific region has been steadily increasing, surpassing the initial budgeted allocation. The team wants to use the analytics portal to identify the main contributors to this increase and adjust their consumption strategy accordingly. As the HPE GreenLake Administrator, how should you proceed to efficiently pinpoint the source of the increased consumption and address it?

A) Use the 'Resource Usage' report to view detailed consumption data by service type and region.

B) Access the 'Cost Forecast' feature to predict future spending trends in the Asia-Pacific region.

C) Utilize the 'Consumption Trends' dashboard to monitor month-over-month resource usage changes.

D) Implement the 'Optimization Recommendations' to automatically reduce unnecessary resource usage.

E) Analyze the 'Consumption by Application' report to identify which applications are driving usage.

F) Enable 'Usage Alerts' to receive notifications when consumption exceeds a set threshold.

Answer: E

Explanation: To effectively address the increased resource consumption in the Asia-Pacific region, the best approach is to identify the root cause of the consumption. The 'Consumption by Application' report provides detailed insights into which applications are driving the resource usage, allowing Globex Inc.'s IT team to pinpoint the specific applications contributing to the increase. This report is invaluable because it breaks down the consumption by each application, offering a clear view of where resources are being most heavily used. Once the contributing applications are identified, the team can develop targeted strategies to optimize or limit resource usage for those specific applications, ensuring that they stay within their allocated budget. This method is more precise than general usage reports or forecasts, which may not provide the granular data needed to make informed decisions.

Q465: True or False: The HPE Consumption Analytics Portal allows administrators to set custom cost allocation rules to reflect their organization's internal financial policies.

A) True

B) False

Answer: A

Explanation: The statement is true. The HPE Consumption Analytics Portal offers administrators the ability to set custom cost allocation rules, which is an essential feature for aligning IT spending with organizational financial policies. This functionality allows organizations to tailor cost reports to reflect internal budgeting and financial reporting requirements, providing a more accurate representation of how resources are utilized across different departments or projects. By using custom allocation rules, administrators can ensure that IT costs are distributed in a way that mirrors the company's financial structure, thereby facilitating better financial management and accountability.

Q466: While using the HPE Consumption Analytics Portal, an administrator wants to create a report that includes both current and historical data to analyze trends over the last fiscal year. Which feature should they use to achieve this?

A) Real-Time Analytics

B) Historical Data Export

C) Trend Analysis Dashboard

D) Integrated Cost Reports

E) Custom Report Builder

F) Data Retention Management

Answer: C

Explanation: To analyze trends over the last fiscal year using both current and historical data, the administrator should utilize the 'Trend Analysis Dashboard'. This feature is specifically designed to provide insights into usage patterns over time, helping administrators to identify trends and make data-driven decisions. The Trend Analysis Dashboard aggregates historical data and presents it in a format that highlights changes and patterns, making it easier to understand how resource consumption has evolved. This is crucial for strategic planning and budgeting, as it allows organizations to anticipate future needs based on past behavior. While other features may offer some reporting capabilities, the Trend Analysis Dashboard is uniquely suited for longitudinal analysis.

Q467: An HPE GreenLake Administrator needs to ensure that the organization's resource consumption remains within budget. They decide to set up alerts to notify them when usage approaches the budgeted limits. Which type of alert should they configure in the HPE Consumption Analytics Portal to achieve this?
A) Anomaly Detection Alert

B) Threshold-Based Usage Alert

C) Budget Deviation Alert

D) Capacity Planning Alert

E) Predictive Spending Alert

F) Real-Time Monitoring Alert

Answer: B

Explanation: The best type of alert to configure for ensuring that resource consumption remains within budget is a 'Threshold-Based Usage Alert'. This type of alert allows administrators to set specific usage thresholds that, when exceeded, trigger notifications. By configuring these alerts, administrators can proactively monitor their resource usage and receive warnings before they surpass their budgeted limits. This approach enables timely interventions, such as adjusting resource allocations or implementing cost-saving measures, to prevent overspending. While other alerts may provide valuable insights, threshold-based alerts are directly aligned with monitoring and controlling budget adherence.

Q468: A company is analyzing its energy consumption data through the HPE Consumption Analytics Portal to improve its sustainability practices. They want to identify which data centers have the highest energy usage relative to their compute output. Which report should they generate to obtain this information?

A) Energy Efficiency Report

B) Compute Output Comparison

C) Data Center Performance Dashboard

D) Sustainability Metrics Analysis

E) Power Usage Effectiveness (PUE) Report

F) Resource Allocation Efficiency

Answer: E

Explanation: To identify which data centers have the highest energy usage relative to their compute output, the company should generate the 'Power Usage Effectiveness (PUE) Report'. PUE is a key metric used to determine the energy efficiency of a data center, calculated by dividing the total energy used by the facility by the energy used by the IT equipment alone. This report provides insights into how effectively a data center is using energy, with a lower PUE indicating greater efficiency. By comparing the PUE across different data centers, the company can pinpoint those with higher energy usage relative to their compute output and target them for energy efficiency improvements. This approach not only supports the company's sustainability goals but also helps reduce operational costs associated with energy consumption.

Q469: Scenario-based question Your company, Tech Innovators Inc., has recently adopted the HPE GreenLake platform to manage its IT infrastructure. The IT team is keen on ensuring maximum uptime and efficiency. As part of this initiative, they want to leverage HPE's proactive support tools to anticipate and resolve potential issues before they impact operations. You are tasked with leading this initiative. After an initial assessment, you realize that the team is not utilizing the predictive analytics capabilities to their full potential, particularly with respect to hardware components. Which proactive support tool should the IT team focus on to enhance predictive maintenance and avoid hardware failures?

A) HPE InfoSight

B) HPE OneView

C) HPE iLO Amplifier Pack

D) HPE Smart Update Manager

E) HPE Insight Remote Support

F) HPE Synergy Composer

Answer: A

Explanation: HPE InfoSight is a powerful AI-driven platform designed for predictive analytics and proactive support in the HPE ecosystem. It leverages machine learning to analyze vast amounts of data, identifying patterns and predicting potential hardware failures before they occur. By focusing on HPE InfoSight, Tech Innovators Inc. can significantly enhance their predictive maintenance capabilities, thus avoiding downtime and ensuring consistent performance. While tools like HPE OneView and HPE Synergy Composer offer valuable management capabilities, they do not specialize in the predictive analytics required for proactive maintenance.

Q470: True/False question HPE's proactive support tools can automatically initiate hardware replacements without any user intervention when a failure is predicted.

A) True

B) False

Answer: B

Explanation: While HPE's proactive support tools, such as HPE InfoSight, can predict potential hardware failures and provide alerts, they do not automatically initiate hardware replacements. Instead, they generate actionable insights and recommendations that the IT team can use to proactively address issues. This ensures that the process is controlled and validated by IT professionals, maintaining oversight and accommodating any business-specific requirements or constraints.

Q471: Multiple-choice question Which feature of HPE proactive support tools is most beneficial for reducing the time spent on troubleshooting by IT staff?

A) Automated ticket creation and management

B) Real-time performance monitoring

C) Predictive analytics and recommendations

D) Detailed hardware health reports

E) Firmware updates and patch management

F) Remote access and control

Answer: C

Explanation: Predictive analytics and recommendations are pivotal in reducing troubleshooting time. By identifying potential issues before they become critical, these tools enable IT staff to address concerns proactively, rather than reactively. This not only reduces downtime but also frees up IT staff to focus on strategic initiatives rather than constant firefighting. While other features like automated ticket creation and real-time monitoring are beneficial, they primarily support existing issues rather than preventing them.

Q472: Multiple-choice question A company is experiencing frequent network bottlenecks and suspects that the issue might be related to their storage systems. Which HPE proactive support tool feature would best help identify the root cause of the performance issue?

A) Network topology mapping

B) Storage capacity forecasting

C) Workload optimization analytics

D) Historical performance analysis

E) Device utilization alerts

F) Automated incident escalation

Answer: D

Explanation: Historical performance analysis is essential for identifying trends and patterns that may contribute to network bottlenecks. By examining past performance data, IT teams can pinpoint when and where issues began, leading to a more accurate diagnosis and resolution. This feature allows comparison across different time frames and configurations, revealing underlying causes that may not be apparent through real-time monitoring alone. Other options, such as workload optimization and device alerts, are useful but do not provide the comprehensive historical view needed for root cause analysis.

Q473: Fill-in-the-gap question To maximize the benefits of HPE's proactive support tools, it is crucial to ensure that all systems are _____ and properly configured to communicate with the central analytics platform.

A) Networked

B) Virtualized

C) Licensed

D) Synchronized

E) Monitored

F) Updated

Answer: A

Explanation: For HPE's proactive support tools to function effectively, all systems must be
networked and properly configured to communicate with the central analytics platform.
This connectivity ensures that data from various components is transmitted and integrated,
allowing for comprehensive analysis and accurate predictions. Without proper networking,
the tools cannot collect the necessary data to deliver insights, thereby limiting their
effectiveness in proactive maintenance and support. Other options, like virtualization and
licensing, are important but do not directly impact the connectivity required for data
analysis.

Q474: Scenario-Based Question Your company, a mid-sized e-commerce
platform, is experiencing rapid growth. The development team frequently
deploys updates and new features to the application. These deployments are
initially tested in a development environment before moving to production.
However, the infrastructure that supports the dev/test and production
environments is often stretched, leading to performance bottlenecks, especially
during peak usage times. You are evaluating HPE GreenLake to optimize
resource allocation and ensure seamless transitions from dev/test to
production. Which strategy would be the most effective in managing these
workloads with HPE GreenLake?   ---

A) Implement a fixed resource allocation for both dev/test and production environments to
prevent resource contention.

B) Utilize HPE GreenLake's capacity planning tools to dynamically allocate resources
between dev/test and production based on real-time demand.

C) Set up separate HPE GreenLake instances for dev/test and production to isolate
workloads and eliminate resource contention.

D) Schedule dev/test workloads during off-peak hours to ensure production workloads have priority.

E) Use HPE GreenLake's metering tools to limit resource usage in dev/test environments automatically.

F) Increase overall infrastructure capacity in HPE GreenLake to accommodate peak usage across all environments.

Answer: B

Explanation: In a growing e-commerce platform, dynamically managing resources is crucial to maintaining performance and cost-efficiency. HPE GreenLake offers advanced capacity planning tools that allow for real-time resource allocation based on current demand. This ensures that both dev/test and production workloads receive the resources they need when they need them, minimizing bottlenecks. Fixed allocations (A) or separate instances (C) might not be as flexible or cost-effective. Off-peak scheduling (D) can help but doesn't address real-time demand fluctuations. Metering tools (E) and increasing capacity (F) might provide temporary relief but don't address the core issue of dynamic resource management.

Q475: True/False Question In HPE GreenLake, you can configure automatic scaling for both dev/test and production workloads to optimize resource utilization.   ---
A) True

B) False

Answer: A

Explanation: HPE GreenLake is designed to offer flexible, scalable solutions that adapt to the evolving needs of businesses. Automatic scaling is a key feature of HPE GreenLake, allowing organizations to optimize resource utilization by automatically adjusting resources in response to workload demands. This feature is especially beneficial for dev/test and production environments, where workload demands can vary significantly. By enabling automatic scaling, businesses can ensure that they have the necessary resources to handle peak loads while minimizing costs during periods of lower demand.

Q476: When transitioning workloads from development/test to production in HPE GreenLake, what is a critical consideration to ensure a seamless transition?

A) Ensuring that production workloads have dedicated IP addresses different from dev/test.

B) Utilizing HPE GreenLake's analytics to predict potential bottlenecks in production.

C) Implementing a strict change management process to prevent unauthorized modifications.

D) Using the same network settings for dev/test and production to simplify the transition.

E) Maintaining a constant resource allocation across both environments.

F) Relying on manual monitoring to ensure performance standards are met.

Answer: B

Explanation: Predicting potential bottlenecks with HPE GreenLake's analytics is crucial for a seamless transition from dev/test to production. These analytics provide insights into resource usage patterns and potential performance issues, allowing administrators to proactively address them before they impact production workloads. While dedicated IPs (A) and change management (C) are important, they do not directly address performance issues during transitions. Using the same network settings (D) might simplify some aspects but doesn't address resource needs. Constant resource allocation (E) and manual monitoring (F) are less efficient compared to leveraging advanced analytics for proactive management.

Q477: Which feature of HPE GreenLake is most beneficial for balancing the demands of dev/test and production workloads?   ---
A) Static resource partitioning

B) Network traffic shaping

C) Real-time performance monitoring

D) Automated workload prioritization

E) Fixed cost billing

F) Pre-configured workload templates

Answer: D

Explanation: Automated workload prioritization is a key feature in HPE GreenLake that helps balance the demands of dev/test and production workloads. This feature automatically prioritizes workloads based on predefined rules and current demand, ensuring that critical production workloads receive the necessary resources without completely starving dev/test environments. Static resource partitioning (A) and fixed cost billing (E) are less flexible solutions. Network traffic shaping (B) and pre-configured templates (F) address different aspects of workload management. While real-time performance monitoring (C) is important for oversight, it doesn't directly manage resource allocation.

Q478: In the context of HPE GreenLake, which practice should be avoided to ensure optimal performance of both dev/test and production workloads?

A) Regularly reviewing resource usage reports

B) Allowing dev/test workloads to run on the same infrastructure as production without any limitations

C) Implementing automated alerts for resource thresholds

D) Conducting periodic performance audits

E) Leveraging HPE GreenLake's burst capacity feature during peak times

F) Utilizing historical data for capacity planning

Answer: B

Explanation: Allowing dev/test workloads to run on the same infrastructure as production without any limitations should be avoided to ensure optimal performance. Unrestricted dev/test workloads can consume resources needed by production environments, leading to performance degradation during critical operations. Regular reviews (A), automated alerts (C), and performance audits (D) are necessary to maintain oversight of resource usage. Burst capacity (E) ensures additional resources are available during peak demand, and historical data (F) helps in accurate capacity planning. Properly managing dev/test environments is essential to prevent them from impacting production services.

Q479: Scenario-Based Question You are an HPE GreenLake administrator for a mid-sized technology firm, and your company is planning to expand its cloud services to meet increased customer demand. The executive team has decided to partner with an HPE reseller to optimize their infrastructure costs and enhance service delivery. The reseller has proposed several solutions, but your team is unsure about the strategic fit. You need to evaluate the reseller's proposal against your company's long-term business goals, which include scalability, cost-efficiency, and security compliance. Which of the following actions would be the most appropriate initial step in working with the HPE reseller to ensure alignment with your business objectives?

A) Immediately negotiate for the lowest possible pricing with the reseller.

B) Request a detailed proposal from the reseller including case studies of similar implementations.

C) Conduct a workshop with the reseller to align on strategic goals and technical requirements.

D) Choose the solution with the most advanced features offered by the reseller.

E) Perform a comprehensive risk assessment of each proposed solution.

F) Schedule a meeting with the reseller's technical team to discuss integration challenges.

Answer: C

Explanation: When engaging with an HPE reseller, especially in a strategic partnership, it is crucial to ensure that both parties are aligned on business objectives and technical requirements. Conducting a workshop allows for a collaborative setting where your company can communicate its long-term goals, and the reseller can tailor their proposal to meet those needs. This step helps mitigate misunderstandings, ensures that all parties have a clear vision, and lays the foundation for a successful partnership. While pricing, risk assessment, and technical discussions are important, alignment on strategic goals should be the priority to ensure that subsequent actions are relevant and effective.

Q480: True/False Question HPE GreenLake administrators must always choose the cheapest solution offered by HPE resellers to ensure cost-efficiency for their organization.

A) True

B) False

Answer: B

Explanation: Cost-efficiency is a crucial consideration, but it should not be the sole factor in selecting a solution from an HPE reseller. The cheapest solution may not always align with the organization's needs for scalability, performance, or compliance with industry standards. It is important to evaluate solutions based on a holistic view of total cost of ownership (TCO), which includes not only initial costs but also ongoing maintenance, potential for future expansion, and any hidden costs that might arise. A strategic approach ensures that the solution will deliver value over time, rather than just minimizing immediate expenses.

Q481: Standard Multiple-Choice Question Which of the following is the primary role of an HPE reseller in the context of the HPE GreenLake model?

A) Developing proprietary software for HPE GreenLake deployments.

B) Providing third-party cloud services in addition to HPE products.

C) Offering support and maintenance services for HPE GreenLake solutions.

D) Acting as a financing partner for HPE GreenLake subscriptions.

E) Serving as a strategic advisor to optimize and align GreenLake solutions with business needs.

F) Manufacturing hardware components for HPE GreenLake solutions.

Answer: E

Explanation: HPE resellers play a vital role in the HPE GreenLake model by acting as strategic advisors. They help organizations tailor GreenLake solutions to fit their business needs, ensuring that the services align with strategic objectives such as scalability, efficiency, and compliance. While resellers may offer additional services like support and maintenance, their primary value lies in their ability to provide insights and guidance that optimize the deployment and utilization of HPE GreenLake solutions within the specific context of the customer's business environment.

Q482: Fill-in-the-Gap Question When collaborating with HPE partners, it is essential to establish clear communication channels to manage expectations and ensure project success. Which of the following is NOT a recommended practice when establishing these communication channels?

A) Defining roles and responsibilities clearly at the start of the partnership.

B) Setting up regular progress meetings to discuss developments and issues.

C) Only communicating via email to maintain a written record.

D) Using collaborative tools for real-time project updates and feedback.

E) Encouraging open dialogue to resolve conflicts and align on goals.

F) Establishing a single point of contact for streamlined communication.

Answer: C

Explanation: While maintaining a written record through email is important, relying solely on email for communication can lead to misunderstandings and delays. A mix of communication methods, including regular meetings, collaborative tools, and open dialogue, helps ensure that all parties stay informed and can respond quickly to changes or issues. These practices help in managing expectations, aligning objectives, and ensuring that all stakeholders are engaged and contributing to the success of the partnership.

Q483: Standard Multiple-Choice Question An organization is considering multiple HPE resellers for a GreenLake deployment. What is the most critical factor they should evaluate to ensure the reseller can meet their specific industry compliance requirements?

A) The reseller's pricing model and cost structure.

B) The reseller's track record with other similar organizations.

C) The reseller's ability to provide custom solutions tailored to their industry.

D) The reseller's geographic location and availability.

E) The reseller's partnership level and certifications with HPE.

F) The reseller's marketing strategies and outreach programs.

Answer: C

Explanation: Industry compliance is a critical requirement for many organizations, particularly those in regulated sectors such as finance, healthcare, or government. When evaluating HPE resellers, it is crucial to assess their ability to provide custom solutions that adhere to specific industry standards and regulations. This ensures that the deployment will not only meet technical and performance needs but also comply with legal and regulatory requirements. While other factors like track record and partnership level are important, the ability to deliver industry-specific solutions is paramount for compliance.

Q484: Scenario-Based Question Your company, Tech Innovators Inc., has decided to expand its cloud infrastructure using the HPE GreenLake platform to better manage its multi-tenant environment. The goal is to optimize resource allocation and maintain strict access controls for different departments. As the primary GreenLake administrator, you are tasked with setting up a new project for the R&D department, which requires significant computational resources for AI model training. The project needs to remain isolated from other departments but should allow for collaboration with trusted external vendors. What is the first step you should take in setting up this project within the GreenLake platform?

A) Immediately provision all required computational resources for the R&D department.

B) Create a new organization for the R&D department within the GreenLake platform.

C) Set up a project under an existing organization and configure network isolation.

D) Initiate a security audit to identify potential vulnerabilities in the R&D network.

E) Develop a detailed budget plan for the project's resource consumption.

F) Configure role-based access control (RBAC) to restrict resource access to authorized personnel.

Answer: B

Explanation: In the HPE GreenLake platform, it is crucial to first create an organization to effectively manage and isolate resources and permissions for a specific department, like R&D. By setting up a new organization, you can ensure that the resources are allocated exclusively to the R&D team, while maintaining the ability to configure specific access controls for external vendors. This step is foundational and precedes any resource provisioning or security configurations. Once the organization is established, you can proceed with creating projects, provisioning resources, and setting up RBAC to ensure that only authorized personnel have access.

Q485: In the GreenLake platform, which of the following best describes the relationship between projects and organizations?

A) Projects and organizations are independent and have no effect on each other.

B) Projects are subsets of organizations and inherit their access controls.

C) Organizations can only exist within a project and not independently.

D) Projects define resource limits, while organizations define user access.

E) Organizations are created automatically when a new project is set up.

F) Projects and organizations must be managed by separate administrators.

Answer: B

Explanation: In the HPE GreenLake platform, projects are subsets of organizations, meaning that they are created within the context of an organization and inherit the organization's access controls and resource policies. This hierarchical relationship allows administrators to efficiently manage resources and user permissions, ensuring that all projects within an organization adhere to the same governance rules. This structure facilitates streamlined management of resources and security across multiple projects within the same organization.

Q486: True or False: In the HPE GreenLake platform, an organization can contain multiple projects, but a project cannot span multiple organizations.

A) True

B) False

Answer: A

Explanation: This statement is true. In the HPE GreenLake platform, an organization serves as a container for various projects, which allows for centralized management of resources and policies within that organization. Each project is confined to a single organization to maintain clear boundaries and prevent cross-organization data or resource sharing. This design ensures that projects remain isolated to their respective organizational contexts, thus simplifying access control and resource management.

Q487: When setting up a new project in an existing organization within the GreenLake platform, which of the following is a critical step to ensure compliance with data governance policies?

A) Enable automatic resource scaling.

B) Configure data encryption settings.

C) Set up automated billing alerts.

D) Assign a project manager to oversee tasks.

E) Develop a detailed project timeline.

F) Establish a direct support line with HPE.

Answer: B

Explanation: Configuring data encryption settings is a critical step in ensuring compliance with data governance policies when setting up a new project. Encryption helps protect sensitive data from unauthorized access and breaches, which is particularly important when handling proprietary or sensitive information. By implementing encryption, organizations can adhere to regulatory requirements and maintain a high level of data security, which is essential for compliance and safeguarding organizational data integrity.

Q488: As a GreenLake administrator, you need to ensure that a specific project does not exceed its allocated budget. Which feature of the GreenLake platform would you use to monitor and control project spending effectively?

A) Project Access Logs

B) Resource Usage Reports

C) Billing and Invoicing Alerts

D) Cost Management Dashboard

E) User Activity Monitoring

F) Security Compliance Reports

Answer: D

Explanation: The Cost Management Dashboard in the HPE GreenLake platform provides a comprehensive view of project spending and resource consumption. This feature enables administrators to monitor costs in real time, set budget thresholds, and receive alerts when spending approaches or exceeds predefined limits. By using the Cost Management Dashboard, administrators can make informed decisions to optimize resource usage and stay within budget, ensuring financial control and accountability for each project.

Q489: Scenario-Based Question Your company, Tech Innovators Inc., is planning to migrate its on-premises data center to HPE GreenLake using Terraform for infrastructure as code. You have been tasked with ensuring that the deployment is automated, efficient, and easy to manage. The company needs to deploy multiple virtual machines with specific CPU, memory, and storage configurations for different departments. Additionally, security compliance requires that all resources must be tagged appropriately for auditing purposes. How should you structure your Terraform configuration files to meet these requirements effectively?

A) Use a single large Terraform configuration file to manage all resources, ensuring all VMs and tags are defined in one place.

B) Create separate Terraform configuration files for each department, with modules for VM configurations and tagging.

C) Use Terraform workspaces to create different environments for each department, handling configurations in one file.

D) Integrate Terraform with a configuration management tool to automate tagging and resource creation.

E) Utilize Terraform's provider block to automate resource tagging across all configurations in one file.

F) Implement a CI/CD pipeline to apply Terraform configurations and manage tagging through scripts.

Answer: B

Explanation: In this scenario, creating separate Terraform configuration files for each department (Option B) is the most efficient approach. This allows for modular management of resources, making it easier to maintain and update configurations as needed. By using modules, you can define the VM configurations and tagging once and reuse them across different departments, ensuring consistency and reducing duplication. This approach also aligns with best practices for infrastructure as code, promoting reusability, and maintainability. Although a single configuration file (Option A) might seem simpler, it becomes difficult to manage as the number of resources increases. Using workspaces (Option C) is more suited for managing different environments (e.g., dev, test, prod) rather than departmental configurations. Integration with a configuration management tool (Option D) or using a CI/CD pipeline (Option F) could enhance automation but doesn't directly address the need for structured, modular configurations and tagging within Terraform itself. Lastly, Terraform's provider block (Option E) is not designed for managing tagging alone.

Q490: True/False The Terraform "plan" command is used to apply the changes required to reach the desired state of the configuration and its resources.

A) True

B) False

Answer: B

Explanation: The statement is false. The Terraform "plan" command is not used to apply changes; instead, it is used to generate and show an execution plan. This plan outlines what actions Terraform will take to achieve the desired state as defined in the configuration files. It is a preview of the changes that will be made to the infrastructure, allowing administrators to review and verify the plan before any actual changes are applied. The command used to apply the changes is "terraform apply," which executes the actions proposed in the plan to modify the infrastructure.

Q491: Which Terraform feature allows you to safely and predictably create, change, and improve infrastructure while providing a consistent workflow for provisioning resources in HPE GreenLake?

A) Terraform Providers

B) Terraform Modules

C) Terraform State

D) Terraform Plan

E) Terraform Apply

F) Terraform CLI

Answer: B

Explanation: Terraform Modules (Option B) are the feature that allows you to safely and predictably create, change, and improve infrastructure. Modules encapsulate configurations into reusable, shareable components that promote consistency and best practices across multiple projects. They provide a consistent workflow by enabling the reuse of resource configurations, thus simplifying complex provisioning tasks, and reducing the risk of human error. While Terraform Providers (Option A) enable interactions with cloud providers and other APIs, and Terraform State (Option C) tracks the state of the infrastructure, Modules specifically offer the framework for organizing and managing reusable components. Terraform Plan (Option D) and Apply (Option E) are commands used in the execution workflow, and the CLI (Option F) is the tool interface itself.

Q492: In a situation where multiple developers are working on Terraform configurations for HPE GreenLake, what strategy should be employed to prevent conflicts and ensure seamless collaboration?

A) Use a single shared Terraform state file for all developers.

B) Implement remote state storage with locking enabled.

C) Assign each developer a separate Terraform workspace.

D) Use version control to merge all configuration changes manually.

E) Allow developers to apply changes directly to the infrastructure without review.

F) Employ a peer-review process for all Terraform configuration changes.

Answer: B

Explanation: Implementing remote state storage with locking enabled (Option B) is the best strategy for preventing conflicts when multiple developers are working on Terraform configurations. Remote state storage, such as using a backend like Terraform Cloud or AWS S3 with DynamoDB for state locking, ensures that only one developer can modify the state at a time, preventing race conditions and conflicts. This setup provides a centralized location for the state file, enabling collaboration while maintaining the integrity of the infrastructure. Using a shared state file without locking (Option A) can lead to inconsistencies, and separate workspaces (Option C) are more suitable for managing different environments rather than collaboration. Manual merging (Option D) and direct changes without review (Option E) can increase the risk of errors and conflicts. A peer-review process (Option F) is beneficial for code quality but does not address state management directly.

Q493: When working with Terraform to provision resources in HPE GreenLake, which practice should be followed to ensure that sensitive information, such as passwords or API keys, is not exposed in configuration files?

A) Store sensitive data directly in the Terraform configuration files, but ensure files are encrypted.

B) Use Terraform environment variables to handle sensitive information securely.

C) Encrypt Terraform configuration files using a third-party tool before applying.

D) Utilize Terraform's built-in encryption feature for sensitive data.

E) Incorporate a secrets management tool to securely store and access sensitive information.

F) Avoid using sensitive information in Terraform configurations altogether.

Answer: E

Explanation: Incorporating a secrets management tool (Option E) is the best practice for securely storing and accessing sensitive information, such as passwords or API keys, when working with Terraform. Tools like HashiCorp Vault, AWS Secrets Manager, or Azure Key Vault are designed to manage secrets securely and integrate well with Terraform. This approach ensures that sensitive data is not exposed in plaintext within Terraform configuration files and offers robust access controls and auditing capabilities. Storing sensitive data in environment variables (Option B) provides some level of security but may still expose data if not handled correctly. Encrypting configuration files (Options A and C) adds complexity and doesn't inherently protect data during processing. Terraform itself does not have a built-in encryption feature for sensitive data (Option D). Avoiding sensitive information in configurations (Option F) is impractical, as some level of sensitive data is often required for provisioning.

Q494: A mid-sized company, TechCore Solutions, is looking to expand its data analytics capabilities to better handle seasonal spikes in demand. They've recently adopted HPE GreenLake and are considering utilizing the HPE GreenLake Marketplace to procure additional services. Their IT team is inexperienced with cloud marketplace models and is concerned about cost management and service integration. As the administrator, you need to guide them on how to best leverage the HPE GreenLake Marketplace to meet their needs efficiently.

A) Recommend a pay-as-you-go model to handle seasonal spikes.

B) Suggest committing to a 3-year subscription for better pricing.

C) Advise them to use the marketplace's trial services to evaluate solutions.

D) Propose hiring a consultant to manage their marketplace interactions.

E) Recommend using only on-premises solutions to avoid cloud costs.

F) Suggest creating a hybrid environment with services from multiple vendors.

Answer: A

Explanation: The HPE GreenLake Marketplace offers flexible consumption models, including pay-as-you-go, which is ideal for businesses like TechCore Solutions experiencing fluctuating demand. This model allows them to scale their resources according to their needs without long-term commitments, providing cost-efficiency during off-peak periods and the ability to handle increased demand during spikes. While long-term subscriptions might offer cost benefits, they lack the flexibility required for seasonal variations. Trial services are useful for initial testing but aren't sustainable for ongoing needs. Hiring a consultant might add unnecessary costs, and solely relying on on-premises solutions could hinder scalability. A hybrid environment might be complex and isn't directly related to leveraging marketplace offerings.

Q495: True or False: In HPE GreenLake Marketplace, all services procured are automatically integrated with existing infrastructure without any additional configuration required.
A) True

B) False

Answer: B

Explanation: While the HPE GreenLake Marketplace provides a streamlined process for procuring services, not all services are automatically integrated with existing infrastructure. Some services may require additional configuration and integration efforts based on the existing IT setup and specific service requirements. The level of integration varies based on the service's nature and compatibility with the company's current environment. Administrators must assess each service's integration requirements to ensure seamless operation.

Q496: When using the HPE GreenLake Marketplace, which of the following is a primary benefit for IT administrators managing resource allocation?

A) Unlimited resources without any cost controls.

B) A predictive cost model based on future growth.

C) The ability to provision resources on-demand.

D) Fixed resource allocation preventing flexibility.

E) Mandatory approval processes for all resource changes.

F) Automatic scaling with zero manual intervention.

Answer: C

Explanation: One of the primary benefits of the HPE GreenLake Marketplace is the ability for IT administrators to provision resources on-demand. This feature allows them to quickly adjust to changing business needs, ensuring that resources are available when required and reducing the risk of over-provisioning. Unlike fixed resource allocation, which limits flexibility, on-demand provisioning offers agility in resource management. While automatic scaling is advantageous, it typically requires some level of configuration to align with business policies and may not apply universally to all services.

Q497: An enterprise customer using the HPE GreenLake Marketplace wants to ensure compliance with industry regulations while deploying new cloud services. Which feature of the marketplace should they leverage to meet their compliance needs?

A) Default security settings provided by HPE GreenLake.

B) The ability to customize service configurations.

C) Built-in compliance reports for industry standards.

D) The use of third-party compliance tools outside the marketplace.

E) Automatic encryption of all data by default.

F) The marketplace's SLA guarantees.

Answer: C

Explanation: The HPE GreenLake Marketplace includes built-in compliance reports that align with various industry standards, providing a valuable tool for organizations seeking to meet regulatory requirements. These reports help IT teams verify that their deployed services comply with necessary regulations, reducing the burden of manual compliance checks. While customizing service configurations and using default security settings are important, they do not directly address compliance reporting. Third-party tools and automatic encryption may enhance security but aren't specific to compliance tracking. SLAs focus on service performance rather than regulatory adherence.

Q498: Fill in the gap: When using the HPE GreenLake Marketplace, administrators can utilize _____ to gain insights into usage patterns and optimize resource allocation.

A) HPE OneView

B) HPE InfoSight

C) HPE iLO

D) HPE SIM

E) HPE Performance Advisor

F) HPE Capacity Advisor

Answer: B

Explanation: HPE InfoSight is a powerful analytics tool integrated with the HPE GreenLake Marketplace that provides insights into usage patterns and resource utilization. By leveraging machine learning and predictive analytics, HPE InfoSight helps administrators make informed decisions about optimizing resource allocation, improving operational efficiency, and anticipating future needs. It goes beyond basic monitoring by offering actionable insights and recommendations, unlike tools such as HPE OneView or HPE iLO, which focus on different aspects of IT management.

----

www.ingramcontent.com/pod-product-compliance
Lightning Source LLC
LaVergne TN
LVHW051428050326
832903LV00030BD/2964